José Esteban Muñoz

Sexual Difference

D1570134

Theories of Representation and Difference

GENERAL EDITOR, TERESA DE LAURETIS

Sexual Difference

A Theory of Social-Symbolic
Practice

The Milan Women's Bookstore Collective

INDIANA UNIVERSITY PRESS
Bloomington and Indianapolis

Translated from *Non credere di avere dei diritti: la generazione della libertà
femminile nell'idea e nelle vicende di un gruppo di donne* by Patricia Cicogna and
Teresa de Lauretis
© 1987 by Rosenberg & Sellier, Via Andrea Doria 14, 10123 Turin

The paper used in this publication meets the minimum requirements of American
National Standard for Information Sciences—Permanence of Paper for Printed
Library Materials, ANSI Z39.48-1984.

 ™

Manufactured in the United States of America

Library of Congress Cataloging-in-Publication Data

Non credere di avere dei diritti. English
  Sexual difference : a theory of social-symbolic practice
/ by the Milan Women's Bookstore Collective.
    p. cm.—(Theories of representation and difference)
  ISBN 0-253-33826-3 (alk. paper).
  —ISBN 0-253-20605-7 (pbk. : alk. paper)
    1. Feminism—Italy—History. 2. Women's rights—Italy.
I. Libreria delle donne di Milano. II. Title. III. Series.
HQ1638.N66 1990
305.42'0945—dc20   89-46324
1 2 3 4 5   94 93 92 91 90

CONTENTS

The Practice of Sexual Difference and Feminist Thought in Italy

An Introductory Essay

by Teresa de Lauretis

Italian feminism is not well known in North America. With very few, very recent exceptions, its critical texts are not translated, discussed, or cited by American and other anglophone feminists.[1] In presenting this text to them and others concerned with the development and elaboration of feminist thought and its relations to history and cultural practices, I shall especially resist the temptation of providing even a brief overview of a social, political, and intellectual movement whose history is still as ever in process, multifaceted, overdetermined, contradictory—in a word, emergent. The book you are about to read, however, is not only a major theoretical text of Italian feminism but one which, in elaborating a critical theory of culture based on the practice of sexual difference, also reconstructs *a* history of feminism in Italy from the particular location, the social and political situatedness, of its authors.

That this is only one possible history, one story that may be told out of the many documents and social memory of Italian feminism, and the experiential recollections of individuals and groups, is clearly stated in the book's original title, *Non credere di avere dei diritti: la generazione della libertà femminile nell'idea e nelle vicende di un gruppo di donne* [Don't Think You Have Any Rights: The Engendering of Female Freedom in the Thought and Vicissitudes of a Women's Group]. The partiality and situatedness of the book's theoretical and historical project—a project *at once* theoretical *and* historical—are further emphasized by its attribution of collective authorship to the Milan Women's Bookstore [Libreria delle Donne di Milano], which one infers must be roughly coextensive with the "women's group" referred to in the subtitle. They are reiterated in the authors' introduction: "This book is about the need to make sense of, exalt, and represent in words and images the relationship of one woman to another. If putting a political practice into words is the same thing as theorizing, then this is a book of theory, because the relations between women are the subject matter of our politics and of this book."

The events and ideas recounted in the book, the authors continue, took place between 1966 and 1986, mainly in Milan; they commonly go under the name of feminism. But in reassessing them retrospectively, in rewriting its history, the book renames it *genealogy:* "In the years and places we mention, we saw a genealogy of women being charted; that is, women appeared who were legitimized by referring to their female origin. . . . We are not certain that the history reconstructed in this book will really produce what we wanted, that is, to be inscribed in a female generation. We cannot be sure that, put to the test, our experience will prove to be only one of the many historical vicissitudes of the fragile concept of woman."

The bold injunction of the title, "Don't think you have any rights" (a phrase of Simone Weil's, cited in the epigraph), with its direct address to women and its unequivocal stance of negativity, sharply contrasts with the subtitle's affirmation of a freedom for women that is not made possible by adherence to the liberal concept of rights—civil, human, or individual rights, which women do not have *as women*—but is generated, and indeed en-gendered, by taking up a position in a symbolic community, a "genealogy of women," that is at once discovered, invented, and constructed through feminist practices of reference and address. Those practices, as the book later specifies, include the reading or rereading of women's writings; taking other women's words, thoughts, knowledges, and insights as frame of reference for one's analyses, understanding, and self-definition; and trusting them to provide a symbolic mediation between oneself and others, one's subjectivity and the world.

The word *genealogy*—whose root links it with *gender, generation,* and other words referring to birth as a social event—usually designates the legitimate descent, by social or intellectual kinship, of free male individuals. The intellectual and social traditions of Western culture are male genealogies where, as in Lacan's symbolic, women have no place: "Among the things that had no name [prior to feminist discourse] there was, there is, the pain of coming into the world this way, without symbolic placement." In this sense, Virginia Woolf's "room of one's own" may not avail women's intellection if the texts one has in it are written in the languages of male genealogies. A better figure of symbolic placement [*collocazione simbolica*] is Emily Dickinson's room, as Ellen Moers describes it, filled with the insubstantial presence of women writers and their works—a symbolic "space-time furnished with female-gendered references [*riferimenti sessuati femminili*]" which mediate her access to literature and poetry. Only in such a room may the woman "peculiarly susceptible to language," as Adrienne Rich has put it, be able to find, or to look for, "*her* way of being in the world."[2] In other words, the authors suggest, the conceptual and discursive space of a female genealogy can effectively mediate a woman's relation to the symbolic, allowing her self-definition as female being, or female-gendered speaking subject. And lest it be misconstrued, let me anticipate right away that this notion of genealogy is not limited to literary figures but reaches into relationships between women in everyday life.

Woolf, Dickinson, and Rich are major points of reference in the critical genealogy of feminism in Italy, which, while distinct in its historical and political specificity from both Anglo-American and French feminisms, nonetheless retains significant connections with them. Thus, if the terms *symbolic, genealogy, freedom,* and others, all newly inflected and recast in this text, come from the philosophical tradition of Nietzsche, Benjamin, Sartre, de Beauvoir, Lévi-Strauss, Lacan, Kristeva, Irigaray, Foucault, et al., the sense of their recasting can be traced to Rich's 1971 essay "When We Dead Awaken: Writing as Re-Vision," published in the collection *On Lies, Secrets, and Silence* (1979), which was translated into Italian in 1982. See, for instance, the passage I cited above about

> the girl or woman who tries to write because she is peculiarly susceptible to language. She goes to poetry or fiction looking for *her* way of being in the world, since she too has been putting words and images together; she is looking eagerly for guides, maps, possibilities; and over and over in the "words' masculine persuasive force" of literature she comes up against something that negates everything she is about: she meets the image of Woman in books written by men. She finds a terror and a dream, she finds a beautiful pale face, she finds La Belle Dame Sans Merci, she finds Juliet or Tess or Salomé, but precisely what she does not find is that absorbed, drudging, puzzled, sometimes inspired creature, herself, who sits at a desk trying to put words together. So what does she do? What did I do? I read the older women poets with their peculiar keenness and ambivalence: Sappho, Christina Rossetti, Emily Dickinson, Elinor Wylie, Edna Millay, H. D. (p. 39)

The notions of a woman's relation to the symbolic marked by "peculiar keenness and ambivalence," of a female genealogy of poets, makers of language, and of their active role in mediating the young woman's access to poetry as a symbolic form of being (female being or being-woman) as well as writing (authorship, author-ity), are all there in Rich's passage, although the first two are stated, the last one only suggested by negation. Nearly two decades later, the Milan feminists turn the suggestion into positive affirmation.

In her reading of Rich over and against a comparably influential text in the male genealogy of poststructuralist criticism, Barthes's "The Death of the Author," Nancy K. Miller uses this very essay by Rich to argue for a double temporality of intellectual history unfolding concurrently, if discontinuously, in the "women's time" of feminist criticism and in the "standard time" of academic literary criticism. With regard to Rich's later work, however, Miller questions the "poetics of identity" grounded in a community of women exemplified by "Blood, Bread, and Poetry" (1983) and the limitations set to feminist theory by what she takes to be "a prescriptive esthetics—a 'politically correct' program of representation."[3] Instead, Miller proposes irony as a mode of feminist performance and symbolic production.

Now, there definitely is irony—whether intended or not—in a theory of sexual difference such as the one proposed by the Italian feminists that draws as much on the philosophical and conceptual categories of poststructuralism and the critique of humanism as it does on the classic texts of Anglo-American feminism—and recasts them all according to its partial, political project; an irony most remarkable in that it underscores precisely the effectivity of the concept of genealogy. For while both Miller and the authors of *Sexual Difference* are feminist theorists fully conversant with poststructuralist critical thought, the latter trace their descent from Irigaray rather than Barthes. It is Irigaray's reading of woman's oblique, denied, repressed, unauthorized relationship to the symbolic order from Plato to Hegel and Lacan that resonates, for the Italian theorists of sexual difference, with Rich's "peculiar keenness and ambivalence" to language, and motivates their shared political standing as (in Rich's words again) "disloyal to civilization." Here is, for example, another Italian feminist, the philosopher Adriana Cavarero, writing "Toward a Theory of Sexual Difference":

> Woman is not the subject of her language. Her language is not *hers*. She therefore speaks and represents herself in a language not her own, that is, through the categories of the language of the other. She thinks herself as thought by the other. . . . Discourse carries in itself the sign of its subject, the speaking subject who in discourse speaks himself and speaks the world starting from himself. There is thus some truth in man's immortality, which I mentioned earlier as a joke: in universalizing the finitude of his gendered being [*della sua sessuazione*], man exceeds it and poses himself as an essence that of necessity belongs to the "objectivity" of discourse.[4]

The history of philosophy, Cavarero continues, records in various ways the finitude that the thinking subject carries in itself *qua* thinking being, but is extraordinarily blind to the finitude of its sexual difference. While it would have been possible to start from a dual conceptualization of being-man [*l'esser uomo*] and being-woman [*l'esser donna*] as originary forms of being, Western philosophy has started from the hypothesis of the one and from the assumption of a "monstrous" universal, at once neuter and male, whose embodiment in individuals of two sexes does not concern its essence as thinking being but remains external to it. "The task of thinking sexual difference is thus an arduous one because sexual difference lies precisely in the erasure on which Western philosophy has been founded and developed. To think sexual difference starting from the male universal is to think it as already thought, that is, to think it through the categories of a thought that is supported by the non-thinking of difference itself" (48).

The question, then, for the feminist philosopher is how to rethink sexual difference within a dual conceptualization of being, "an absolute dual," in which both being-woman and being-man would be primary, originary forms. This is a question that subverts the categories of Western thought which, precisely, elide sexual difference as primary—as "being there from the beginning" in both woman and man—and relegate it to the status of a secondary difference contained in the gender marking [*sessuazione femminile*] of the being-woman: "Woman is thus the repository of sexual difference, which constitutively belongs to her (and thus constitutes her) since the process of universalization has excluded it from the male" (62). It is a question quite similar to the one posed by Irigaray throughout her readings of Western philosophers in *Ethique de la différence sexuelle,* and similarly located, framed from inside the philosophical discourse they both mean to subvert.

I will come back later to the notion of an originary or primary character of sexual difference. For the moment, I return to the Milan Bookstore and its history of feminism in Italy, where the critical reflection on sexual difference has been going on since the early, activist days of the women's movement but, in the more self-reflexive writings of the '80s, has been taking shape as both a theory of sexual difference and a theory of social practice: the theory of that particular and specifically feminist practice now emerging in Italy, which the book names *the practice of sexual difference* [*la pratica della differenza sessuale*] and proposes as the conceptual pivot of its critical and political project.

The first document of Italian feminism, in this history, was a manifesto issued in 1966 by a group known as Demau (acronym for Demystification of Patriarchal Authoritarianism). While centered on the contradictory position of women in society—which at the time and in the terms of its most progressive social thought, Marxism, was called "the woman question"—the Demau manifesto contained the suggestion that no solution could be found to the problem women pose to society as long as women themselves could not address the problem that society poses to women; that is to say, as long as the terms of the question were not reversed, and women were not the subject, rather than the object, of "the woman question." A further step in the development of what the Milan book calls "the symbolic revolution," namely, the process of critical understanding and sociocultural change whereby women come to occupy the position of subject, was the celebrated pamphlet by Carla Lonzi first published in 1970 with the title *Sputiamo su Hegel* [Let's Spit on Hegel]. Not coincidentally it is a philosopher, and a philosophy of history and culture, that are targeted in Lonzi's critique ("*The Phenomenology of Mind* is a phenomenology of the patriarchal mind," she wrote unhesitantly), rather than an anthropological or sociological notion of patriarchy, though she was not a philosopher but an art historian and later a feminist theorist whose influence on the development of Italian feminist thought has obviously continued long after her untimely death. Also not coincidentally, therefore, her writing resonates not only with Marx's *Communist Manifesto* but even more distinctly with the manifestoes of the Futurist movement, which ushered into Italy and into Europe the very image of a cultural revolution, the avant-garde, in the first two decades of this century.

The idea of women as a social subject, the "Subject Unexpected by the master-slave dialectic," recurs in Lonzi's impassioned pamphlet, as it did in the first feminist manifesto, their stylistic and ideological differences notwithstanding; but Lonzi articulates it further, in a dimension at once utopian, historical, and philosophical. "The unexpected destiny of the world lies in its starting all over with women as subjects," she wrote. Yet, with regard to the political strategies of feminism, she argued against equality and for difference:

> Equality is a juridical principle . . . what is offered as legal rights to colonized people. And what is imposed on them as culture. . . . Difference is an existential

principle which concerns the modes of being human, the peculiarity of one's experiences, goals, possibilities, and one's sense of existence in a given situation and in the situations one may envision. The difference between women and men is the basic difference of humankind.[5]

Hence, feminism's fight for women's equality with men is misdirected since equality is "an ideological attempt to subject women even further," to prevent the expression of their own sense of existence, and to foreclose the road to women's real liberation.

Evident in the above passages are the roots of the current concept of sexual difference as constitutive of one's sense and possibilities of existence. Elsewhere the ideal of a female symbolic or symbolic mediation is implied by negation ("the equality available today is not a philosophical but a political equality"), and the necessity of a politics of radical separatism is adamantly asserted against the grain of the Marxist analysis of culture that has shaped all of Italy's recent social movements, the women's movement included: women, Lonzi states, who for two centuries have tried to express their demands by joining in the political demands of men, first in the French revolution and then in the Russian revolution, but obtaining only a subservient role, now see that "the proletariat is revolutionary with regard to capitalism, but reformist with regard to the patriarchal system" (29). "Women's difference is in their millenary absence from history. Let's take advantage of that difference. . . . Do we really want, after millennia, to share in the grand defeat of man?" (20).

During the '70s, the better part of Italian feminism took the latter road, a radical anti-institutional politics, even as large numbers of women continued to work within the parties of the Left for women's rights and social equality, achieving major social reforms such as the legalization of abortion in 1978. But even for those women (and they were many) who continued to be active in Left party and union politics, the development of a feminist consciousness took place in small women's groups, in the form of the separatist feminist practice known as *autocoscienza;* and because the two forms of activism were necessarily and strictly separated in time and place, not only during the first decade of the movement but well into the '80s, Italian feminism was characterized by the widespread phenomenon of "the double militancy," a particular variant of what here was called "the double shift," with its distinctive contradictions and difficulties.

Autocoscienza [self-consciousness or consciousness of self, but the Italian word suggests something of an auto-induced, self-determined, or self-directed process of achieving consciousness] was the term coined by Carla Lonzi for the practice of consciousness-raising groups which Italian women adapted from North American feminism to suit their own sociocultural situation. They were intentionally small groups, unattached to any larger organization, and consisting exclusively of women who "met to talk about themselves, or about anything else, as long as it was based on their own personal experience." And while this form of gathering could easily be grafted onto traditional cultural practices in a country more deeply conscious of gender and pervasively gender-segregated yet more thoroughly politicized than the United States, the impact of this first, specifically feminist, political practice was perhaps stronger and ultimately more significant for the development of feminist theory in Italy than in North America.

Here, easier institutional access and a less gender-segregated history of white women in the public sphere (e.g., in education, social work, and what is now called pink-collar work) favored the diffusion, much earlier on, of the sites and modes of feminist consciousness. From the relatively private environment of small women's groups, feminism could move into more public ones—academic Women's Studies programs, publishing and media enterprises, social service and law firms, etc. Concurrently, a greater social and geographical mobility made life in separatist communities seem more of a realizable possibility than it ever could in Italy—or than it actually can be in the United States, for that matter. Whence the different meaning and relative weight of the term *separatism* itself in feminist discourse in Italy and North America: there, it is mostly a "good" word, almost synonymous with feminism, and with positive connotations of intellectual and political strength for all feminists, regardless of sexual orientation or class differences. It lacks, in other words, most of the negative connotations that have accrued to separatism in this country and that, in my opinion, are due to more or less founded fears, on the part of feminists, of loss of professional status, loss of heterosexist privilege, or loss of community identity.

In Italy, on the other hand, if it valorized women's interactions with one another and the sharing of personal experience by conferring upon the latter an unprecedented social significance and analytical power, nevertheless the relatively privatized practice of *autocoscienza* could not fulfill the need for immediate political effectivity in the larger world that was the goal of the movement (and hence the practice of the double militancy); nor could it promote the public recognition of feminism as a critical analysis of society and culture, and not merely a narrowly political one. Above all, it could not envision (as this book's authors now can) a different symbolic order by reference to which women could be legitimated as women. Thus feminist thought found itself in a bind: it needed conceptual tools to develop itself and its relation to the world but, wishing to guard its own authenticity, it could use none except *autocoscienza*. Which for many had become insufficient.

In a sense, it can be argued retrospectively, the "static" separatism of the small group practice that marked the Italian movement in the '70s, in contrast with the more dynamic separatism (or "diffuse feminism") of the present day, reproduced and solidified the split between private and public existence typical of women's lives in general: a painful and contradictory rift between, on the one hand, the experience of a shared language and apprehension of female subjectivity and existence that occurred inside the movement, and, on the other, the daily confirmation of its incompatibility with, its utter otherness and alienation from, all other social relations outside the movement, where women's new critical knowledge—their "sense of existence" or their "ways of being in the world"—were neither legitimated nor recognized. And where, on the contrary, sexism and a pronounced disregard for feminism continued to pervade, as they still do, all social intercourse. Yet, I would suggest, that experience of a harsh and protracted separateness, of social-symbolic defeat—in the impossibility for women to achieve what Lonzi called "philosophical equality" and to gain self-representation in the established symbolic order—may be just what enabled the subjects of that experience to reach the present-day critical understanding of their own different subjecthood (the theory of sexual difference) and to attempt to define the modes of its possible existence, the ways of living it out in the practice of everyday life (the practice of sexual difference).

Eventually, then, under the pressure of its own contradictions, the practice of *autocoscienza* evolved into other, more open and conflictual practices that expanded or created new spaces of female sociality: cultural activities, parties, dances, conferences, journals, group holidays and travel, teaching, and direct contacts with feminists in other countries, notably the "Politique et psychanalyse" group in France (also known as "Psych et po" from its former name, "Psychanalyse et politique"). This more dynamic and interactive, though no less separatist, mode of sociality and communication among women is regarded by the Milan authors as a breakthrough in the development of their theory of feminist practice. For among the results of the new practice of female relationships [*pratica dei rapporti tra donne*] was the necessity of coming to terms with the power and the disparity—the social and personal inequality—inherent in them, as well as with the erotic dimension of all relationships between women and *its* relation to power. This proved to be especially conflictual, indeed "scandalous," in view of the ethos of parity (equality among women), nonaggressivity, and sisterhood in oppression that had characterized the past practice and self-image of the movement. Not surprisingly, these issues are still live as coals, and the views of the Milan authors very much contested.

A first formulation of the issues and perspective that inform *Sexual Difference: A Theory of Social-Symbolic Practice* appeared in 1983 as a pamphlet of the Milan Bookstore publication *Sottosopra* [Upside Down] entitled "Più donne che uomini" [More Women Than Men] but better known as "the green *Sottosopra*" from the color of its print. It was this text, by national consensus, that marked a definitive turning point for all Italian feminists, whatever their positions, pro or against or ambivalent about its authors' position.[6] Several years of intense debate ensued, in many Italian cities and with many groups representing various tendencies within the movement. The debate has been rekindled since the publication of the book.

One of the major points at issue is the notion of *entrustment* [*affidamento*], a term proposed to designate a relationship between two women which, though recorded and variously accounted for in feminist and women's writing, had not yet been named or formally addressed in feminist theory. Briefly, the relationship of entrustment is one in which one woman gives her trust or entrusts herself symbolically to another woman, who thus becomes her guide, mentor, or point of reference—in short, the figure of symbolic mediation between her and the world. Both women engage in the relationship—and here is the novelty, and the most controversial aspect of this feminist theory of practice—not in spite but rather because and in full recognition of the disparity that may exist between them in class or social position, age, level of education, professional status, income, etc. That is to say, the function of female symbolic mediation that one woman performs for the other is achieved, not in spite but rather because of the power differential between them, contrary to the egalitarian feminist belief that women's mutual trust is incompatible with unequal power.

Sexual Difference questions this belief on the basis of the experience of social defeat and personal disempowerment that women in the movement have admitted to, and that led to a weakening of energy, a leveling of women's fantasies, and a stifling of female desire ("within feminism, the politics of equal rights had no theoretical grounding but was nourished by the weakness of female desire, in its reluctance to expose itself, in its lack of symbolic authorization"); and it forcefully argues that the disparity, which does exist in the world as constructed and governed by the male social intercourse, is invested in women by dint of their subjection to the institutions of the male social contract, i.e., by their being objects of the male symbolic exchange. To confront that disparity and to practice it in the relationship of entrustment establishes the ground of a symbolic exchange between women, a female social contract whose terms can be defined autonomously from the male social contract.

> Naming the fact of disparity among women was certainly the decisive step. It meant breaking with the equalization of all women and their consequent submission to the distinctions set by male thought according to its criteria and the needs of men's social intercourse [*dei commerci tra uomini*]. It meant that among women there can and must be established a regime of exchange [so that] from being objects of exchange, as they were in the male world, women can and must become subjects of exchange.

Only a generalized social practice of entrustment through disparity, the book implies, can change the affective contents, symbolic meaning, and social value of women's relations to one another and to themselves, and produce another structure of symbolic exchange and other practices of signification. But how can trust be given to the powerful (woman) when power has been the means of women's oppression, by other women as well as men?

The examples of the relationship of entrustment given in the book range from the biblical story of Naomi and Ruth to the relationships between H. D. and Bryher in Greece described in H. D.'s *Tribute to Freud,* between Virginia Woolf and Vita Sackville-West, Emily Dickinson and (the writings of) Elizabeth Barrett Browning, Mme du Deffand and Mlle de l'Espinasse, and from the "Boston marriages" back to the myth of Demeter and Persephone. What these have in common, besides the intimately complex and often erotic nature of the bond between the women, is the symbolic recognition, the value or valuation of human, gendered worth that each one is capable of conferring upon the other, their formal social differences notwithstanding. Although their roles and symbolic functions with respect to one another may have been as different as their social or personal powers, yet each woman of each pair validates and valorizes the other within a frame of reference no longer patriarchal or male-designed, but made up of perceptions, knowledges, attitudes, values, and modes of relating historically expressed by women for women—the frame of reference of what the book calls a female genealogy or a female symbolic. The recognition of mutual value is thus made possible by their inscription in a symbolic community for which the authors again borrow a phrase from Adrienne Rich, "the common world of women" (and here Mlle de l'Espinasse serves as the negative example). But all this does not yet explain the concept of entrustment through disparity, in which consists the originality of this theory of female social-symbolic practice as well as its major difficulty, and on which are predicated two other crucial notions—the notions of female freedom [*libertà femminile*] and of the originary nature of sexual difference.

Again, since this theory of sexual difference is also a theory of social practice, we must go back to the history of the women's group whose critical autobiography, as it were, is written in *Sexual Difference*. By the early '80s, as women's politics had effectively pushed social legislation toward a degree of emancipation unprecedented in Italy, the process of women's assimilation into (male, or male-directed) society was well on its way, and the need for a discourse that could account for sexual difference by concepts other than victimization and emancipation was all the more urgently felt. The group began a project of reading literary works by women, especially novels, hoping to find in their contribution to Western culture some expression of "what human culture does not know about the difference in being a woman. What it was exactly, we could not know then, because what was missing was a 'language,' that is, a symbolic structure of mediation."

Their method, therefore, was "experimental," from the perspective of literary criticism. Very simply, they treated the texts as they would have their own words, as parts of a puzzle to be solved by disarranging and rearranging them according to extratextual, personal associations and interpretations, and thus erasing the boundaries between literature and life. This practice of reading (based on the group's previous experience of a collective, wild form of psychoanalysis, which they named "the practice of the unconscious") led to a division in the group regarding the preferred writers and the contest of interpretations: some women, like their favorite writers, were seen as authoritarian "mothers" prevaricating over the preferences and interpretations of the others, who thus felt cast in the role of daughters. The admission of disparity among women—if only, in this case, in matters of literary authority or critical persuasiveness—was at first shocking but subsequently liberating. "We were not equal. . . . Mentioning the disparity present in our relations apparently freed us from the constraint of representing them according to an ideal of neutral, genderless justice, and cleared our minds of the image of this kind of justice as well as of the guilt feelings and the resentment that this neutral authority introduced into our relations." And not by chance, the authors remark, the inequalities among the members of the group emerged and were named in connection with the mother.

The next step, though not an easy one, was to understand that the source and point of reference of women's worth as female-gendered subjects was a female-gendered one—in other words, to understand that, while figures of authority such as God, the Father, the party, or the state delegitimate and erase all actual difference, a figure of female authorization or symbolic mediation is necessary to "legitimate female difference as an originary human difference." That figure, inscribed in the writings and words of other women, and embodied in the gestures and practices of female relationships in daily life, was named *the symbolic mother [la madre simbolica]*, the term signifying at once its power and capacity for recognition and affirmation of women as subjects in a female-gendered frame of reference, and its transcendence with regard to individual women's subjectivities and differences. "Our favorite authors helped us to represent the female source of authority and to represent it together with the revelation of our diversity. . . . Included in the common horizon of sexual difference, different female words could be affirmed, and even clash, without fear of destroying each other."

As a theoretical concept, the symbolic mother is the structure that sustains or recognizes the gendered and embodied nature of women's thought, knowledge, experience, subjectivity, and desire—their "originary difference"—and guarantees women's claim to self-affirmative existence as subjects in the social; an existence as subjects not altogether separate from male society, yet autonomous from male definition and dominance. As a guiding concept of feminist practice, in the relationship of entrustment, the notion of the symbolic mother permits the exchange between women across generations and the sharing of knowledge and desire across differences. It enables, as the book's authors put it, the alliance "between the woman who wants and the woman who knows," that is to say, a mutual valorization of the younger woman's desire for recognition and self-affirmation in the world, and the older woman's knowledge of female symbolic defeat in the social-symbolic world designed by men. For there, the relation of daughter to mother is thought of as "natural . . . variously overlaid with affect and loaded with emotions, but without symbolic translation, that is to say, without figures or rules"; whereas, in redefining the mother-daughter relationship as a symbolic one, the concept of the symbolic mother extends it beyond the confines of the "natural" and the domestic to enable an alliance, a social contract between them. Without that social contract and the structure of symbolic mediation that supports it, no freedom or self-determination exists for women: "as long as a woman asks for reparation, no matter what she may obtain, she will know no freedom."

Freedom, here, is not understood in libertarian terms as freedom from all social constraint. On the contrary, the female freedom which the Milan group envisions for women entails a personal and social cost, a symbolic debt. For if, on the one hand, women owe nothing to men—since women's social survival has required the acceptance of both subordination and irresponsibility on their part, and hence, they state, "there is no social contract between women and men"—it is not the case, on the other hand, that women owe nothing to no one, a belief fostered by the politics of victimization prevalent in the movement. On the contrary, women owe women, and the price of female freedom is the symbolic debt each woman has toward other women, i.e., toward the symbolic mother. "The relationship of female entrustment is a social relation, and we make it the content of a political project. The symbolic debt toward the mother must be paid in a visible, public, social manner before the eyes of everyone, women and men." It is paid in "the responsibility [a woman] assumes toward other women out of her belonging to the female sex." Moreover, as the politically and consciously assumed practice of disparity brings to light the hidden or unconscious conflicts and emotions of the ancient (patriarchal) relationship with the mother, it opens up the possibility and the critical elaboration of new symbolic forms of female authority that can effectively legitimate a woman's subjecthood and thus render unto her not emancipation (under the law of the Father) but full social agency and responsibility as a woman. That is the meaning of the book's original subtitle, "the engendering of female freedom."

A freedom that, paradoxically, demands no vindication of the rights of woman, no equal rights under the law, but only a full, political and personal, accountability to women, is as startlingly radical a notion as any that has emerged in Western thought. It is bound to appear reductive, idealist, essentialist, even reactionary unless one keeps in mind, first, the paradox on which it is founded and which has been the first task of feminist thought to disentangle—the paradox of woman, a being that is at once captive and absent in discourse, constantly spoken of but of itself inaudible or inexpressible, displayed as spectacle and yet unrepresented; a being whose existence and specificity are simultaneously asserted and denied, negated and controlled. And hence the task of feminist philosophy: "thinking sexual difference through the categories of a thought that is supported by the non-thinking of difference itself." Second, one should be mindful that this paradox is not solely discursive, but is grounded in a real contradiction for women in the world designed and governed by men, a conceptual and experiential contradiction in which women are necessarily caught as social beings, and which no other political or social thought but feminism has seen fit to consider. And third, one cannot read the book and not be constantly reminded that its radical theory of sexual difference is historically and culturally located. The authors openly admit the limited, partial, and situated nature of their knowledge, embodied in the "vicissitudes," the history and the practices, of their group: "We see the necessity of entrustment because it appeared to us, but we cannot demonstrate it completely because we do not see it completely. This admission does not weaken our arguments. It means that our arguments have partly been dictated to us [by] the power of things which are not under our control, but which are favorable to us."

The book's closing remark that female freedom comes about neither by historical necessity nor by pure chance, but by a kind of favor, of *kairós,* a particular historical convergence, suggests to me an unwonted connection. The concepts that articulate this theory of sexual difference (genealogy, symbolic mother, female freedom, female subject—terms drawn from Western critical discourse but otherwise inflected and drastically recast) and the original feminist practices which ground the theory and to which the theory gives formal expression (*autocoscienza*, entrustment, disparity, female relations) mark an epistemological rupture in the continuum of Western thought. This rupture, it seems to me, has the quality of that "leap in the open air of history" which, according to Benjamin, "blast[s] a specific era out of the homogeneous course of history," where the latter is understood as "progression through a homogeneous, empty time."[7] Seen in this light, the conception of sexual difference as "originary human difference" proposed by *Sexual Difference* is less an essentialist—biological or metaphysical—view of woman's difference (from man) than a historical materialist analysis of "the state of emergency" in which we live as feminists. An emergency that, as Benjamin says of other oppressed and revolutionary classes, "is not the exception but the rule" (257).

In other words, this is not the sexual difference that culture has constructed from "biology" and imposed as gender, and that therefore could be righted, revisioned, or made good with the "progress of mankind" toward a more just society. It is, instead, a difference of symbolization, a different production of reference and meaning out of a particular embodied knowledge, emergent in the present time but reaching back to recognize an "image of the past which unexpectedly appears to [those who are] singled out by history at a moment of danger" (255). I offer that suggestion simply for further thought, and turn briefly to consider some of the responses, objections, and reverberations that *Sexual Difference*, like the green *Sottosopra* before it, has sparked across the spectrum of Italian feminism.

The magnitude of the debate and its repercussions at all levels of feminist politics, including the oldest and strongest women's organization in the Italian Communist Party (PCI), are evidence of the importance, timeliness, and theoretical strength of a feminist political theory based on a radical separatist stance. Which is also, of course, its major difficulty in obtaining consensus (to say nothing of implementation) as a theory of political and social practice. The objections have ranged from the personal, *ad foeminam* charges of authoritarianism, prevarication, and intellectual elitism brought against the authors by a subset of the Milan Bookstore collective itself, to more general objections of political vanguardism and (bourgeois) class bias.[8] Especially intense has been the debate around such notions as the wish to win, the symbolic mother and the symbolic debt to the mother, the practice of disparity and its correlative, entrustment, with their explicit reference to social hierarchies and personal inequalities. On the other hand, this theory's unprecedented influence on progressive political thought, as represented by the second-largest party of Italy, the PCI, is stated in no uncertain terms by Livia Turco and Rossana Rossanda in the first issue of *Reti*, a new cultural journal of communist women published in Rome by Editori Riuniti under the editorship of Maria

Luisa Boccia. The terms *feminist* and *feminism, sexual difference, female authorization, female reference,* [symbolic] *mediation,* even *female society* ("La società femminile" is the amazing title of Boccia's editorial in the inaugural issue) recur throughout the journal, whose project is to elaborate the positions stated in the "Women's Charter" [*Carta delle donne*], an official intervention by women members of the PCI in the direction of the party itself.

Reversing or subverting over sixty years of PCI theory and praxis on "the woman question," the Charter and the journal demand not only equality but also difference for women, insisting on the necessity for communist women to be both communists and feminists at once: "women are not a constituency to be added on [to party membership] but a different constituency, whose centuries-old history of difference, positively exploded in the past few years, entails a reconstitutive *self-consciousness* and thus a rethinking of the *entire* horizon and method of the party. . . . This is historically new, one of the problems facing a left-wing party today," writes Rossanda. But, she immediately adds, "the men of the party, who are still *the* party today," have not yet registered this fact or seen the necessity of a radical transformation of society that will prioritize the gendered subjects, rather than the objects, of social development.[9] Then, addressing herself specifically to *Sexual Difference,* Rossanda compares it with the political method implicit in the "Women's Charter": whereas the latter brings feminist issues and theory into direct confrontation with the party as the crucial political institution of Italian social life, she argues, the practice of entrustment is a simpler form of social relations, which shifts the emphasis away from the economic, the institutional, the mass levels, and toward an elitist, interest-group, and potentially hierarchical model of political practice based on dyadic relationships between "female-gendered individuals [*individui donne*]" (42).

The interesting thing about Rossanda's article is not her ideological objection, which follows predictably from the historical contradiction of PCI women, as she herself describes it, unable to be both communists and feminists at once. It is rather her strategic move to grant political status to the theory of sexual difference, to take its feminist critical lesson to heart, and then to appropriate or absorb its conceptual novelty into her preferred position (the Charter's) while reducing the book's concept of a *diffuse social practice* of sexual difference to a *political model,* or "method," of narrow, personal, and hierarchical proportions. This strategy is not unique to her, though as a major figure of the Italian Left, Rossanda commands a higher degree of persuasiveness and national visibility than most of the other women who have publicly engaged in this debate.[10]

Other objections have been less guarded and more impassioned, revealing their stakes in rather transparent ways. For example, Grazia Zuffa, also writing in *Reti,* laments the turn of feminism from the " 'free' feminist politics" of the early *autocoscienza* groups to the current "necessary and thus obligatory" practice of disparity and symbolic mediation. The appeal of entrustment, she fears, is all too reminiscent of the appeal that the psychoanalytic relationship has on women, with its controlling definition of subjectivity. Isn't the symbolic mother really a projection of paternal authority vested in its familial enforcer, the social or real mother? That, one infers, would be bad enough. Worse still if the symbolic mother is the figure of a female social contract (as it indeed is), for then the whole theory is founded on a "radically separatist practice" and on refusing the male-female dialectic (or, as she awkwardly puts it, "on affirming the non-dialectic with the masculine [*nell'affermazione della non dialettica col maschile*])."[11] Such "homosexual fundamentalism," she concludes, is a very long way and quite a different thing from "separatism as traditionally understood" in feminist politics. In other words, when the meaning of separatism shifts from the "traditional," socially innocuous, women's support group, in which women could let down their hair and commiserate with one another on personal matters, to a new social formation of women with no loyalty to men and intent on changing the world on their own—this is going too far.

Here we find ourselves on more familiar terrain, as Zuffa's homophobic sentiment lends itself easily to transcultural translation into Anglo-American feminism, where the term *separatism* has always carried the connotation she bluntly acknowledges, even as it is seldom stated in so direct a way as to reveal the heterosexual fundamentalism that motivates the objection. But unlike North America, where lesbianism has been a visible—if by no means unopposed or undivided—presence within the women's movement, and an acknowledged influence on the development of feminist thought, Italy has had no history of lesbian feminism, though it has a lesbian history that is now beginning to be told, and though lesbians have been active in the movement all along as women and as feminists, if not as lesbians.[12]

In a very intelligent essay entitled "Double Movement," published in a special issue of *DWF* on "Belonging" [*Appartenenza*], Ida Dominijanni does not so much object or adhere to the theory of sexual difference as take up its implications in her critical reading of the history (again, *a* history) of the movement and the current stakes of feminism in Italy. And in one of the rare honest statements I have encountered in the pervasive silence that enshrouds lesbianism in Italian feminist writings, Dominijanni admits: "I will not even mention here [among the various forms of women's political identity or 'belonging'] the most unnamed of all belongings, if we can call it that: women's homosexual or heterosexual choice, on which Italian feminism has rightly chosen not to split itself, as happened in other countries, but which today is becoming a major cause of opacity in the theoretical and political debate."[13] And she goes on to another topic. But again extraordinarily, the same journal issue runs an article by Simonetta Spinelli, "Silence Is Loss," which argues for the necessity of coming out and theorizing lesbian identity and subjectivity as distinct from feminism. For the material specificity of lesbian desire and the embodied knowledges that can sustain a collective lesbian identity have remained "the unsaid of the movement," as she puts it, and the price to lesbians has been the nonbelonging to oneself as well as others, the loss of identity and finally of community.[14]

Whether or not Italian feminists are right (as Dominijanni believes) in not splitting the movement over what might well be called the lesbian question, Spinelli's intervention in the current debate on sexual difference hits very close to home when she indicts the inadequacy of a theory "that starts from me but in some oblique way also avoids me." Although she does not seem to be speaking directly about *Sexual Difference,* a passage from the book actually sustains her objection: "Living in a community of women was an extraordinary experience. The most amazing discovery was the intense eroticism present there. *It was not lesbianism, but sexuality no longer imprisoned in masculine desire*" (emphasis added). This is a troubled statement—and the only one where the word *lesbianism* appears in the book. What is meant by lesbianism, then, if it is not a female sexuality unfettered or autonomous from masculine desire and definition? Two are the possible readings of the statement.

One is that lesbianism is still understood, by the authors as by Italians in general, in terms of Havelock Ellis's sexology: as a form of sexual inversion whereby a woman would assume a masculine identification vis-à-vis her (female) sexual object choice. This is not only a prefeminist notion that does not recognize lesbianism as a form of autonomous *female* sexuality, although it has gained some credibility even among lesbians since its inscription in Radclyffe Hall's famous novel *The Well of Loneliness;* but, more important, it is also a notion that would contradict the rest of the statement, for it forecloses the possibility of *any* form of female sexuality autonomous from the masculine. Havelock Ellis's definitions of homosexuality and inversion are in fact predicated on the male-centered conceptual structure that Irigaray cleverly called "hom(m)osexuality" or "sexual indifference," where "the object choice of the homosexual woman [can only be understood as] determined by a *masculine* desire and tropism."[15] The point of her pun was precisely to make visible the male-centeredness of the structure and its absolute negation of female sexuality in itself. However, in view of the bearing that Irigaray's thought has had on the authors of *Sexual Difference,* I should add that her more recent positions on the issue of feminist politics have taken quite a different turn from what her earlier works suggested, and caused the distance between Irigaray and the Milan collective to become more clearly visible.

In a public conversation held at the Virginia Woolf Center in Rome, not coincidentally a few months before delivering an invited address to the 1989 National Congress of the Italian Communist Party, Irigaray stated: "Promoting homosexuality to [the status of] a political problem seems extremely ambiguous to me. This, in my opinion, is a cause of paralysis in the women's movement." And in response to the question from the floor "How long will lesbians have to hide their sexual choice?" she answered, "Forever!"[16] The great value of Irigaray's thought for the Milan Women's Bookstore collective consisted primarily in her emphasis on the articulation of sexual difference in the symbolic; in this sense, her work not only served very effectively the Milan collective's effort to counter the rights-oriented, sociological arguments of much Italian feminism, but also contributed significantly to the Milanese theorization of sexual difference as a social-symbolic practice and to their project of delineating or (re)constructing a female symbolic. However, Irigaray's long-known dissociation from any feminist political practice, as well as her more recent insistence on an ethics of sexual difference that will favor the final, and optimal, union of woman and man (both of which may account for her elision of lesbianism from the political/ethical domain and for her recent paradoxical rapprochement with the PCI), is in striking contrast with the political positions publicly reiterated by the authors of *Sexual Difference* and explicitly articulated in the book.

The other, perhaps closer reading of the passage from *Sexual Difference* cited above is the one suggested by Spinelli: that the authors' conception of an autonomous female sexuality avoids lesbianism "in some oblique way," bypasses it, circumvents it, or disclaims it. In other words, one might ask more bluntly, is this a theory that dare not speak its name? The authors' insistence in public debates that their theory is not lesbian but rather homosexual—that is to say, predicated on the notion of social-symbolic practices and same-sex relationships between and among women—may be seen as a considered political choice and an appeal for hegemony on the part of a militant social movement which, after all, potentially involves all women. Or it may be seen, perhaps concurrently, as yet another effect of the social and discursive dominance of the institution of heterosexuality which, even in a radically separatist theory of social practice, imposes the excision of the very figure of female subjectivity that is most capable of signifying the resistance to that dominance and the unqualified rejection of that institution.[17] Thus, Spinelli's essay is a powerful ironic counterpart to the homophobic objections that have met the Milanese proposal of a radically separatist theory of social practice. For if that proposal does in fact articulate a position that, at least in the North American context, might be read as a lesbian feminist position, yet its consistent dodging of the crucial questions of sexuality, fantasy, and the erotic in the definition of sexual difference all but drops the lesbian specification by the wayside. Whether this will, itself, end up "splitting the movement," or whether it will cause *Sexual Difference* to lose its most radical, antipatriarchal edge, and thus lend itself to appropriation by dominant social-symbolic discourses, remains to be seen.

A third reading, or explanation, of that troubling statement was offered by one of its authors, Luisa Muraro, in a personal letter she wrote to me on September 12, 1989, in response to a manuscript version of this introductory essay which I had sent to her. It is not only fair but also useful to the reader that her views on this particular issue be given space in this introduction. Muraro writes:

> The essay you cite by Ida [Dominijanni] is truly intelligent, but the argument about not splitting the movement is not applicable to us [the Milan Women's Bookstore collective], who have notoriously authored conflicts and splits in it (even though we are sorry about that). Moreover, it is wrong (in our opinion, of course) to claim that not mentioning choice (hetero- or homosexual) is a "major cause of opacity" in the

current debate. . . . Why? (1) for the reason fairly obvious, although not to be disregarded, that many of the differences between women, like this one, are induced or overdetermined by a social order that is not autonomous; (2) for the reason that we are working exclusively toward female freedom, which is the only thing that can constitute a goal common to all women, and hence the reason of a politics *of* women; and this makes us *relatively* indifferent to the possible consequences and possible uses of that freedom. That a woman may freely love no one or the whole of humanity, that she may make love with other women, with men, with nobody, with children or animals—these are but consequences, each worthy of attention and respect as a source of experiences and knowledges valuable in strengthening female freedom.

From the way you speak of lesbianism, it almost seems as if you are making sexual choice a principle or a cause or a foundation of freedom. If that were what you thought, I would say to you: no, the principle of female freedom is of a symbolic nature. It is not an actual behavior, however valid and precious such behavior may be toward the empowering of women in society. Did I manage to make myself clear?

You see, the two opposite kinds of criticism (represented by Spinelli and Zuffa in your references) both come from a lack of understanding of this point: that in order for us to enter the symbolic order we must start from silence, we must clear everything out—*the place of the other must be empty.*

On the other hand, I realize, I do more and more every day, that it is difficult (impossible?) to transform a symbolic order and create freedom by political activism; but this is our gamble, and you are among the few who have understood that this indeed is the gamble. This is why I insist and ask you to think about it precisely in relation to this question of lesbianism.[18]

And think about it I shall, and so will other readers of this book, whose provocative answers open up each time a more difficult and crucial question.

Up to now, in its effort to define female desire and subjecthood in the symbolic, without sufficient attention to the working of the imaginary in subjectivity and sexual identity, *Sexual Difference* has provoked very serious objections and opposition from all sides, as well as wide support, including support among women in the PCI. As has been pointed out, this theory of female social-symbolic practice makes little space for differences and divisions between—and especially within—women, and so tends to construct a view of the female social subject that is still too closely modeled on the "monstrous" subject of philosophy and History. However, this is not biological or metaphysical essentialism, but a consciously political, materialist formulation of the specific difference of women in a particular sociohistorical location where, for instance, race or color has not been at issue; and where, if sexuality is now emerging as an issue, it is not merely against, but in part owing to, the very strength of this theory of sexual difference.

As another contributor to the theory well said it, "by essential and originary difference I mean that, for women, being engendered in difference [*l'essere sessuate nella differenza*] is something not negotiable; for each one who is born female, it is always already so and not otherwise, rooted in her being not as something superfluous or something more, but as that which she necessarily is: female."[19] If the project of this feminist philosophy can be rightly criticized for its unquestioning acceptance of the classic, unified subject of philosophy, nevertheless the notion of essential and originary difference represents a point of consensus and a new starting point for feminist thought in Italy.[20]

And here it could as well, I would suggest, for without this basic feminist assumption—basic, that is, to feminism as historically constituted at the present time—the still-necessary articulation of all other differences between and within women must remain framed in male-dominant and heterosexist ideologies of liberal pluralism, conservative humanism, or, goddess forbid, religious fundamentalism. Finally, then, the partial, bold, provocative, contradictory, controversial, and highly original theoretical proposals of this book should prove to be of much value to the ongoing elaboration of feminist theory in English-speaking contexts, as well as to the reflection on the limits and possibilities of our increasingly difficult feminist political practice.

TERESA DE LAURETIS

NOTES

1. Two recent books have been published in the United States on Italian feminism, Lucia Chiavola Birnbaum, *Liberazione della donna: Feminism in Italy* (Middletown, Conn.: Wesleyan University Press, 1986), and Judith Adler Hellman, *Journeys among Women: Feminism in Five Italian Cities* (New York: Oxford University Press, 1987); and one in Britain on feminist film, Giuliana Bruno and Maria Nadotti, eds., *Off-Screen: Women and Film in Italy* (London: Routledge, 1988). Also in Britain some extracts from a publication of the Milan Bookstore were recently edited and introduced by Rosalind Delmar, "Writers and Readers," *Red Letters*, no. 9 (n.d.): 17–34. Delmar is also the translator of the Italian classic feminist novel, Sibilla Aleramo's *A Woman* (Berkeley and Los Angeles: University of California Press, 1980). An earlier article by Mary Russo, "The Politics of Maternity: Abortion in Italy," *Yale Italian Studies* 1, no. 1 (1977): 107–27, is a rare example of American feminist theoretical writing dealing with the Italian women's movement in the '70s.

2. Adrienne Rich, *On Lies, Secrets, and Silence: Selected Prose, 1966–1978* (New York: W. W. Norton, 1979), p. 39.

3. Nancy K. Miller, "Changing the Subject: Authorship, Writing, and the Reader," in *Feminist Studies/Critical Studies*, ed. Teresa de Lauretis (Bloomington: Indiana University Press), pp. 109–11.

4. Adriana Cavarero et al., *Diotima: Il pensiero della differenza sessuale* (Milan: La Tartaruga, 1987), pp. 45 and 49; my translation. Diotima, the collective author of the homonymous volume, is a "philosophical community" of academic feminists which has, however, some significant overlap with the more militant feminism of the Milan Libreria delle Donne. The members of the collective and authors of *Diotima* are Adriana Cavarero, Cristiana Fischer, Elvia Franco, Giannina Longobardi, Veronica Mariaux, Luisa Muraro, Anna Maria Piussi, Anita Sanvitto, Wanda Tommasi, Betty Zamarchi, Chiara Zamboni, and Gloria Zanardo.

5. Carla Lonzi, *Sputiamo su Hegel* (Milan: Scritti di Rivolta femminile, 1974 [1970]), pp. 20–21; my translation.

6. No individual authors' names appear in the pamphlet, or in *Sexual Difference,* as customary in the Italian movement practice of collective authorship, a practice no longer followed as strictly as it was in the '70s except by long-standing groups such as the Milan Libreria delle Donne. Any Italian feminist, however, would be able to name at least some of the individuals in the group and knows that the authors of both the green *Sottosopra* and *Sexual Difference* include the two women most directly associated with the Libreria, Luisa Muraro and Lia Cigarini. For a full documentation of the movement in Milan, see Anna Rita Calabró and Laura Grasso, eds., *Dal movimento femminista al femminismo diffuso: Ricerca e documentazione nell'area lombarda* (Milan: Franco Angeli, 1985).

7. Walter Benjamin, *Illuminations,* ed. and with an introduction by Hannah Arendt, trans. Harry Zohn (New York: Schocken Books, 1969), pp. 263 and 261. For this very interesting connection between radical feminist theory and Benjamin's "Theses," I am indebted to the original work in progress of Kathy Miriam, doctoral candidate in History of Consciousness at the University of California, Santa Cruz.

8. See, for example, Laura Lepetit et al., *Una libreria e i suoi doni: Lettera aperta dalla Libreria delle donne di Milano,* pamphlet dated Ottobre 1987.

9. Rossana Rossanda, "Politica: significati e progetti. Le diverse strade della Carta e dell'affidamento," *Reti: Pratiche e saperi di donne* 1 (1987): 40–41; my translation.

10. Only two men thus far have publicly expressed their opinions in the debate spurred by the Milan collective: the philosopher Franco Rella was highly critical, while Mario Tronti, philosopher and politician of the Left wing of the PCI, was more favorable (personal communication by Luisa Muraro).

11. Grazia Zuffa, "Tra libertà e necessità. A proposito di *Non credere di avere dei diritti,*" *Reti: Pratiche e saperi di donne* 1 (1987): 52; my translation.

12. A valuable contribution to the history of lesbian activism and its relation both to the women's movement and to the "diffuse feminism" of the '80s is Bianca Pomeranzi's "Differenza lesbica e lesbofemminismo," published in *Memoria,* a journal of women's history. But it is sadly remarkable that the most comprehensive and up-to-date account of lesbianism in Italy is a paper in English by Liana Borghi, Gloria Corsi, Simonetta Spinelli, and Alessandra Perini, "Italian Lesbians: Maps and Signs," presented at the International Conference on Gay and Lesbian Studies at the Free University of Amsterdam (December 15–18, 1987) and published in its proceedings, *Homosexuality, Which Homosexuality?,* pp. 112–25. Borghi is also the author of one of the first texts of lesbian fiction in Italy, a wonderful and funny novella, *Tenda con vista* [Tent with a View], published in 1987 by Estro Editrice in Rome (one of the two lesbian small presses currently operating in Italy, the other being Felina Editrice). Estro is also the publisher of the major contribution to lesbian cultural history that has appeared in Italy, Rosanna Fiocchetto's *L'amante celeste: La distruzione scientifica della lesbica* [Heavenly Lover: The Scientific Destruction of the Lesbian], 1987. The only other lesbian publication is the monthly bulletin of CLI [Collegamento fra le lesbiche italiane], a national organization based in Rome.

13. Ida Dominijanni, "Doppio movimento," *DWF [DonnaWomanFemme]* 4 (1986): 25; my translation.

14. Simonetta Spinelli, "Il silenzio è perdita," *DWF [DonnaWomanFemme]* 4 (1986): 52; my translation.

15. Luce Irigaray, *Speculum of the Other Woman,* trans. Gillian C. Gill (Ithaca, N.Y.: Cornell University Press, 1985), p. 99. On the paradox of what I call *sexual (in)difference* and how it works in lesbian representation and self-representation, see Teresa de Lauretis, "Sexual Indifference and Lesbian Representation," *Theatre Journal* 40, no. 2 (1988): 155–77.

16. *Incontro con Luce Irigaray,* Dispense [Working Papers] del Centro Culturale "Virginia Woolf," Rome, 1988, pp. 8–10; my translation.

17. See Rosanna Fiocchetto, "Quattro luoghi comuni," *Squaderno,* no. 1 (giugno 1989): 5–9.

18. I thank Luisa Muraro for this and other very useful comments, and for several points of information and clarification that I also incorporated into the final version of the essay as it appears here.

19. Adriana Cavarero, "L'elaborazione filosofica della differenza sessuale," in *La ricerca delle donne: Studi femministi in Italia,* ed. Maria Cristina Marcuzzo and Anna Rossi-Doria (Turin: Rosenberg & Sellier, 1987), pp. 180–81; my translation.

20. See Rosi Braidotti, "Commento alla relazione di Adriana Cavarero," in *La ricerca delle donne: Studi femministi in Italia,* ed. Maria Cristina Marcuzzo and Anna Rossi-Doria (Turin: Rosenberg & Sellier, 1987), pp. 188–202.

Note on Translation

Any act of translation is fraught with problems. The dense substratum of connotations, resonances, and implicit references that the history of a culture has sedimented into the words and phrases of its language is often simply untranslatable; thus the act of translation is often a rewriting of the original language (in this case, Italian) and a reconfiguration or interpretation of its plurivocal meaning by means of connotations and resonances built into the words and phrases of the second language (in this case, American English). For example, Italian does not normally use the word *gender* for the sex-based distinction between female and male, as English does. Instead, Italian uses *sesso,* "sex," and the adjective *sessuato/sessuata,* "sexed," where the English would say "gendered," as in the phrase "gendered thinking" *(pensiero sessuato)* or "gendered subject" *(soggetto sessuato).* The phrase "sexed subject" is also used in English, however, with a meaning distinct from "gendered subject." The translation "gendered subject" was preferred here because it better conveys the sense of the original Italian. As for the common phrase *il sesso femminile,* it was more often rendered by the traditional English equivalent, "the female sex." Another problem is posed by the adjective *femminile,* which is translated as "female," although it also corresponds to the English "feminine." The latter, however, is strongly resonant with "femininity," the ideological construct of woman's "nature," which feminism has taken pains to deconstruct; alternatively, outside the context of feminist discourse, the phrase "feminine freedom" sounds rather like an advertisement for "personal hygiene" products. Thus, in spite of the biological connotations that hover around the term *female,* that term was preferred in most instances: *libertà femminile,* for example, is translated as "female freedom."

Don't think you have any rights. That is, don't obscure or deform justice, but don't think that one can legitimately expect that things happen in a way that conforms with justice; especially since we ourselves are far from being just.

Vertical superimposition.

There is a bad way of believing we have rights, and a bad way of believing we do not have any.

—Simone Weil, *Notebooks*, II

INTRODUCTION

This book is about the need to make sense of, exalt, and represent in words and images the relationship of one woman to another. If putting a political practice into words is the same thing as theorizing, then this is a book of theory, because the relations between women are the subject matter of our politics and of this book. It is a book of theory, then, but interspersed with stories. We believe that to write theory is partly to tell about practice, since theoretical reasoning generally refers to things which already have names. Here we are dealing partly with things that had no names.

The events and ideas we talk about took place between 1966 and 1986, mainly in Milan. They generally go under the name of feminism. We would now like to bring to light their true meaning and therefore their name as well. That name is "genealogy." In the years and places we mention, we saw a genealogy of women being charted; that is, women appeared who were legitimized by referring to their female origin.

Saying this is exciting, because the outcome is still uncertain. We are not certain that the history reconstructed in this book will really produce what we wanted, that is, to be inscribed in a female generation. We cannot be sure that, put to the test, our experience will prove to be only one of the many historical vicissitudes of the fragile concept of woman.

The study of linguistics informs us that the root *gen* in words such as *genus, genealogy, generation* characterizes words traditionally associated with birth as a social event, and, strictly speaking, it refers to the legitimate birth of free male individuals.[1] In our culture, as Luce Irigaray has pointed out, the representation of the mother-daughter relationship is missing; a mother always carries a son in her arms.[2]

Among the things that had no name, there was, there is, the pain of coming into the world this way, without a symbolic placement. Human beings are made up of mind and body, they are born and find themselves by chance in a given place at a given time, and their minds begin trying to place themselves, to search for reference points. The body is physically located, but the mind must decide its own location for itself, with the help of those who came before. If you are born a woman, what help do you get? Society intends for the female mind to be located with the body and like the body. Either there or no other place.

Anthropologists tell us that human society is based on the exchange of signs, goods, and women.³ It is a strange way of representing things, an artificial, scientifically simple way of hiding the horrible disorder caused by the domination of one sex by the other, the violent destruction of relations between women, starting with the mother-daughter relationship, which is often accompanied by a woman's not being able to control her own production, and which is nearly always connected with a woman's difficulty in producing original signs: with whom, after all, can she exchange them; what can they signify?

When we think about women's condition, we are usually aware of the confusion caused by their/our being transplanted into masculine genealogies, the confusion between a woman's corporeal being and her conceptual being. This brings about a state known as female hysteria, which is female almost by definition. In the streets of your city, you too must have noticed young women, often very young, mere teenagers, walking by themselves, concentrating, as if on a definite errand. But they do not have one; they are just walking purposefully to and fro. However, they take the same route day after day after day.

According to accepted terminology, these are the rituals of obsessional neurosis, rituals which, in this case, are more female than male, although little is known about female obsessional neuroses. What we do know is that those women are trying to find a space-time in which to locate themselves symbolically, and their coming and going like that is an attempt to obtain a rational body for themselves, to design a topology where they can get their mental bearings.

Virginia Woolf maintained that in order to do intellectual work, one needs a room of one's own.⁴ However, it may be impossible to keep still and apply oneself to work in that room because the texts and their subjects seem like extraneous, oppressive blocks of words and facts through which the mind cannot make its way, paralyzed as it is by emotions which have no corresponding terms in language. The room of one's own must be understood differently, then, as a symbolic placement, a space-time furnished with female gendered references, where one goes for meaningful preparation before work, and confirmation after.

Like Emily Dickinson's room was for her. Her solitude, writes Ellen Moers, was broken only by the spiritual presence of women writers. Emily knew them solely, though intimately, from reading their works and anything else she could find out about their lives. She was scandalously ignorant of the great male writers: it seems she never read a line by Poe, Melville, or Irving. Instead she read and reread all the English and American women writers of her time: Eliot, Barrett Browning, the Brontë sisters, and then Helen Hunt Jackson, Lydia Maria Child, Harriet Beecher Stowe, Lady Georgina Fullerton, Dinah Maria Craik, Elisabeth Stuart Phelps, Rebecca Harding Davis. Between them and her, as another scholar of this great American poet has pointed out, one feels a close relationship, a sort of familiarity coming from close association.

Emily Dickinson had memorized almost all of the poem *Aurora Leigh* by Elizabeth Barrett Browning. She referred to its author as "the world's Aurora" and considered her her mentor. According to Moers, Dickinson created some of her verses by elaborating emotional content, not from her own personal life, but which she learned about by reading *Aurora Leigh*. "Emily Dickinson was self-consciously feminine in poetic voice, and more boldly so than is often recognized. It was here, I suspect, that Mrs. Browning meant the most to Dickinson, in her confident use of female experience and female accessories—the clothes, the looks, the domestic chores of a woman—for universal purposes."[5]

We have discovered that the search for symbolic reference points provided by other women is a very ancient search and has often taken the same form as the one we have given it: a relationship of entrustment, as in the story of Naomi and Ruth told in the Bible.[6] The Book of Ruth tells us that at the time of the Judges, a man from Bethlehem left his town because of a famine and went to the land of Moab with his wife, Naomi, and their two sons. The man died, and the sons married two Moabite women, Orpah and Ruth. After ten years, the sons died, and Naomi was left, a widow in a foreign country, with two widowed daughters-in-law. Later, having learned that her country was again flourishing, she decided to return there.

Naomi set out and, having gone halfway, she kissed her daughters-in-law and told them: "Go, return each to her mother's house: the Lord deal kindly with you, as ye have dealt with the dead, and with me. The Lord grant you that ye may find rest, each of you in the house of her husband." The two young women burst into tears and asked her to let them stay with her. Naomi reasoned with them: "I am too old to have a husband. If I should say, I have hope, if I should have a husband also to-night, and should bear also sons; Would ye tarry for them till they were grown?" Orpah kissed Naomi and went back. Ruth did not move. "Behold," said Naomi, "thy sister-in-law is gone back unto her people, and unto her gods: return thou after thy sister-in-law." "Entreat me not to leave thee," answered Ruth; "whither thou goest, I will go; and where thou lodgest, I will lodge: thy people shall be my people, and thy God my God. Where thou diest, will I die, and there will I be buried: the Lord do so to me, and more also, if aught but death part thee and me."

Naomi, seeing her so determined, took her along, and they reached Bethlehem, where the women recognized Naomi in spite of the many years that had passed. The barley harvest had just begun, the Book of Ruth tells us, and it goes on to explain how Ruth, carefully following Naomi's instructions, succeeded in becoming the wife of a good rich man, Boaz, and bearing him a son and heir. After the birth of the child, the neighbors said to Naomi: "Blessed be the Lord, which hath not left thee this day without a kinsman. . . . And he shall be unto thee a restorer of thy life, and a nourisher of thine old age: for thy daughter-in-law, which loveth thee, which is better to thee than seven sons, hath borne him." Naomi lifted up the child and placed him on her lap, and the neighbor women congratulated her, saying: "There is a son born to Naomi."

We have given a name to the relationship between Ruth and Naomi; we have called it "entrustment." It must be remembered, in fact, that in the many languages springing from a millenary culture, there were no names for such a social relationship, or for any other relationship between women for themselves.

The name "entrustment" is beautiful; it contains the root of such words as *true, trust, entrust, troth, truth*. However, some women do not like it because it has come to connote a social relationship which our legal system envisions between an adult and a child. The entrustment of one woman to another can, in fact, involve a female child and an adult woman, but this is only one of its possible forms. We have envisioned it as primarily a kind of relationship between adult women. It offended some women that in such a relationship, one of the two partners is thus put in the same position as a little girl.

No one who objected to the word, however, made an issue of it, and we could overlook it. Yet that drawing back from a word that in itself is beautiful, simply because of the way others use it, is a symptom of impotence in front of what has already been thought by others, in this case what has already been thought about the relationships between children and adults, and what would or would not be proper for an adult woman.

It often happens that language imposes on us the domination of others' experiences and judgments in many areas. Language in itself does not imply the dominance of one kind of experience or thought to the exclusion of others. However, language is part of the fabric of social relations, and these are not favorably disposed to a woman's experiencing and wanting things for herself in her difference from man.

It is very likely that none of us were taught that we needed to take special care of our relations with other women and to consider them an irreplaceable source of personal strength, originality of mind, and social self-assurance. And it is difficult even to have any notion of how necessary this is because in the culture we receive, a few products of female origin have been preserved, but not their symbolic matrix, so that they appear to us as regenerated by male thought.

Now, our political experience of relations between women has allowed us to examine past events more carefully. Thus, to our great surprise, we discovered that from the earliest times, there have been women who worked to establish social relationships favorable to themselves and to other women. And female greatness was often (perhaps always?) nourished by the thought and energy which circulated among women.

During the years when Jane Austen was becoming a supreme writer of English prose, her letters show that her daily "nourishment" consisted of the fiction written by women of her day. She read Harriet Burney, Jane West, Anna Maria Porter, Anne Grant, Ann Radcliffe, Laetitia Matilda Hawkins, Elisabeth Hamilton, Helen Maria Williams. . . .[7]

The disparity between Jane Austen and these authors is so great as not to leave any doubt about the way they must have been of help to her. Like her, they were women who wrote and were published. They were the trailblazers and provided a useful comparison in her effort to portray in words reality as it appeared to her, a woman. She did not look for a model among the few male writers with whom she was familiar, such as her beloved Samuel Johnson or the famous Walter Scott. She preferred the women writers because she felt the most elementary kind of harmony with them, on the levels of reality where the great artist, male or female, works and excels. The results were seven perfect novels that make Jane Austen a master of English prose and of the modern novel.

In spite of this, a woman in our society today can reach the highest level of education or perform the most demanding tasks in almost any field without knowing anything about the way in which Jane Austen became so great in her field. Without realizing, that is, what mental vigor a woman can acquire by associating with her fellow women.

In emancipated societies, the limits imposed on female desires have been enlarged, but the necessary strength to actualize them has not increased. The matrix of female strength is acted against even in emancipated societies, thus erasing past events as well as present considerations. An ancient myth alludes to this opposition, the myth of Persephone, or Proserpine, taken away from her mother, Demeter, by Pluto, who carried her off to the underworld. In modern times there is the story of Madame du Deffand and Mademoiselle de l'Espinasse.

In the eighteenth century, for a long time, Madame du Deffand had the most famous salon in Paris. At that time, the salon was a place of more power and pleasure for women than we can imagine today, because in that century even men's politics were based on personal relationships, and the salons were a strategic locale for political plotting. Not for long, however. Political parties and other forms of political organization were coming to the fore. In Paris, the party of the "philosophers," the rationalists of the Enlightenment, was being formed. Madame du Deffand opposed it. She shared many of their ideas and was a friend of many of the philosophers, especially Voltaire, but she opposed their party, which was beyond her range of action and her way of thinking about politics.

Benedetta Craveri, author of a detailed historical study entitled *Madame du Deffand and Her World,* tells us about the complicated and subtle maneuvers that Madame du Deffand used in order to get one of her brother's illegitimate daughters, Mademoiselle de l'Espinasse (whose intelligence and sensitivity had charmed her), to come to Paris and be her companion. The story is then told of their relationship, which lasted ten years and finally broke up because the younger woman went against the wishes of her protectrix and met D'Alembert and others in the philosophers' party on her own.[8]

Madame du Deffand was the perpetuator of a tradition of female knowledge and prestige which had been formed over time, starting with such other great ladies as Madame de la Fayette and Madame de Sevigné. Mademoiselle de l'Espinasse breaks with that tradition, which she misunderstood rather than rejected. With her begins the long series—not yet ended—of intelligent, passionate women who fight for a cause or an ideal that is almost always just, but which has no relation with the concerns of their fellow women—the Saint Theresas, founders of nothing, as George Eliot calls them.[9]

No one intervened violently between the old lady and her young friend as

Pluto did with Demeter and Persephone. Their bond broke because the young woman preferred the authority of the thought that dominated the historical scene of the time to the authority of female thought. Naturally. However, the consequences were that she did not understand what was happening on the historical scene, because, without the ideas given by her belonging to the female sex, her being a woman ceased to be enlightening and returned to being a shadowy part of a history enlightened exclusively by the plans of men.

Thus we see that female descendence can be threatened by women themselves. This possibility was written about in novel form in *The Bostonians* by Henry James. He tells the story of Olive Chancellor, a wealthy and determined Boston feminist, who is full of ideas. She meets Verena, a young woman of charismatic communicative power. Olive perceives that she is gifted and teaches Verena her new ideas. She makes a great orator out of her, and takes her into her home until the day when Basil Random, a Southern gentleman who is Olive's cousin, convinces Verena to leave Olive in order to marry him.

The circumstances in which Verena makes her final decision are incredibly theatrical. The situation described reflects a social reality which was typical of New England, where many female friendships had some of the characteristics of matrimony—so much so that they were referred to as "Boston marriages." These were stable relationships between two women who were economically independent, sometimes lived together, and were often active in struggles for social justice. James was well informed about this new kind of social relationship, because in the last ten years of her short life, his sister, Alice, was united to a woman, Katherine Loring, in one of these so-called Boston marriages.

The way the relationship between Olive and Verena ends is portrayed as James imagined it might. The relationships about which we have historical information were usually solid. He is, however, correct in pointing out the structural fragility of this type of social relation, imperiled not by one single man's charm, but by that of male sexuality—by a sexuality, that is, based on the social homosexuality of the father-son relationship extolled in all dominant forms of knowledge and power.

After one or two generations, in the same country that had watched female friendship be transformed into a solid and coherent social relation, we find the friends of Mary McCarthy's *The Group*, educated but confused women, without plans for themselves and without a trace of the vigor of their ancestresses. Can one ever forget the figure of the Vassar graduate who, though almost flat-chested, painfully persists in breastfeeding her newborn son to please her husband, who is a scientific supporter of natural feeding?

It seems as if the matrix of female strength can be lost with the passing of one generation. But then in other circumstances, in other ways, it comes back into existence. This may be because of the irrepressible need to find a faithful mediation between oneself and the world: someone similar to oneself who acts as a mirror and a term of comparison, an interpreter, a defender and judge in the negotiations between oneself and the world. The circumstances and the ways are almost always those of personal friendship, because there are no other social forms in which a woman can satisfy her need for self-verification through a fellow creature.

It is perhaps for this reason that women take care of their friendships and are more expert in the art of giving shape to a friendship—as Vita Sackville-West wrote in a letter to Virginia Woolf, after she had been her friend for three years. Vita, the "beautiful aristocrat," author of books of uncertain merit but certain sales, was thirty years old when she first met Virginia Woolf, who was forty, a renowned writer and owner (along with her husband, Leonard) of a small, sophisticated publishing house, the Hogarth Press. Even before she met her, Vita thought of Virginia as her "gentle genius." When they met, Virginia suggested an arrangement which would be profitable to both of them, that is, that Vita publish her books through the Hogarth Press.

From then on, Vita had to submit her facile, superficial prose to the criticisms made by Virginia, who became and remained the only person in the world capable of telling her with brutal frankness what was wrong with her writing—and what was right. Vita accepted that and was grateful. Both women recognized Virginia's superiority. It was not, however, a teacher-student relationship in which one person tries to pattern the other on herself. On the contrary, Virginia extolled Vita's diversity; she thought her way of writing sumptuous and full-bodied; sometimes she was openly envious of her ease with language.

Virginia and Vita backed each other up publicly for years. Vita reviewed and praised Woolf's books in articles and on radio programs. Although they were both very busy women, when one of them had to appear in public at a conference or a ceremony, the other would be present to support and congratulate her. This went on until the war intervened and Virginia, the more fragile of the two, died. To Vita she dedicated *Orlando*, the only novel she had written happily and almost easily.

Hence we see that the symbolic matrix which was torn apart reestablished itself and began to nourish the female mind again. Concurrently, the sexual difference, which does not consist in this or that content but in the references and relations inside which existence is inscribed, began to signify itself again.

It is more important to have authoritative female interlocutors than to have recognized rights. An authoritative interlocutor is necessary if one wants to articulate one's own life according to a project of freedom and thus make sense of one's being a woman. Without a symbolic placement, the female mind is afraid; exposed to unpredictable events, everything befalls it from outside the body. Neither laws nor rights can give a woman the self-confidence she lacks. A woman can acquire inviolability by creating a life which has its starting point in herself and is guaranteed by female sociality.

Having observed and weighed these things, we came to the conclusion that the entrustment of one woman to another is the stuff of political struggle. So we also decided to write this book, which documents our political history. One factor outweighed the others: seeing that women entrust themselves spontaneously to each other but almost without understanding the power of this act. For example, the women who enter male organizations often help each other by entrustment in order to acquire self-confidence and to get some ideas of their own about their situation, more or less as Vita and Virginia did in their literary careers.

To entrust herself to another woman is often, if not always, indispensable if a woman is to achieve a social aim. It is therefore a primary political form for her, and this must be known and asserted, if necessary, even against forms judged to be primary by men in their organizations. The politics of claiming one's rights, no matter how just and how deeply felt it is, is a subordinate kind of politics, and a politics of subordination, because it is based on what seems just according to a reality designed and supported by men, and because logically it uses their political form.

A politics of liberation, as we have called feminism, must give a foundation to women's freedom. The social relationship of entrustment between women is both a content and an instrument of this most basic struggle. Of course, when entrustment is no longer a secondary personal relation or one silent with regard to other social relations, and becomes itself a social relation, the ways and the consequences of practicing it will change too.

The masculine forms of politics, as of various other things, are not simply different from the forms which are closer to women's experience. They are often different and hostile because they aim at universality and therefore are against the signification of sexual difference. It is an unequal battle: power, tradition, the material and symbolic means are all on one side; no need to say which. But on the women's side there remains, indestructible, the fact that a woman cannot be unaware of the human difference involved in being born a woman.

The problem is to unite this knowledge of gendered duality to great human demands and achievements. Some women have done it. They are few, however; more often a woman aware of her difference interprets it as meaning that she must either give it up or subordinate herself, while the woman who wishes neither to give it up nor subordinate herself ends up denying that she belongs to the female human race.

Every time that a woman's great demands and achievements have been united to the knowledge of sexual difference, we find that she had recourse to another woman as a point of reference. Among the stories that come to mind, there is one which in some ways is the strangest, as well as the simplest and the most explicit: the story of the writing-on-the-wall. The protagonist of this story was the poet H. D. (Hilda Doolittle, 1886–1961), and she herself tells about it in her short book dedicated to Freud: *Tribute to Freud*.[10] Here it is in her own words.

". . . as the Professor picked on the writing-on-the-wall as the most dangerous or the only actually dangerous 'symptom,' we will review it here." The Professor is Freud, whom H. D. consulted in 1930 for analysis. "The series of shadow- or of light-pictures I saw projected on the wall of a hotel bedroom in the Ionian island of Corfu, at the end of April 1920, belong in the sense of quality and intensity, of clarity and authenticity, to the same psychic category as the dream of the Princess, the Pharaoh's daughter, coming down the stairs."

H. D. went to Corfu together with a young acquaintance. Previously she had explained how, a year before, she had been close to losing her health and her life. "The material and spiritual burden of pulling us out of danger," she tells us, "fell upon a young woman whom I had only recently met. . . . Her pseudonym is Bryher. . . ." Bryher organized a trip to Greece for both of them; ". . . she would take me . . . to the land, spiritually of my predilection, geographically of my dreams." "Perhaps my trip to Greece, that spring, might have been interpreted as a flight from reality. Perhaps my experiences there might be translated as another flight—from a flight. There were wings anyway."

According to the Professor's interpretation, the vision of the writing-on-the-wall meant that she desired to remain united to her mother. "I may say that never before and never since have I had an experience of this kind. I saw a dim shape forming on the wall. . . ." It was an indistinct human figure—"It was a silhouette cut of light, not shadow, and so impersonal it might have been anyone. . . ."

The vision then became more distinct and was transformed in front of H. D.'s attentive, immobile eyes. "But here I pause or the hand pauses—it is as if there were a slight question as to the conclusion or direction of the symbols." "That is in myself . . . —a wonder as to the seemliness, or the safety even, of continuing this experience or this experiment. For my head, although it cannot have taken very long in clock-time for these pictures to form there, is already warning me that this is an unusual dimension, an unusual way to *think*, that my brain or mind may not be equal to the occasion."

While she is reconstructing that faraway event, she remembers the interpretation Freud gave it in 1930, and thinks: perhaps the Professor was right, perhaps it really was a "dangerous symptom." She had always considered it an "inspiration," a poetic inspiration in a pure state, a vision of "writing which writes itself."

The story continues. "But it is no easy matter to sustain this mood, this 'symptom' or this inspiration. And there I sat and there is my friend Bryher who has brought me to Greece. I can turn now to her, though I do not budge an inch or break the sustained crystal-gazing stare at the wall before me. I say to Bryher, 'There have been pictures here—I thought they were shadows at first, but they are light, not shadow. They are quite simple objects—but of course it's very strange. I can break away from them now, if I want—it's just a matter of concentrating—what do you think? Shall I stop? Shall I go on?' Bryher says without hesitation, 'Go on.'"

The vision is disturbed however, by a buzzing mass of moving black dots. ". . . They were people, they were annoying—I did not hate people. I did not especially resent any one person. I had known such extraordinarily gifted and charming people. They had made much of me or they had slighted me and yet neither praise nor neglect mattered in the face of the gravest issues—life, death. (I had had my child, I was alive.) And yet, so oddly, I knew that this experience, this writing-on-the-wall before me, could not be shared with them—could not be shared with anyone except the girl who stood so bravely there beside me. This girl had said without hesitation, 'Go on.' It was she really who had the detachment and the integrity of the Pythoness of Delphi. But it was I, battered and disassociated from my American family and my English friends, who was seeing the pictures, who was reading the writing or who was granted the inner vision. Or perhaps in some sense, we were 'seeing' it together, for without her, admittedly, I could not have gone on."

The description of the vision goes on until the moment in which, writes H. D., ". . . I shut off, 'cut out' before the final picture, before (you might say) the explosion took place. But though I admit to myself that now I have had enough, maybe just a little too much, Bryher, who has been waiting by me, carries on the 'reading' where I left off. Afterwards she told me that she had seen nothing on the wall there, until I dropped my head in my hands. She had been there with me patient, wondering, no doubt deeply concerned and not a little anxious as to the outcome of my state or mood. But as I relaxed, let go, from complete physical and mental exhaustion, she saw what I did not see. It was the last section of the series, or the last concluding symbol. . . ." "She said it was a circle like the sun-disk and a figure within the disk; a man, she thought, was reaching out to draw the image of a woman (my Niké) into the sun beside him."

Nike, or Victory, was the last of the figures to appear on the wall, and the author had described her minutely: "She is a common-or-garden angel, like any angel you may find on an Easter or Christmas card." She was made of light like the first three symbols, which she also called "my three cards." "But unlike them, she is not flat or static, she is in space, in unwalled space, not flat against the wall, though she moves upward as against its surface. She is a moving-picture and fortunately she moves swiftly. Not swiftly exactly but with a sure floating that at least gives my mind some rest, as if my mind had now escaped the bars of that ladder, no longer climbing or caged but free and with wings."

"The Professor translated the pictures on the wall . . . as a desire for union with my mother." Without contradicting him, H. D. gives a different interpretation, or rather two different interpretations, for the writing which appeared on the wall. "We can read or translate it as a suppressed desire for forbidden 'signs and wonders,' breaking bounds, a suppressed desire to be a Prophetess. . . . Or this writing-on-the-wall is merely an extension of the artist's mind, a *picture* or an illustrated poem, taken out of the actual dream or daydream content and projected from within. . . ."

In any case, it was a fundamental experience, an experience in which the stuff of past life was transformed into writing. It gave H. D. the feeling that she had a poetic vocation, together with the certainty that all this was possible because of the woman who was beside her and who, at the decisive moment, said to her: "Go ahead."

CHAPTER ONE

Now we want to tell how what those great women gained for themselves became a gain for us as well. It will be, necessarily, a partial telling. Among the things we cannot explain, because we have no documentation for them, one at least must be mentioned, and that is the effect that every woman's real mother has on her. Our mothers gave us the idea that the female gender can attain greatness, that first ingenuous idea which we then asked her—almost always in vain—to confirm. Most of the time, she knew nothing more about it, or if she did know something more, she was so confused about it that she made things harder for us.

The first groups: Demau and Rivolta femminile

The first document of Italian feminism is dated December 1, 1966, and is entitled "Manifesto programmatico del gruppo Demau" [Manifesto of the Demau Group's Program].[1] Demau was the abbreviation for "demystification of patriarchal authoritarianism." Actually, neither the group nor its declaration had much to do with demystifying authoritarianism.

The main subject of the declaration, and of the texts that came after it—in 1967, "Alcuni problemi sulla questione femminile" [Some Problems on the Woman Question], and in 1968, "Il maschile come valore dominante" [The Masculine as Dominant Value]—was the contradiction between women and society. There is contradiction, because women are a problem for society. But if it is a contradiction, then it follows that society in turn is a problem for women.

This was the new view put forward by Demau. Women are a social problem, the problem which at the time was called "the woman question," and which cannot be solved until women on their part pose it as the problem which society is for them; that is, it cannot be solved as long as one goes on thinking and reasoning about women from the socio-historical point of view without ever turning the perspective upside down and putting women, putting ourselves as women, in the position of subjects who rethink history and society, starting with ourselves.

The title of the third point in the Manifesto programmatico del gruppo Demau is "Ricerca di una autonomia da parte della donna" [Women's Search for Autonomy]. The gist of it is that "such a search presupposes a new, broader methodology of investigation into women's position in society, one which does not consider it simply in its historical, evolutionary aspect as the 'female condition.' " It is not enough to study women's conditioning; we must consider "woman as both object and autonomous subject of analysis."

Demau's controversial, principal target is the politics of "integrating women into today's society." Their polemic is especially directed against the "numerous women's associations and movements which are interested in women and their emancipation." Demau maintains that these associations try to "facilitate the emancipation of women and insert them into society as it is." They do not put society into question starting from themselves as women, but put themselves into question insofar as they are part of society, "that is, a traditionally male-decisional society."[2]

The authors are consistent in attacking all kinds of favored treatment, laws, or other statutes reserved only for women so that, when they must, or want to, enter the work force, they can go on assuming the traditional female role. It is not by chance that the work women do outside the home is called "extra-domestic." In essence, a woman remains "a reproducer of the species and a worker in the domestic sphere." The society into which she enters this way teaches her that the feminine is "without any social value." The consequences are that every woman, confronted "by the masculine world," has only two alternatives: "masculinizing herself," or taking refuge in the traditional feminine role. In any case, the "essence of male power and of the society which is based on it" remains unchanged.

The politics of integration is therefore said to "be a placebo for the real ill." It "gives women external assistance in order to integrate them into a masculine world," but "this world remains opposed to them because it is masculine, that is, founded on women's exclusion, while women are at the center of another, clearly separate kind of world."

In the Demau texts, little is said about "this clearly separate other world" and about "the real ill." Both things—the separateness of a woman's experience and the division she experiences on entering social life—are alive and present in those who are writing the texts, one feels, but as yet have no expression. In just this way, by their material but wordless presence, the other world and the real ill surface in the texts—for example, in the difficult passage in "Conclusioni rapidissime" [Quick Conclusions] at the end of "Alcuni Problemi," where an answer is sought for the question "What does all this mean insofar as feminist issues are concerned?" The answer is: "It means that a woman should, first of all, disregard her gender, which should be, and is, a secondary accident of her being and existence, in order to repudiate everything that, theorized, affirmed, and desired by the structure of a male chauvinist society, ties her to it and confirms it." This is then amended: "Not in order to repudiate sex and its fruits, but to free herself from the snares and limitations that these two terms (*sex* and *children*), as interpreted by others and not by herself, have constituted for woman in the history of her evolution."

Female experience is extraneous because others dictate its meaning according to their own experience, in lieu of the person who lives through it and who therefore finds herself ensnared in it like an animal in a trap. This is a sexual difference which marks the female body without leaving signs, words, reasons, and thus her body itself becomes a trap for her, or part of one. Hence the terrible invitation to "repudiate" a part of her own experience, the part that others have defined and used in order to dominate her. And hence, as well, later on in the article, the invitation to women to find "the courage to start over again" in order to become conditioners instead of remaining "conditioned," to become "subjects of history," subjects who "make history."

The drastic determination which, when negative, forces one to repudiate experience, when positive calls forth a surprising, precious idea, that of a female "transcendence." This idea is not to be found in later feminist literature, with one notable exception which we will encounter shortly.

"As long as we are concerned only with solving women's problems," the 1967 text reads, "we will go on focusing on the female who, even if she has evolved, will never be a woman (a human being) with an autonomous transcendence." When women will no longer be assigned, by definition, to reproduction, when "the consequences of difference, of the duality of the sexes" will be "evaluated and equably sustained by both sexes," then, "basing herself on herself, thus liberated, a woman will be able to discover in herself and for herself a veritable and just transcendence." This is then explained as being an "achievement of consciousness which alone can assert itself as power and will in the history of humanity," in contrast with past history, where women "do not appear in a decisional context." The article goes on to ask women "to find the courage to start over again," the courage needed to make a radical reversal in the woman question and, finally, "a social revolution" based on women's freedom.

Some of these new ideas were destined to be widely accepted by women and developed further. Not immediately, however. Membership in the Demau group (organized in 1965) was small at the beginning. In 1968, this already small membership was halved. It was a favorable time for the pursuit of freedom, even for women; however, then, as on other similar occasions, many women preferred to go about this task by joining male groups and movements which were larger and (so it seemed at the time) more likely to attain their goals.

It must be said that the Demau analyses were difficult to assimilate not only because of their novelty but for another reason as well; that is, the idea of sexual difference was missing in them. These texts deal with that difference insofar as it is a biological fact, which is recognized as meaningful because it is necessary for the reproduction of the human species. That meaning, they say, is distorted by society when it puts the female sex in bondage: in fact, historically, women have been allocated to procreation as opposed to men, who "have had the opportunity to interpret their different sexual role" and in this way have been able to "transcend it" at women's expense.[3]

This conception of sexual difference, valid in itself, does not, however, explain the fact that that difference itself already speaks in the texts, with the consequence that the texts press for more radical conclusions, such as complete change, starting anew, social revolution. This imbalance causes the argument to proceed by turning round on itself like a screw, giving it substantial depth but making it difficult to understand.

In 1970, the "Manifesto di Rivolta femminile" [Manifesto of Women's Revolt] was published in Milan and Rome along with an essay by Carla Lonzi, *Sputiamo su Hegel* [We Spit on Hegel]. The language and content of the two texts show that the first one was written by her as well. A free thinker, Carla Lonzi had a lively way of expressing herself. The language of these two texts is inflammatory: short statements first pile up, one on top of another, then separate suddenly, just like the flames of a roaring fire. Her "Manifesto" is very different from that of the Demau group in language and in many other aspects, but they agree about the basic question.

"Man has interpreted woman," she writes, "according to an image of femininity which is an invention of his. . . . Man has always spoken in the name of the human race, but half of the human race now accuses him of having sublimated a mutilation. . . . we consider history incomplete because it was written, always, without regarding woman as an active subject of it." She goes on, "We have watched 4,000 years; now we have seen!"[4]

Woman carries out a symbolic revolution by putting herself in the position of the subject. Lonzi also considers this to be "starting over." As she says in *Sputiamo su Hegel*: "The unexpected fate of the world is to start its journey all over again in order to make it with woman as subject."[5]

The texts of Rivolta femminile state that the logical result of this revolution is the concept of sexual difference. In fact, the difference between man and woman is presented as something which cannot be left out of consideration. There is neither freedom nor thought for woman without the thought of sexual difference. The "Manifesto" starts with the idea that "woman must not-be defined in reference to man. Both our struggle and our freedom are based on this consciousness. Man is not the model for woman's process of self-discovery. Woman is other with respect to man. Man is other with respect to woman."[6]

The plan for equality between the sexes which claims to secure full human dignity for women is harshly rejected: "Equality is an ideological attempt to enslave woman at a higher level. To identify women with men is to eliminate their last road to liberation. Liberation, for women, does not mean accepting man's kind of life . . . but expressing their own sense of existence."[7]

In *Sputiamo su Hegel*, Carla Lonzi writes about the same subject, but with milder words: "Equality is a legal principle: it is the common denominator present in every human being to whom justice must be rendered. Difference is an existential principle that has to do with the modes of being human, the particularity of one's experiences, goals, possibilities, and one's sense of existence in a given situation and in the situations one wants to create. The difference between woman and man is the fundamental difference."[8]

It is in the last pages of this essay that we find, before it disappears for years, the idea of a female transcendence which had been formulated by the Demau women. "Man," Lonzi asserts, "searches for the meaning of life beyond and in opposition to life itself; for woman, life and its meaning overlap continually." Philosophy has spiritualized "this hierarchy of destinies" by saying that "woman is immanence, man transcendence." Contempt for the feminine is thus rationalized: "If femininity is immanence, man has had to negate it in order to start the process of history." Man, Lonzi comments, "has prevaricated, but about a necessary given," that is, the opposition between immanence and transcendence. To counter that, "woman need only pit her transcendence against his." "On what bases have philosophers acknowledged the act of masculine transcendence and denied it to woman?" The answer is that they have looked for "confirmation in the establishment of power"; that is, women's lack of power in patriarchal society was the reason philosophers did not perceive "a different kind of transcendence" of which woman can be the originator, but which in actual fact has "remained repressed."[9]

Here, as in the Demau articles, we have a theoretical frame which connects *consciousness of self, the desire to be free,* and *the will to exist,* woman's body and mind, beyond the limits of a condition determined by nature as well as by society. Culture springs from human beings' capacity for transcending themselves. In actual fact, this capacity is exercised by man at woman's expense, both in a material sense, by a division of labor in which woman is given the most repetitive daily tasks of survival, and in a symbolic sense, by a culture of subordination of the female to the male. Sexist domination is therefore an integral part of human culture. Even the concept of transcendence is marked by it, Lonzi tells us, but it should not be rejected, only corrected, by interpreting it according to sexual differences. The act of female transcendence is missing in human culture as well as in women's freedom—that extra act of existence that we can acquire by symbolically surpassing the limits of individual experience and of natural living.

In the '70s, with the widespread growth of collective political consciousness, the idea of transcendence disappears from the frame, with the result that the other two terms (i.e., the desire to be free and the will to exist) also lose part of their semantic power. The development of consciousness was, above all, in the sense of a consciousness of oppression, and on this basis the first identification with the oppressed female gender was carried out. Thus acquired, this new consciousness was not immediately consciousness of the self in a constitutive relationship with the world without any limits preset by nature or society. The scope of the liberty desired shrank correspondingly.

To explain that shrinking, one must realize how difficult it is to grasp and subsequently develop the concept of that "different kind" of transcendence. Besides, there was the most important problem of what political practice to follow. The women's movement started with the practice of small consciousness-raising groups, which was also its first political form. In these small, women-only groups, women could talk freely about their experiences, provided that they remained within the limits of what they had personally lived through. It was thanks to this strict adherence to personal, lived experience that women's difference was finally able to appear. But what did not, could not, appear was the idea that a woman has in herself the will to exceed the limits of her personal experience precisely in order to be faithful to it—which is her true, proper transcendence.

The practice of *autocoscienza* began to spread at the beginning of the '70s, in part thanks to Rivolta femminile, which followed the example and ideas of American feminism. The "Manifesto di Rivolta femminile" borrowed several ideas from American feminism as well as the certainty that it was interpreting an incipient mass movement. However, it did not depend on the practice of consciousness-raising for either its content or its language, just as the Demau articles did not, for obvious chronological reasons.

Autocoscienza, the first invention of feminist politics

The political practice of consciousness-raising was invented in the U.S., we do not know by whom, toward the end of the '60s. In Italy it was called *autocoscienza* [self-consciousness], a term adopted by Carla Lonzi, who organized one of the first Italian groups to adopt that practice. Groups of women met to talk about themselves, or about anything else, as long as it was based on their own personal experience. These groups were intentionally kept small and were not part of larger organizations. From 1970 on, groups of this kind were formed in every part of the industrialized world. The women's movement cannot be identified with the practice of *autocoscienza*, but the latter certainly contributed in a decisive way to make feminism a mass movement. It was a simple, ingenious practice.

Equality had not yet been attained when women began to have to bear the brunt of their new social standing as equals of men, together with that of continuing discrimination. It was too much; suddenly the prospect of becoming real equals with the opposite sex lost its attraction. Many turned their backs on that possibility and blazed an entirely different trail, that of women's separatism. Women have always been accustomed to meeting among themselves to talk about their problems far from masculine ears. *Autocoscienza* was grafted onto this widespread, though little-appreciated, social custom, and gave it political dignity. This is the way, it was said, that we participate in politics; other ways do not suit us, neither those of the great organizations nor those of democratic representation—and not even the new ways invented at that time by the youth movements to participate directly in the political process. In the one, as in the others, what we know and want is denied expression, or the necessary freedom of expression.

The small *autocoscienza* group was the social site where, for the first time, women could talk about their experience openly, and where this talk had acknowledged value. Before, that experience had been invisible, lost human material which the social body consumed almost without knowing it and to which it attached no value; it de-valued it. In Milan, *autocoscienza* was the predominant political practice between 1970 and 1974. Even groups such as Demau that had been formed with different characteristics adopted this technique.

Three publications which came out in those years attest to this: *Donne e' bello* [Woman Is Beautiful], which was published in 1972 by the Anabasi group organized two years earlier, and the first and second issues of *Sottosopra* [Upside Down], which came out in 1973 and 1974 respectively, on the initiative of several Milanese groups. The Anabasi magazine, which came out only once, contains almost nothing but American and French texts. The two issues of *Sottosopra* are devoted mainly, as the subtitle explains, to the "experiences of feminist groups in Italy."

The editorial that introduces *Donne e' bello* expresses the general feeling which is associated with the practice of *autocoscienza*. "We women," it begins, "have never really communicated with one another." Our first reaction is to "feel that problem as something personal," but it is a mistake to do so. In reality, our isolation derives from the "divisions between women created by men." Masculine culture has imposed on women an "oppressive straitjacket of models." Because of the "solitude" of our lives, these models have given each of us "the feeling that we are misfits, antisocial, neurotic, hysterical, crazy." "Isolated and unhappy," women tend to "think of their problems as personal defects." Those problems are, instead, "a social and political phenomenon," because they are common to all women. This discovery "has led to the movement," a great movement: women have begun "taking action all over the world."

However, the press falsifies the meaning of the movement; it attributes "ridiculous aims" to it in order to "mask the real reasons for our struggle." Men are not willing to modify "the present social status quo that guarantees them the monopoly of power." On the other hand, the editorial states, "we are not at all interested in sharing this competitive kind of power. . . . The masculine models are completely extraneous to our interests." We do not want to imitate men; on the contrary, we are pleased to "have been born female." "A new solidarity" has been created among women, one "from which we want to exclude antagonism, competition, and the mania for commanding and over-powering others." What we want is "to be able to experience the pleasure" of being women, and naturally "without having to submit to the yoke of subjugation and oppression which now afflicts us all."

They refuse, adamantly, to use others' ideas: "We want no intermediaries, no interpreters," that is, men. "We no longer believe what men, politicians or journalists, scientists or husbands, say about us, about our destiny, about our desires and duties" (the whole sentence is underlined). But what if the intermediaries were women, like the authors of the editorial and the essays they are presenting? This hypothesis is not taken into consideration. The collection of essays is merely "an invitation to women to express themselves," an aid in "overcoming their initial inhibitions." Feminism makes an exciting proposal: "Let us get rid of unacceptable structures and assumptions, so that true thoughts and feelings can flow freely." Women must no longer conform to others' opinions; we have finally attained the "freedom to think, say, do, and be what *we decide to,* including the freedom to make mistakes," which for some women was "the most liberating thing." The editorial ends by asking its readers for contributions. Like the *autocoscienza* groups, this journal offers "a space for talk, where everything that each of you says is important and increases the level of your, and other women's, consciousness."[10]

The practice of *autocoscienza* was backed by a partly explicit, partly implicit theory which is evident in the text we have been quoting. First of all, there is the notion of the small group, which was fully developed by American feminists. The editorial does not mention it, but the journal includes several essays on the subject. Second, there is the thesis that personal experience (and therefore also the words that express it) has intrinsic authenticity. That authenticity is thought to be absolute, in the sense that there is no possible authenticity for women except in what they experience themselves. This position conflicts with the fact that, according to the editorial, there are women who spontaneously think and act in wrong ways (for example, they are competitive, or they feel guilty when they dedicate time to themselves). This apparent difficulty is solved by the positing of an external agent: women are subject to these conflicts within themselves or in their relationships because of what men say and do.

The idea of a female mediation between oneself and the world is not, as we saw, taken into consideration, in spite of the fact that the journal is committed to explaining the ideas (of which some are theoretical) of women to other women. In the context of *autocoscienza,* this was no incongruity. The practice of *autocoscienza,* in fact, presupposed and promoted a perfect reciprocal identification. I am you, you are me; the words that one of us uses are women's words, hers and mine. Of course, this is valid to the extent that the woman who is speaking has attained self-consciousness, since consciousness is the political act in which one discovers and affirms women's common identity. When that common identity is recognized, it has the power of uniting women among themselves as much as, and better than, any organization could.

Lastly, *autocoscienza* groups thought that words have a liberating effect. That idea may have come from psychoanalytic therapy, in a revised version. In fact, the liberating effect comes from words exchanged in groups and among women, without the help of interpretation, because what women suffer from, basically, is not speaking for themselves, not saying by themselves what they are and what they want, but saying it instead to themselves, with the words of others.

Look at yourself and change

If we compare the content of the first feminist documents (those of Demau and Rivolta femminile), which were not inspired by *autocoscienza*, with the content which this practice caused to emerge, it is striking how much more the theme of women's oppression is stressed in the latter and how, on the contrary, thought devoted to reality is not expressed there, except for matters having to do with women's condition of subordination to men. It must, however, be added that the theory-practice of *autocoscienza* was devised in such a way as to be able to be shaped by individual women. There were some groups, starting with Demau and Rivolta femminile, that limited the consideration of experiences with men so as to focus attention on other relationships or to illuminate moments of autonomy in women's lives.

In the first issue of *Sottosopra*, there are relatively few articles which reflect the practice of *autocoscienza*. These are very good, as are the things we sometimes say without having to search for the right words. The other, more numerous essays are discussions of feminist politics.

Some feminists had wanted this "newspaper," as it was called, in order to satisfy the "most important need, for knowledge and exchange among already extant groups," and thus to be the means for the formation of "a feminist *movement* which is something more than the more or less well known existence of various groups of women." The introductory note explains that they propose to "construct a reality that differs from the small group, something vaster, more complex, which is not an alternative, of course, but simply has different functions from those of the small group." The small group is where self-consciousness is attained, while the movement must satisfy the "need to do something which has an effect on the reality in which we ive."[11]

The desire to modify social reality existed, therefore, but according to the authors of this introduction, the small group was not able to satisfy it. Rivolta femminile contradicts this view in that same issue: it claims to exist and consist exclusively in "its *autocoscienza* groups."[12] So does an article by Demau that says: "we do not want to turn away from women; hence we will continue to exist as a small group."[13]

The journal contained several other contradictions as well. It could do so because its intention was to "faithfully reflect the true state of the movement," which it presented, however, not as riddled by internal contradictions but as "made up of many unconnected groups doing very different things." The journal proposed to both reflect and change this state of affairs by fostering knowledge and confrontation between the groups.

Faithful reflection was therefore understood to be an instrument of change for the reality it mirrored, an idea which arose from the very heart of the practice of *autocoscienza*. Each woman, finding her exact reflection in a fellow woman, discovers that she is different from what she thought she was and recognizes in her new image what she had always been without knowing it. *Autocoscienza* had that power and that limit: it could not show differences between women because "I am you, you are me." If differences arose, they were noted insofar as they were able to bring about reciprocal change, so that reciprocal identification could be again set up and was reinforced by this experience. Those were the years when sexual difference was confirmed this way: by the search for oneself in one's fellow women.

Although rarely mentioned explicitly, the practice of *autocoscienza* influenced the tone of the whole first *Sottosopra,* as it did the Anabasi review; both were conceived from the practice of a small group where every woman could speak knowing that her words would be listened to and not judged. According to the explicit statement of the editors, any woman and any group of women not connected to male organizations could publish material in *Sottosopra.* The editors promised not to turn down any articles. All those sent to them were guaranteed publication. This was done, and new, unforeseen problems cropped up.

The second issue, which came out in 1974, opened with a "debate on the role of *Sottosopra.*" The first article was written by Lotta femminista [Feminist Struggle], a political group well known because it fought for salaries for housewives. In this article they affirm peremptorily that if the review wants to talk about "experiences," as its subtitle proclaims, then it must talk above all "about feminist activism in factories, in neighborhoods, in consulting rooms; and make use of all available information about the actual state of oppression and exploitation of the female masses."[14]

This is followed by the troubled "contributions of several Milanese feminists who have followed the progress of *Sottosopra.*" By "followed the progress" must be understood: packaged. They are editors in the sense we explained above, that is, those women who were wholly responsible for the venture, from printing to distribution, but who had no editorial powers. They had given these up as a calculated political risk. One woman reaffirms the idea: "Making a collection of experiences will serve as an incentive to personal responsibility and activity." Others begin to have doubts because the first issue of the journal did not attain the results hoped for: "A year has passed since *Sottosopra* first came out, and the expanded debate we need so desperately has not yet taken place. . . ."

Doubts about the paper itself are also expressed. "When we were discussing the first issue as well as the second," one woman writes, "I was one of those who insisted that *Sottosopra* had to publish everything," but there are some "risks: for example, the risk of boredom (because of articles which are too long or old hat), of repetition (several pieces on the same subject), of giving too much space to those who are stubborn enough to demand it." This may be an allusion to Lotta femminista, which, though it had its own publications, sent *Sottosopra* long articles which were all a bit alike, and moreover defended positions, such as salaries for housewives, which the editors opposed. Another woman put her finger on the real problem, the contradiction which is created by the fact that, in guaranteeing space to women's words, you may end up impoverishing them owing to the effect of a "static coupling of proposals and views which are angled differently."

In spite of these doubts, it was decided to bring out the second issue "more or less following the same project as the first."[15] The result was more voluminous and more boring than the first. It included quite a few articles which, taken singly, would have been lively and original. But as the aforementioned reader observed, their static coupling stifles them. As a matter of fact, it proved impossible to find enough people to produce *Sottosopra* according to the original formula. A "journal group" survived which, however, did not succeed in producing anything concrete. There were other issues of *Sottosopra*, but their project was different.

The original idea of producing something new by adjoining different views was abandoned for reasons that had less to do with the journal than with the politics that shaped it. The effect of boredom, or worse, of powerlessness, generated by this collection of so many different experiences began to weigh on even the small *autocoscienza* group.

The sense of growing dissatisfaction is evident in many texts published in the second *Sottosopra*. They mostly say that *autocoscienza* is all well and good, *but* it is not enough. So they try to figure out what to add or how to strengthen and develop it. To take only one example, "Esperienza alla Feda" [An Experience at the Feda Factory], written by women who had joined women workers in an occupied factory: "Going personally to see what was happening fulfilled the need we felt to go beyond the work of *autocoscienza* done in groups. We recognize that that is an essential method of attaining consciousness individually and collectively, but by itself it is not enough," because "it makes us aware, but does not give us the instruments for change; it does not help us develop the contractual power we need to transform society, but only consciousness and anger."[16]

Actually, by now the practice of *autocoscienza* was producing a feeling of impotence for the simple reason that it had exhausted its potential. It was a limited political practice which could not be prolonged after it succeeded in making women conscious of being a separate sex, a sex neither subordinate nor assimilable to the male. It had removed woman's difference from the position of being spoken (by others), and had put her in the position of speaking for herself. Problems and contradictions grew out of this practice which the practice itself could not deal with, much less solve. Its very way of working—women listening to each other tell about feelings and events they had experienced in common— was limited. It was fascinating, by virtue of the fascinating discovery of her own self which each woman made in the mirror that was her fellow woman. There was certainly no hint of boredom or feeling of impotence in that act of discovery. But the appearance of boredom was a signal. Something new, not repetition, had to follow a discovery to keep it alive.

There are many signs of dissatisfaction in the essays which document this phase of passage, but no real criticism of *autocoscienza,* at least not by those who had thoroughly practiced it. They abandoned it simply because they had found something new to follow it. It must be said, however, that not everyone abandoned it. Rivolta femminile and many recently set-up groups kept the practice for several more years.

Those were years of triumphant feminism when new groups were continually being formed. Because it was so well known and ingeniously simple, *autocoscienza* was a practice that many women adopted spontaneously as they came close to feminism, so much so that in the women's movement *autocoscienza* was considered a sort of initiation rite throughout the '70s (though not later).

This practice left women's minds with an enduring delight in reasoning while remaining in contact with perceptible reality, and with the ability to use that contact with reality in elaborating theoretical thought. Without that delight and that ability, the original forms of "female transcendence" referred to by our first theorists might not have been discovered. The first issue of *Sottosopra* gives a good example of this in the article entitled "La nudità'" [Nudity].[17] There are others, such as "La violenza invisibile" [Invisible Violence],[18] in the second issue.

"La violenza invisibile" takes a position which is more anguished yet closer to the disappearing practice of *autocoscienza*. As it was dying out, the practice of women getting together to talk about their personal experiences generated, as we saw, a sense of dissatisfaction. Some said this was because it did not furnish us with the means to change the reality around us. But the article on "invisible violence" points to another, quite different complication. Out of those now-repetitive discussions, that harping on the painful aspects of the female condition, grew a dimly perceived anguish which had roots deep in places where the reasoning of political consciousness did not reach. This anguish was the fear of solitude, dependence on men, the absence of mother's love, the weakness of desire. . . .

In search of concepts: our meetings with the French women

The *autocoscienza* phase ended with a double, opposite movement of the female mind: introversion toward its obscure regions ("La violenza invisibile") and extroversion toward society ("Esperienza alla Feda"). Two theories, Marxism and psychoanalysis, could aid the female mind in its double movement. At the time, quite a few people thought that these two theories were compatible in some ways, in spite of their obvious differences. However, they presented an additional, serious, and unsolved problem for us. In both theories, the difference of being women was conceived of from a neutral-masculine point of view. For Marxism, women make up an oppressed social group whose liberation depends basically on the class struggle. For Freudian psychoanalysis, our difference from men is reduced to our lacking something men possess. In other versions, our difference disappears in an ideal complementarity between the sexes.

The details are not important here. The point is that the female mind needed concepts with which to think itself and the world, but the concepts which human culture offered were such that they denied that she was (inasmuch as she was female) a thinking principle.

In order to show that woman is the original principle of herself, the theory of *autocoscienza* excluded, as we know, any form of mediation. "From now on, we want no screen between ourselves and the world," reads the manifesto of Rivolta femminile, because "behind every ideology, we glimpse the hierarchy of the sexes."[19] Thus feminist thought was in a bind: it needed instruments with which to relate to itself and the world, but in order to save its own authenticity, it could use only the one, *autocoscienza,* which had become, however, unsatisfactory for many women.

In Milan, the women who found themselves in this situation did the following: they used the theoretical instruments that their culture offered and thought up a political practice that would adjust them so that they could serve to signify the original human difference in being a woman. In doing this, the Milanese women were inspired by the example of a group of French feminists known as Politique et psychanalyse (Politics and Psychoanalysis) which was organized in Paris in 1968.

The 1973 *Sottosopra* has a section devoted to foreign experiences where a brief article, "A proposito di una tendenza" [Concerning a Trend], by the French women was published. We are not a group, they write, but a current within the women's movement which is characterized by a social and ideological practice. "These two different levels of practice, in order not to be blind, anarchical, dogmatic, falsely revolutionary, idealist," must come to terms with Marxism and psychoanalysis. "Inventions are not made out of nothing; spontaneous generation does not exist." They therefore rejected *autocoscienza,* which, in fact, they had never practiced. They specify that it is not a question of privileging other theoretical discourses over our own political practice, but of "going through them again": "The available instruments of thought are already stamped with the masculine, bourgeois mark, just like everything else that surrounds us, for example, the most ordinary language. (Neutral language does not exist)." And they will stay this way "until we take them apart and analyze them so that we can go beyond them." How? "Starting from concrete contradictions on the ground level, on the level of the body, we will work hard to transform this social, political, ideological reality that censors us. . . . That transformation is a process of continual production of knowledge by and about women in themselves/for themselves."[20]

In 1972, the French women organized two international meetings, one of which lasted a whole week, at La Tranche (Vendée) under the auspices of the MLF [Mouvement de libération des femmes], and a five-day meeting near Rouen, which was organized entirely by Politique et psychanalyse. Several Italian women participated, and were thus able to get a concrete idea of the "laborious transformation" which the above article mentions; they were greatly impressed by it, both intellectually and emotionally.

A woman who calls herself "a comrade from Milan" ends the account of her stay at La Tranche (an account that appeared in the 1973 *Sottosopra*) with these words: "I became thoroughly convinced that we women, myself included, are not simply an oppressed caste that rebels; we are not only capable of making a correct analysis in order to work out an effective strategy; we are not just comrades in a struggle for liberation. . . . There is all of that, but it is leavened, you might say, made splendid and happy and powerful, by the evidence, which I experienced, that women for women can be creatures on whom you can depend, to whom you can entrust yourself, with whom you can play flutes and tambourines all night long, and have fun dancing, discussing, making plans and making them come true." Up till then, the writer tells us, she had done these things only in male company.

"I discovered," she ends by saying, "that one can, that one really needs to, 'fall in love' with women," and she adds a note to say that she uses quotation marks because the expression "fall in love" is often misused, but she cannot think of any other. "This was the first, completely new, step forward with respect to our old consciousness of common oppression, a step which led me to joyously recognize *myself too* in other women, and to reconstruct my identity, not just in pain and anger but with enthusiasm and laughter."[21]

The relationship of one woman to another is unthinkable in human culture. The female instrument which transforms the world is the practice of relationships among women: this is, in short, the invention of the women of Politique et psychanalyse. They theorized about and practiced female relationships of such human complexity that nothing was excluded—body, mind, pleasure, money, power. . . . All of the human potentialities in a woman were admitted, and everything was observed most attentively. The analysis of what took place among women was made with theoretical instruments, especially those of psychoanalysis, which were, however, adapted to this unforeseen use.

Again in the 1973 *Sottosopra*, there are comments by several Milanese women who had participated in the Rouen meeting and then met to discuss it. Living in a community of women was an extraordinary experience. The most amazing discovery was of the intense eroticism present there. It was not lesbianism, but sexuality no longer imprisoned in masculine desire. "We talked very little about our relationships with men," and a lot instead about the relationship with the mother. That was not a new theme: "we had come to consider it the fundamental relationship," but without considering its "sexual dimension." "The first censorship, the first repression of sexuality, takes place in the relationship with the mother." Even in women-only groups, sexuality is involved; in a relationship with other women there are "traces of one's relationship with the mother." Love between women "is a recouping of female sexuality."

"Many of the women we met," the Milanese women continue, "openly asserted they were homosexuals" and gave their political work as the reason for this choice: "the French women say: our demonstrations of affection serve to reclaim our sexuality." One woman comments: "The atmosphere was certainly not particularly pleasant; it was, instead, one of contradiction and tension. My anguish derived from the fact that I found myself face to face with women who were honestly trying to find themselves and who were not afraid to lose themselves, striving in a constant search, a constant critique." Another woman, less inclined toward anguish, realized that "those women have an easier way of moving, talking, and above all *projecting a different life for themselves,* something almost never done in our country. They are women who give you the sensation that they can reshape the world." Alluding to a problem that was beginning to torment feminists, the problem of "the other women," she notes that "the French women did not need to talk about others because they were themselves already important."[22]

In contrast with the prevailing opinion, one of the Milanese women said that the French group gave her a "feeling of unreality owing to the absence of an engagement with reality which is, in fact, a masculine reality." According to her, "many women struggle to encounter male reality, to change it, and want to *keep* this dialectic going." She says "keep," whereas, as someone else noticed before, "the French women say that historically there has never been a true dialectic between the sexes." The latter is also the position of Demau and Rivolta femminile. More specifically, Carla Lonzi theorized that there is no possibility of a dialectic between woman and man and that the liberation of women comes from their assertion of difference, not from overcoming it.

The woman who said "keep" felt (something which at the time was not noticed or discussed) that "the issue of homosexuality—proposed by the French women—is not a theoretical matter but a kind of affective, sexual life of the whole group." From this "life," during the five days of the meeting, she received an "ambivalent sensation" of attraction, envy, and uneasiness, and she concludes that "to repropose the question of the mother in such a radical, sexual form may mean being swallowed up again for many women, turning back" (to the primitive forms of the relationship with the mother).[23]

In order to understand her ambivalence, perhaps we should keep one circumstance in mind. The French group was headed by a woman who was not in a position formally distinct from the others, and yet had a personal prestige and an eminence within the group which no one, neither she nor the others, tried to hide. The Italians noticed this and were surprised by it: "We asked, 'Antoinette'—that was the woman's name—'seems to be your leader. How come?' 'That's true,' one of them answered, 'she is our leader; she's the one who has a certain power, we admit it. Let us also point out, however, that what we want to do is face this contradiction.' " The Italian commented: "They are aware of the problem, of the decisive role this woman plays"; she, on her part, "is all intent on her own liberation and continually unloads her own contradictions onto the group." The conclusion is that "Antoinette is the leader of the group; however, she is also the promoter of her own destruction as leader: this fact is rather dramatic. . . ."[24]

The idea that one woman might occupy a preeminent position with respect to others had no place in feminism. The theory and practice of *autocoscienza* was such that it did not need it in order to work. It is true that in actual fact the women's groups were almost always set up by decision of one or two individuals, who then, precisely for this reason, occupied a position in the group which was not comparable to that of the others.

The Italians were aware of this. However, it did not constitute "something to be theorized," but was simply an aspect of the "life" of the whole group, unmentioned therefore, and negligible to the extent that the classical feminist group did not express the sexual component of women-only meetings, except in the form of sisterly affection, in accordance with the well-known concept of sisterhood theorized by American feminists. The French, instead, took note of the sexual component in all of its manifestations, including that of power.

Some of the Italians understood that there was strength well worth appropriating in this ability to act politically without idealizing women and their relationships, and they tried to find a way to learn what the French had to teach. In 1973, the French were invited to a small meeting at Varigotti, on the Ligurian coast. Five or six of them came, as well as about fifty Italians, mainly from Milan and Turin. Homosexuality and relationships between women were discussed, in French. There was dancing to the beat of the usual tambourines: the French women preferred them to other musical instruments. During the day, one talked; in the evening, one danced. The same format was followed a year later at the large national meeting at Pinarella di Cervia.

During those years, 1972–74, *autocoscienza* was practiced a great deal and, as a matter of fact, was a new experience for many women who, having heard the message of feminism, wanted to translate it into political action. There was nothing new in feminist politics at that time except its growing in number. The predominant political form of Italian feminism was, and continued to be, the small group of women who meet to talk about their most ordinary experiences in order to understand themselves and the world.

But through this form of political practice, and without replacing it, a new practice was being elaborated: it was called the practice of relationships among women. The phrase was mentioned for the first time in a text published at the beginning of 1974: "Feminism's protest against the male-master is visible, but the rest is not, that is, our existence as women together, the practice of relationships among women, the possible liberation of our bodies which has already begun to take place, of emotions hitherto frozen or fixed univocally on the male world, and the struggle to find a language for [women's] joy."[25]

The text, entitled "Mater mortifera," published in *L'erba voglio*, no. 15 (one of the journals of the antiauthoritarian movement), was a polemic against the importance being given to the fantasy of an imaginary "mother who satiates and devours." In masculine thought, this figure was called in to explain, in psychoanalytic terms, the harmful phenomena typical of consumer society. As we have seen, it was a figure that could be used against feminist groups and female relationships in order to try to negate their rational political significance.

Our meeting with the French women helped us to find answers to several pressing questions. Other effects were to follow more slowly. The main problem was to understand the significance of, and decide how to use, the female energy that had been released by the attaining of political consciousness. Briefly put, many women no longer devoted to men and to (having) children all the time and energies they had before. What was to be done with them? The answer was in the facts, for time and energies had been spontaneously rerouted in the direction of the women themselves and of other women. However, like every other human act, this rerouting too needed the validation of a meaning, and this was given to it precisely by the politics of relationships among women.

There was less and less talk in women's groups about personal relations with the opposite sex. By now, they were a "problem on the wane" for some, while others considered them rather a secondary problem or one to be put off, as opposed to the "new thing," which was to live and know oneself in relation to one or more women: "It's all new, with a woman" (*Sottosopra* no. 1, 1973). Women joked about slogans such as "Woman Is Beautiful"; they became impatient with the feminism of protest and vindication: "The first phase is one of protest against man, but little by little, as you progress in feminist consciousness, it becomes less and less the main concern."[26]

Under the banner of this new politics, a period of female socialization began which continues to the present day. The early days were exciting, of course. There were, as usual, meetings and discussions, but even more appealing were the parties, dances, dinners, vacations, trips. Everything was organized as well as possible, at times extremely well, and in the midst of all these happenings there were friendships, loves, gossip, tears, flowers, and gifts. It was an unusual way of doing politics, which revealed to many women that the system of social relations could be changed—not in the abstract, as we have all learned is possible, but in the concrete, inventing new ways to spend our own energy.

The practice of the unconscious

Compared to women's meetings in *autocoscienza* groups, the more varied and intimate encounters that were promoted by the new politics produced profound changes in places where the words of *autocoscienza* could not reach. There were new things happening, which only partly corresponded to the political knowledge we had already gained. There were old things, which we had learned in connection with men, and which were identically repeated with women.

Some women turned to psychoanalysis for help when they came up against this difficult nexus of repetition and modification. This occurrence, almost irrelevant if one considers the small number of persons involved, was, however, a sign that there must be a bigger problem: we were shifting something without knowing what it was—"the change that we expect from our political action comes from elsewhere," for example, in a session of psychoanalytic therapy. There was "a risk in turning things upside down," the risk, that is, of doing politics with our "personal fantasies" while "the real political problems connected to our condition as women" are treated in analysis "as a personal illness and neurosis" (*Sottosopra* no. 3, 1976).[27]

Some women followed the example of Politique et psychanalyse and invented a new technique which was called "the practice of the unconscious." Two Milanese groups worked on it for two years, 1974–1975, and then two other groups did, in Turin and Rome. It was a practice difficult in itself and difficult to explain. It was invented in order to endow women's speech with those experiential contents which affected it unconsciously and, consequently, threatened to weaken it. We knew that this was true, because of certain ideological stresses and strains in our discourse, because listening to each other was boring, because we oscillated between inside and outside without finding the connection between the two, but what was blocking out the speaking of experience remained somewhat of an enigma.

It was decided to work on this by transferring the psychoanalytical technique of listening into the political context of relationships among women. We analyzed those behaviors which revealed the greatest disconnection between the spoken words and the real motives behind them, such as aggressiveness, the violent rejection of aggressiveness, silence, recrimination. Unspoken or disavowed aspects of women's lives were brought to light, e.g., one's complicity with masculine domination, one's continuing dependence on men, one's anxious search for approval. Above all, fantasies were analyzed, because fantasies "constitute an aspect of reality which is not secondary, but through which both the repetition of the same and the possibility of change have to pass."

On analysis, those fantasies were found to be intrusive and rudimentary, all of them revolving around drastic alternatives. It was evident that the fantasy of acceptance/rejection dominated in relationships between women. Female experience appeared to be a mute body swathed in a cloud of fantasies: a real body in lively, perceptual contact with the real world, but almost altogether lacking the means of symbolic reproduction of itself in relation to that world; human experience given up to the interpretation of others, incapable of self-interpretation. Not knowing how to say it, she prefers to imagine what she is and what she wants. "The symbolic level is precluded to us women."

The existence we are searching for, then, must be sought at the symbolic level, so that we succeed in saying by ourselves what we want, think, desire within ourselves, and not in imitation of, or in reaction to, what others say. The first discovery of feminism was confirmed and made more valuable by this. It is true that women basically suffer by not telling about themselves starting from themselves, and by telling about themselves starting from what others say about them. However, even if man's speech has such a power to interfere in a woman's life, we now saw that this did not depend so much on blatant and forceful dishonesty, or even on our having internalized external violence, as we previously believed. It was subtler than that: man can interfere because he knows the byways, because he knows how to use mediation and thus make his desires felt in a given reality. "Our desire seems to be able to come to light only with the appearance, the imposition of the other's desire."[28]

The problem of the relationship with the mother assumed a central position. If the female mind remains in the power of the most elemental emotions, if there is an unsurmountable infantilism which disappears only with the intervention of masculine authority or imitating men, it means that something of the ancient relationship with the mother remains unresolved within ourselves. There was nothing new in this idea, if one thinks about psychoanalytic theory. However, the context gave it a new meaning. Something had changed in social reality—free relationships between women. And the ancient infantile demand of having the mother all to oneself reappeared in that context: it returned to play itself out toward another destination, a destiny different from the one socially prescribed and made up of loss, disillusionment, recrimination.

We had to interrogate our deepest emotions, start all over again, not resign ourselves to the fact that the male child corners the mother's affection in our culture. Perhaps the mother who bears a female child wants, hopes, to give (her) history a new, different outcome. One sign of this was the fact that women no longer wanted to, or could, banish aggressiveness from women's groups. "By cutting aggressiveness out, everything is kept quiet on the surface, even if inside us, among us, something in the depths of our being becomes ever more menacing; something repressed, and prohibited women from time immemorial, is left out. Women are tenderhearted, they all say. Should we listen to what they all say or to that novel, extraordinary something that is happening among us?"[29]

The practice of the unconscious had a limited following. Its advocates tried to spread information about it, first with a flyer run off on a ditto machine. This was "Rapporto analitico e movimento delle donne" [The Psychoanalytic Relationship and the Women's Movement], which appeared in September 1974 and was followed immediately by a printed article (from which we have quoted) entitled "Pratica dell'incoscio e movimento delle donne" [The Practice of the Unconscious and the Women's Movement], which reproduced part of the previous text and added new material; this was reprinted in full in *L'erba voglio*, nos. 18–19, in January 1975. Lastly, its adherents held a small national meeting at San Vincenzo on the Tuscan coast in the spring of that year.

These repeated presentations are an indication of how difficult it was to explain the concept, on the one hand, and to understand it, on the other. Some women, it must be said, were frankly against it, for instance, the "twenty-two feminists" who expressed their disagreement in a letter addressed to the editor of *L'erba voglio*. They protested above all against the specialized language which "does not jibe with the feeling of sisterhood we looked for in feminists," and they accused the women who use it of "scaring away a large number of women." They were referring, to be exact, to the Feminist Collective of Via Cherubini, which had been organized in Milan in 1972 and of which both the adherents of the practice of the unconscious and the twenty-two signers of the letter were members.[30]

The meeting at Pinarella

Some idea of the work done in those two years was communicated to the women's movement on the occasion of the second large meeting at Pinarella di Cervia held in November 1975. The practice of the unconscious with all its attendant intricate arguments was not explained, but its more immediate political implications were.

A woman who participated in "the large, 'individual-collective: practice of the unconscious' group" tells us that "a new dimension was slowly emerging: I was no longer alone, but neither was I comforted by that unity among women which absorbs one into the affective mire I knew so well, that suffocating sensation of not being able to be different because this would break up that maternal unity which cannot tolerate transgression or any countergroup." The writer, who signs herself Serena (Roma), states that she arrived at Pinarella "exhausted" by the battles she had had with her group in the enlarged collective, battles against "going out" in favor of "finally going inside," without, however, knowing how to do it.

"The new dimension," she goes on, "was being able to be present, wholly, with all my contradictions and schizophrenia, for which I could not ask the group's maternal acceptance. . . . Seeing the others for the first time without the projection of identification we used to make in order to be close, but instead being there, in our differences; we helped each other, criticized each other—I can't seem to convey the idea, but what I mean is that perhaps, after years and years, we finally began to know one another."

The writer keeps on saying that she cannot convey in words what she experienced, and yet she does quite well, for example, when she remarks that "after the first day and a half, something strange happened to me: there were bodies under the heads that spoke, listened, laughed; if I spoke (with what tranquil serenity and unassertiveness did I talk to two hundred women!), somehow in my words there was my body, which had found a strange way of speaking itself."[31]

Serena's is the lead article of *Sottosopra* no. 3, which was published in March 1976 and devoted to the Pinarella meeting and the issues raised by the practice of the unconscious. The "strange way of speaking itself" was nothing but the symbolic representation of self. In the language of the practice of the unconscious, that symbolic birth takes place with the assistance of an "autonomous mother," that is, a mother no longer imagined as good/bad, no longer assailed by the fear of rejection when asking for acceptance, a mother speaking outside the dominant symbolic (the so-called law of the father) because finally interpellated by a female desire that articulates itself in words. This "mother" can be one's real mother or any woman or group of women, or even society as a whole.

More simply said, women are afraid of exposing their own desire, of exposing themselves when they do so, and this induces them to think that others prevent them from desiring; thus they cultivate and manifest desire as that which is prohibited them by an external authority. Female desire feels authorized to signify itself only in this negative form. Just think of the politics of equal rights, carried out by women who never put forward a will of their own but always and only claim what men have for themselves and is denied to women. The figure of the "autonomous mother" meant that, in order to exist, female difference must find legitimation by itself and must take risks for itself.

It is not an accident that the politics of equal rights was being slipped into feminism, even though it was in conflict with its basic ideas and arguments, which are all connected to the thought of sexual difference. Within feminism, the politics of equal rights had no theoretical grounding but was nourished by the weakness of female desire, its reluctance to expose itself, its lack of symbolic authorization.

At Pinarella the problem was addressed under the heading and in the traditional terms of the relation between the individual and the collectivity. But the only thing traditional was the heading; everything else still had to be invented. In fact, as the tapes of the debates show, centuries of masculine thinking about the relation between the individual and the collectivity had gone by almost without touching the female mind. This should not surprise us since that philosophizing was not meant to touch it, and men intended to be personally responsible for women's relation to society. As one woman puts it: "as soon as we draw near to feminism, we deny all the 'normality' there is behind us [in our past], and we place ourselves into a condition of ab-'normality' which we experience and suffer from. We leave behind our relationships with man, who is not only our sexual reference point but also our mediation with all that is social."[32]

At the start, some of the women found it difficult to talk in such a large group and complained about it: "I thought I would be able to talk easily, starting with my personal problems, but instead today . . . I thought it would be possible for me to talk in a group, but I see that it isn't, and I explain this to myself by saying that each of us has specific problems, and the requests she makes don't always arouse immediate interest, so they end up being dropped. . . ." "In the small group," on the contrary, the feedback is "more immediate and much less alienating."

Others noted, and complained still more bitterly, that some women talk without difficulty, in spite of the big group, and prevail over the others: "This morning I felt very bad; I wasn't able to talk, to follow the arguments, to understand . . . some people carry on an argument that the others aren't able to understand . . . [they have] a greater cultural power of verbalization and self-assuredness." The same woman, however, wants to believe that in reality all women are prey to her own feelings of insecurity, and she says so: "I think that actually we are all insecure, but some of us succeed in hiding it better."

Other comparisons and identifications followed: "There was one girl who didn't understand . . . and was anxious to go on discussing a certain issue . . . a terrifying, crazy, aggressive reaction broke out against her." After a vivid report of the facts, the burning question was asked: "Why doesn't this aggressive reaction ever get directed toward the people who are regarded as possessing more valid cultural credentials?" The pain of being treated with contempt, which is tolerated in male society, becomes unbearable in a women's group. Finally. But the appearance of this pain risked overwhelming every other thought.

Judging from the taped debates, the "big group" at Pinarella worked mainly on the creation of forms and reasons for an autonomous female sociality, one, that is, which does not depend on masculine mediation. The word which occurs again and again in these tapes is *immediacy*. "A woman comes here with all the weight of her personal history on her mind and a fundamental need for answers." And rightly so, because our politics are constructed from that history and from that need, but acting politically requires the setting up of a "collective dimension," and there is no collective dimension if each woman is unable to "bear" that "her problem will not be immediately addressed." We want to transform "our lived experience" into political material, and from this wish derives a "contradiction, which must be reconciled, between the immediacy of individual lived experience (desperation, joy . . .) and the collective as a whole." For our discourse to be collective, we must avoid "the immediacy of desire and experience" while succeeding, however, in putting desire and experience into "circulation." "The problem is that desire and the demand for love are presented in an abnormal form so they clash with the different reality of other women." Some say, then, that "acceptance" is necessary. No, reply others, "attention" is necessary.

"If we want to use the material that comes from different people," we must "accept the partiality of our personal experience, and avoid, for example, insisting on the total affirmation or acceptance of ourselves." Demanding to be totally accepted "seems to disguise precisely a desire to be rejected. . . . The collective is created when you succeed in breaking out of the kind of logic that claims your experience is everything."

The obstacle was, therefore, our close tie to what we ourselves felt and lived through. There was also, however, one valuable side to this attachment, and it was a loyalty to one's own sex. The fear of separating from one's own experience and thus losing oneself was not senseless. "We are in a situation in which everything regarding the body and hence affective life in all its various aspects, the fantasies that we carry within ourselves, the compulsion to repeat certain attitudes, all this has been denied and separated from all the rest. Politics and culture have grown, and still grow, out of a basic denial which is the denial of women's bodies, and starting from the body, from sexuality, all possible levels of women's existence have been denied. . . . the separation of politics from psychology, of the personal from the political, is a separation we find already in effect."

A politics which was not called politics

The means for unifying the double, contrary movement of the female mind in search of itself and of existence in the world was not discovered at Pinarella, or anywhere else during those years. On the contrary, the practice of relationships among women had the effect of accentuating divisions, as we realize when we read the observations of Lea (Milano) in *Sottosopra* no. 3, 1976, after she had spent a memorable vacation with some other women in Carloforte, Sardinia.

"The seascape and the company of women remain sweet memories, but a specter of death and madness keeps me from thinking about them. I felt a senseless envy of my friends returning from Portugal [at that time, 1975, an attempt at social revolution was taking place in Portugal], who had seen 'the world,' who preserved a certain familiarity with the world. I felt I was a stranger to their experience, though not indifferent to it. Our consciousness of our reality/diversity as women cannot become indifference to the world without plunging us anew into nonexistence. . . . Our political practice cannot do us the wrong of reinforcing our marginalization. . . . How can we get out of this impasse? Will the women's movement have the strength and originality needed to uncover the *history of the body* without succumbing to the temptation of infantilism (an increase in dependency, omnipotence, indifference to the world, etc.)?"[33]

However, where previously there was oscillation and uncertainty, a new way was now opening up: "now I know the conditions to lay down for relationships," the same woman declares. The way was the one just described, of a female sociality based on relations among women. Man is otherness for woman, the other who both mediates and negates her difference. Not so another woman, who is both different and like. Man can put you in relation with the whole world, indeed, but not with your own self, which is what another woman can do, and this compensates for the fact that she is a social mediatrix of modest proportions. Nevertheless, in the presence of a strong women's movement, she is no longer so modest a mediatrix.

The exercise of female mediation requires each woman to take note of the differences among women and come to terms with them, even when they are differences in power. In the Pinarella discussions of 1975, at a certain point we find a bold affirmation: "It is not a shock to anyone that here too, as everywhere else, relations are power relations."[34] This was false. The fact was shocking, and worse still, it carried the danger of pushing female experience back into its previous silence inside a cloud of fantasies of the kind "in reality, we are all insecure."

Thus progress was slow with respect to the ideas that cropped up every once in a while about female transcendence, about the desire to be social protagonists, about disparity and trust between women, about the symbolic. These ideas remained pending so long as the idea and the practice of a necessary female mediation between women and the world did not take effect. For this is a world, let us not forget, that is not simply unknown to women as it is to every human being born into it; in addition, a woman first apprehends it as a world which neither knows her nor wants to know her, unless she acquiesces to what has already been planned for her by others.

The practice of the unconscious applied to what was "negated" about being a woman, whether it was totally negated or relegated to a chapter on feminine psychology, in order to turn it into political reason. "It is important," the Pinarella records tell us, "that our practice take on this contradiction as well, the contradiction of giving preference to that which has been negated."[35] This meant that our politics would move in a direction contrary to that of every other politics. It also meant parting from those feminists (some were present at Pinarella) who argued for mobilizing around such objectives as the legalization of abortion or the setting up of family planning centers.

Feminism had begun with the hunch that it was possible to engage in political action in a manner that was not called or perceived as politics. As a result of this first gamble, the women's movement gained a momentum that favored those who now wanted to try another experiment: that of giving social form to, and transforming into political content, the very aspect of human female experience that women themselves found difficult to put into words. From 1976 on, this work of transformation took on new forms. It was, in fact, around 1976 that the so-called *practice of doing* among women began.

In its original form, the practice of the unconscious presented several difficulties. We have already talked about how difficult it was to explain its characteristics to others. Worse than this was the fact that it tended to end up in interpretation and commentary instead of direct social change. It had, of course, produced one notable effect in keeping feminism from turning into an ideology which served as a front for a politics of equality. It had pushed the inquiry into female experience beyond conventional representations, including those produced by feminism.

But such critical inquiry was constrained within rather narrow boundaries, because "the context of contradictions"—as we shall see later—was getting smaller: "the one concerning man was hushed up, and the one concerning children was made a private matter, as was the problem of work; all these contradictions remained outside our analysis."[36] To the list of problems which were not faced, we would add the problem of power when it takes female form. Another whole book could be written, with the material on hand, about the vicissitudes of the female mind when confronted with the figures of its own power, real or imagined, loved or hated. The subject matter of discussion was shrinking, and discussion was becoming commentary and interpretation. Women adopted the practice of doing, as we shall see, to change this negative course of events.

The women's movement differs from other political movements in that it rapidly changes its practices. This characteristic is especially evident in Milanese feminism, where it takes the form of downright experimentation. Political practices change for different reasons and in different ways from one time to the next, either to try a new approach to an old problem or because an unforeseen problem crops up. There are practices that are mutually exclusive—such as the practice of the unconscious with respect to *autocoscienza;* there are practices that can coexist, and practices that require other specific ones, like the practice of doing and the practice of relationships among women.

This shifting of practices has not created problems of continuity as yet, possibly because women risk their human wholeness starting from an undeniably partial position. However, problems of existential continuity crop up; almost always, in fact, a change of political practice results in a partial alternation in the group between those who leave a new position because they no longer see themselves in it, and those who instead take it up because they do see themselves in it. This is normal, of course, but causes problems for those who experience human relationships according to the model of the family, where alternations are determined essentially by death and birth.

The custom has been to give a name to each practice. The name, obviously, indicates the new idea that is being tried out. However, it also has the effect of emphasizing the artificiality of the situation. Some experimentation and artificiality is perhaps inevitable in women's struggle for a free social existence. For sexist domination is based on natural and social grounds without solution of continuity. To appeal to nature would be useless, since the answers it gives depend on the social interpretation which deduces women's human destiny directly from female anatomy. On the other hand, it was soon clear that there was no use in appealing to society either, since it contained no contradictions which required the free social existence of women for their resolution.

The latter point needs to be commented on. At the beginning of feminism, women did not think that way, and there are still many fighting for women's liberation who do not think that way. At the beginning, for example, it was thought that men too would have something to gain from the cessation of sexist domination. It was thought, that is, and is still thought by some women, that society as it was needed female freedom, and hence one needed only point out the existing contradictions in order to obtain a free social existence for women. According to them, the current contradictions in a development based entirely on technology are at the forefront of all the other social contradictions that beg for women's presence in the government of society.

An analysis of the evidence proves this view wrong. Society certainly needs women and, in moments of crisis or emergency, also needs to refer to female difference. But the feminine which is invoked in moments of crisis or emergency, today as yesterday, is a feminine without liberty. It is called in in those instances when society needs women more than men because of the sexist division of labor, such as when it needs caretakers rather than owners, conservation rather than exploitation, etc. The social need for a female presence does not go beyond this ambiguous appeal, where one cannot discern what truly corresponds to female experience and what is merely a stereotypical representation of it.

The difference in being a woman has come into free existence not by working through the contradictions pertaining to the social body as a whole, but by working through the ones each woman experienced in herself and which did not have a social form before receiving it from female politics. In other words, it is we who have ourselves invented the social contradictions which make our freedom necessary.

The first and fundamental invention was to open up, within society, the separate spaces, places, and times of an autonomous female sociality.

CHAPTER TWO

The old problem of abortion

As soon as they were formed, women's groups found themselves facing an old problem: abortion. Abortion was illegal; nevertheless, enormous numbers of them were performed clandestinely. Abortion was, in fact, the principal means of birth control in Italy. Illegal abortions, then, were a serious social problem which needed to be solved and which concerned men, women, political parties, Parliament, and the state. This appeared to be, was made to appear to be, a cause, a struggle for freedom, the freedom to have abortions, and thus a struggle to be conducted by both men and women.

As a result, some of the political parties actively challenged women to make abortion one of the primary objectives for which they would fight. Women accepted this challenge en masse: it was the first time that a hidden, inadmissible experience of theirs was placed at the center of the political scene and made visible to society. In struggling for legalized abortion, many women were actually expressing their desire to be protagonists on the political scene, expressing their rejection of the maternal role as the only way for a woman to fulfill herself. They maintained that a woman has the right to separate her sexuality from procreation, with all the social changes that such a separation would bring with it.

The fact that abortion, whether legal or illegal, was an integral part and the sign of a sexuality which was still subordinated to male desire, could seem marginal at a time when thousands of women were demonstrating for a sexuality of their own. Clearly, many of those women who were struggling for legalized abortion were saying something very different. They were demanding autonomy above all, and in their demanding it by way of the legalization of abortion, they disregarded the agonizing contradictions inherent in that immediate objective; they did not suspect what a socio-political mess they were getting into.

This nonchalance was a form of social and political irresponsibility. The more aware women criticized this in the others. However, like every form of irresponsibility which is experienced as a triumph over social constraints, this tended to minimize the problem and the difficulties attending its solution. The women who demonstrated for legalized abortion accepted the criticisms but nevertheless went on demonstrating and feeling pleasantly liberated. Certain groups, however, usually those whose political practice began in *autocoscienza* groups, kept their distance from the political campaign sponsored by the Radical Party. Rivolta femminile declared in July 1971:

> We women of Rivolta femminile maintain that the one to three million clandestine abortions performed in Italy every year are a large enough number to make us consider the law against abortion *de facto* null and void. . . . We refuse to suffer the insult that a few thousand signatures of men and women can serve as a pretext for begging men in power, legislators, to grant a demand that was actually expressed by the lives of billions of women who were butchered in clandestine abortions. We will accede to freedom of abortion, not to new legislation regarding it . . . for only thus will we transform this fundamental aspect of our oppression into the first act of consciousness, aimed at undermining the structure of male domination.
>
> Repeated compulsory reproduction has placed womankind in men's hands, and constitutes the primary basis for their power. But what liberating effect can even a "freely chosen" procreation have today, in a world where culture embodies exclusively the masculine conception of existence, thus conditioning a priori any "free choice" by women? After millennia, do free sexuality and freely chosen maternity, the premises for women's existence as persons, still have to pass through the demand for freedom of abortion? . . .
>
> Man has left woman to face alone, on her own, a law that prohibits her from aborting: alone, disparaged, unworthy of the collectivity. Tomorrow he will end up leaving her to face, on her own, a law that does not forbid her to have an abortion: alone, gratified, worthy of the collectivity. But a woman asks herself: "For whose pleasure did I get pregnant? For whose pleasure am I aborting?" This question contains the seeds of our liberation; by formulating it, women stop identifying with men and find the strength to break away from a conspiracy of silence that is the epitome of colonization.[1]

The *autocoscienza* groups had very valid reasons for keeping their distance from the Radical Party mobilization. These groups were spawned by a contradiction which had not been perceived or foreseen by society: the women who now had access to every kind of job, in every possible workplace and political context, these women had trouble talking, planning, acting, because they were oppressed by something invisible and incomprehensible to everyone. Female difference, which was insignificant in an emancipated world, yet real, was a source of suffering in many women's experience. Attention had to be paid to it. The battle for legalized abortion would now get them involved again in situations, on terms dictated by official politics, situations and terms that had been abandoned in order to form women-only groups where the broken fragments of themselves, of their experience, could be analyzed and put back together again.

Abortion was part of that experience, one of its many fragments. When we talked about it among ourselves, we discovered how varied our experiences were, depending on our different social locations—for example, what quality medical care one could afford. But even more marked were the individual differences between women. Some had never had an abortion because they were sterile, or because they did not have sexual relations with men, or had them in such a way as not to get pregnant, or because they preferred to carry the pregnancy to term rather than abort; others used abortion as their preferred method of birth control. For some having an abortion was untraumatic, nothing at all, while for others it was a tragedy, a mutilation. These various positions were the phenomenal, superficially diversified aspect of female experience; women had not yet managed to get to the heart of the matter, which was: where they stood with respect to sexuality.

It was artificial and forced, therefore, to want the women's movement to unite over the issue of legalized abortion. It was also unacceptable for this to be its prime objective right at the moment when it was felt that the main problem was to interrogate one's sexuality and find a language for it to speak. This position was clearly expressed in a text produced by the Collective of Via Cherubini on February 22, 1973: "For men, abortion is a question of science, law, morals; for us women, it is a matter of violence and suffering. Whereas we demand the abrogation of all punitive abortion laws, and the provision of adequate resources so that abortions are performed in the best possible conditions, we refuse to consider this problem separately from all our other problems, from sexuality, maternity, the socialization of children, etc."[2]

Moreover, according to this text, only the women's movement can guarantee that legalized abortion does not turn out to be "the cynical choice of a state that is starting to see an economic advantage in limiting births." Without the guarantee of women's political strength, the possibility of having a legal abortion would have no positive meaning in women's lives. Many men and women who sided with the legalization of abortion did not understand the necessity for a politics of women.

In an article called "Considerazioni sull'aborto" [Reflections on Abortion], which appeared in the daily newspaper *Il manifesto* on February 23, 1975, Rossana Rossanda observes that the increasing possibility of intervention in procreation calls into question "a responsibility which is not just the individual's," and on that basis, she criticizes the kind of feminism whose position on this question may be summed up in the slogan "The womb is mine" (a slogan which had already been criticized and discarded by part of the feminist movement). The article goes on to say that the human ability to intervene in procreation makes necessary "a new social rule, a new morality . . . in which some power of decision is restored to the female human being. That it be a decision which answers to collective needs is not a question of preventive politics. It is a question of a new scale of values, a new ethics."

The idea in itself would have been right if something essential had not been missing in that passage from the power of decision to a new ethics, after feminism had been quickly disposed of: what was missing was an adequate elaboration of female experience (emotions, needs, social constraints, interests, etc.) by women themselves, an elaboration that had just begun with the advent of *autocoscienza*. The fact that this elaboration was missing (without it the "new ethics" would be, for women, a mixture of constriction and idealization exactly like the ethics of maternity) did not seem to be a problem for Rossana Rossanda, judging from what she writes in this article: "What woman experiences as her own problem of identity, conditioning, and pain, humanity experiences as a problem of its means." For Rossanda, a self-declared "materialist and Marxist" writer, this incongruity "is just fine: in fact, it is a guarantee that for the first time women's liberation will be achieved."[3] Women's liberation without women being subjectively conscious of the collective interests linked with reproduction? Without female sexuality present and active in the social body?

As can be seen, women in the movement took positions on the problem of abortion which were not just different but even radically contradictory. Two issues were involved: that of a political practice in keeping with female reality, and that of the autonomy of the women's movement with respect to groups or movements interested in women's problems.

In a document dated January 18, 1975, and entitled "Noi sull'aborto facciamo un lavoro politico diverso" [We Are Doing a Different Political Work on Abortion], the women of Via Cherubini insist that "mass abortion in hospitals is not an achievement of civilization because it is a violent, death-dealing solution to the problem of pregnancy, and worse, it lays further blame on women's bodies." They add that it is not in woman's interest to support laws meant to regulate an already existent reality which she has to submit to but does not accept, because it satisfies the needs of a sex which is not hers.

Mass mobilizations are traditionally organized by using the political device of finding a unifying objective so as to attract the greatest number of people; they produce demonstrations where men protest together with women. What is the use of these demonstrations, the women of Via Cherubini ask, where men, instead of criticizing their own sexual behavior, march to obtain a free abortion on a body which is not theirs? What advantages do women get from an alliance with the other sex on an issue which concerns sexuality and sexual relations with men?[4]

The Feminist Collective of Santa Croce in Florence and a group in Turin insisted on these same points—abortion as a symptom of an enslaved sexuality, the necessity for autonomy in the analyses and practices of the women's movement, the insignificance of the reforms with regard to sexuality. In their statement, "Non vogliamo piu' abortire" [We Do Not Want to Abort Anymore] (reprinted, like the others, in a special pamphlet called *Sottosopra rosso* [red *Sottosopra*], which was part of the *Sottosopra* published in 1975), the women from Florence emphasize that "the possibility of reclaiming maternity as a positive experience" is "a viable alternative to the present number of abortions." They ask the women's movement to produce a political plan for the step-by-step elimination of the present state of alienation of women from their sexuality and maternity: "The movement must experiment with new practices which will serve as intermediate phases between abortion, the most violent phase, and a total reappropriation of the body which has still to be thought out."[5]

"Some women of the feminist movement" of Turin signed a document entitled "In che modo e' stata colpita la donna nei fatti di Firenze" [How Women Were Affected by the Events in Florence], which analyzes the different positions taken by women's groups on the problem of abortion. It illustrates the contrast between the positions taken by the women's movement on the one hand, and those taken by women involved in mixed political groups (including men). The women from Turin noted that those women who follow an autonomous women's politics differ sharply from the militant "male-communist" women who deny or try to play down the significance of women's politics. It could not be otherwise, because male opinions and decisions about abortion, even when progressive, smack of the worst type of colonialism.[6]

Decriminalization, a proposal which was not heeded

After they rejected that colonizing policy, the *autocoscienza* groups of Turin, Milan, Florence, and other cities found themselves spontaneously agreeing to support only the simple decriminalization of abortion, because they thought that was the only sensible legal action. Basing themselves on female experience, they judged it necessary and sufficient to have a limited law which only abolished the punitive measures against abortion.

Their proposal combined very advanced juridical notions (as the most progressive jurists admit today) with knowledge acquired from a political practice in touch with reality. In fact, women needed time and space to process, among themselves, their individual experience of abortion and its social and subjective significance; above all, they needed time and space to signify to society what they meant by a free, self-determined disposal of their bodies, by a free female sexuality. In that way, they could distance themselves, on the one hand, from the interpretation that the male world had ready for the meaning of female sexual "freedom"—the female body reduced to sex, and the female gender reduced to a body that could be regulated. And on the other hand, they could evade new social rules which, not unlike the old ones, reflect the needs of male experience yet presume to define the correct relationship between the female body and the social body.

The proposal for decriminalization brought forward by the small *autocoscienza* groups, and their reasons for it, were not strong enough to be understood and supported by the majority of the women who were fighting against clandestine abortion. Their proposal was not to mediate between men and women in the conflict about sexuality, and, with abortion decriminalized, to continue to work with the existing contradictions in such a way as to give voice and existence to the choices of the sex which had not been able to express itself.

The *autocoscienza* groups were deeply troubled by the thought that the reform wanted by the majority, though it solved a very real problem for women, would in fact take the place of a solution devised and chosen by women. Besides, since the struggle for legalized abortion had become a crusade for freedom, it seemed to give grandiose significance to what was only a partial solution to that problem: it seemed to bespeak power over one's own body, guaranteed liberation, etc.

That was false. An abortion in a hospital is almost always better than a clandestine abortion, but that fact produces no liberating effects on women's lives. However, it *seemed true,* in the mirror of the great mass demonstrations which had brought to everyone's attention an experience and a problem that directly concerned the female sex, and had given wide resonance and a stage to that experience, that problem. Women could feel, could believe, that they were protagonists.

There was a disproportion between this grandiosity and the subdued voices of the *autocoscienza* groups. The words of the small groups also brought the content of female experience to light, and did so more faithfully, but without the political intensity and immediacy by which the others captured the public imagination. Many other social and political concerns of those years were included in the demonstrations and in the campaign for legalized abortion so that the abortion issue, too, acquired the status of a major social problem; thus women's desire to be at the center of the political stage was at last satisfied, the desire of even those women who have neither the means nor the will to try to compete with men.

As a result, the position of the autonomous groups did not succeed in neutralizing the social and political provocation that was directed at women. Their position was thought to be an interesting theory which provided new approaches to the questions of maternity, sexuality, and female identity. Nothing else. They did not succeed in altering the prevailing political plan, which advocated mobilizing for the legalization of abortion.

Support for this plan was probably added to by the idea that when a certain intensity of social conflict is reached, the most appropriate way of facing and resolving it is to pass a "just" law. Another idea equally popular with those who are not inside the power structure is that behavior is either forbidden or legal; they forget that many kinds of behavior are allowed, or simply possible, and many more can be invented or made possible. So the fact that abortion appeared to be a crime according to the criminal law then in effect, induced people to think that only the law could authorize its practice. In the end, as we know, Parliament approved law number 194/77, which permits abortion in public hospitals only, punishes those who perform abortions privately, and requires the consent of parents or court-appointed guardians if a minor is involved.

When commenting on the proposed bill, in a document dated December 3, 1976, the Women's Courthouse Collective [Donne del Palazzo di Giustizia] in Milan had previously pointed out that the bill was obviously intended to control and repress women's sex lives. Their criticism was primarily directed at the fact that it obliged women to go for their abortions to public hospitals (where, it is common knowledge, physicians and health officials love to show they are against abortion); it was also directed at the punishment ordained for women who have abortions without following the procedure prescribed by law.

When the law was approved and came into effect, even the women who had supported it realized that it reflected the needs, concerns, and compromises of those who had written it, men, who wanted to satisfy a social body clearly dominated by the male point of view. The most violent means of birth control had officially been made part of the norms regulating society. Besides, if we consider the proposed law which some feminists allied to extraparliamentary groups offered as an alternative to the law Parliament was preparing, we find that the problem was not so much a bad or mediocre law but the lack of an autonomous female political philosophy. If, indeed, the law elaborated by those women had been approved, the result would have been the same: damage to women.

The so-called women's law, presented to Parliament by a representative of Lotta Continua [an extraparliamentary Left-wing party], was based on an extreme notion of self-determination—a woman could decide to abort up to term, that is, up to the moment of delivery—with the idea of thus excluding interference and control by the state. But in this way, one fell into an absurd situation whose only justification was the reaction against the state's intentions: the state sets certain limits, we remove them. An abortion which cannot be distinguished from delivery meant that power of life and death over the child was being given to the mother. It was the most unpopular bill one could concoct, because it was a radical negation of the maternal function, and totally emptied the latter of the content and contradictions which are vividly experienced by women in maternity. For women, in fact, maternity is at one and the same time a cause of oppression and a means of survival, a principle of responsibility and a form of social fulfillment, albeit an alienated form: the child's life in place of one's own, maternity in place of any other productive social activity.

The subdued but insistent voices of those women who wanted to participate in politics while keeping faith with female human experience are relevant here. In a document dated December 1976, "Autodeterminazione: un obiettivo ambiguo" [Self-determination: An Ambiguous Goal], some of the women of the Milanese Collective Col di Lana remarked that, if one avoids "questioning oneself about the problem of sexuality, about the man-woman relationship," in order to deal with the issue of abortion and maternity "as a generalized social condition," one actually ends up "proposing the negation of maternity itself as a goal for the masses."

"Procreation as we know it," the document goes on to say, "has undergone such a violent integration into male sexuality that to propose managing it and regulating it is like proposing to fight *inside* alienation rather than freeing oneself from it." To speak of self-determination with reference to abortion makes almost no sense at all; it means only that one needs to defend oneself from the interest, as well as the disinterest, of others: husbands, partners, doctors, priests, laws, etc. Finally, the document points out how contradictory it is to entrust oneself to external regulation by the state and by institutions and reaffirms the principle of absolute self-determination.[7]

The proposal for a law that demanded, quite unrealistically, a mother's right to infanticide was never discussed in Parliament, but had, nevertheless, a positive shock effect. The fight for legalized abortion, in fact, was brusquely abandoned by many women—probably because that proposal, which wanted the law to grant "unlimited limits" to women, made them conscious of the contradictoriness of the desires expressed by women in their struggle for legalized abortion.

Laws that are supposed to be equal for all but in fact are not

At this point it is essential to understand the reason why, when women try to make laws or ask Parliament to resolve some of the social conflicts in which they are implicated, they do damage to their own sex or involve it in agonizing contradictions. That is what happened with the laws on maternity, which created further difficulties for the women who were looking for work. The so-called equal rights laws—such as those mandating equal pay for equal work, or equal access to professions and categories—are useful to women only to the extent that sexual difference is not at issue. Besides being ambiguously formulated (women are made equal to men as if man were the measure of what is best for woman), these laws do not say anything about the relations between the sexes. These are not, to be sure, ungendered laws, either historically (because they were brought into being by women's political struggle) or formally (they are ambiguously male).

However, when sexual difference and the conflict between the sexes are directly at stake, as in the case of abortion and sexual violence, we must keep in mind that what is the norm is always a secondary, derived, figure, which serves to gauge what actually takes place in the social body. Contrary to what some women seem to believe, there are no laws which can give value to female sexuality if such value is not already socially recognized.

Besides, we must remember that within society, women do not make up a homogeneous, socially oppressed group. Here is a preliminary answer to the question posed above: why do the laws in favor of women have an effect contrary to the one intended? Women are a gender rich in diversity, and like the male gender, they are placed in different social locations. Women's struggle to give existence, value, and freedom to the female difference must therefore take note of a multiplicity of interests, paths, actions, and experiences. The women who rely on the instrument of law cannot take into account the complexity of women's choices (of living alone or in a family, having children or not having them, looking for social fulfillment in work rather than in the family, etc.), because the law necessarily anticipates what is going to happen only in an abstract, general way. These women then end up delineating the problems of one category of women, obviously the most disadvantaged, and present them as typical of the female condition in general. This levels the condition of women to their least common denominator, keeps people from perceiving women's different choices as well as the real opportunities they have to improve situations for themselves, and thus denies the existence of the female gender—only a "female condition" exists, with which probably no one really identifies.

A second answer, related to the first, concerns the nature of the means used by women when they deal with legislators. When one thinks about asking for legislative action in favor of women and mobilizes to obtain it, one uses symbolic constructs, such as the state, Parliament, etc., that are not marked by sexual difference. One tends to think of them as neutral (neuter) or nongendered, and therefore such that they may be used indifferently by either men or women. Then one realizes that the symbolic construct believed neutral produces solutions which may perhaps solve problems connected with women, but does not solve the problems of women, and, on the contrary, it sometimes creates new problems for them.

That is because they are, in fact, institutions or concepts created by male thought in order to mediate the conflicts between men, and on the assumption that the male point of view is able to include the whole of social reality, women included. The solutions arrived at reflect this unnoticed unilateral viewpoint, and even when they do not go against women's interests, they are never based on female human experience in all its original diversity. Because of their mediating role between opposing interests, institutions ignore the meaning and value of sexual difference anyway; hence they appear neutral, and even when they do not favor the male sex, they damage the female sex, whose value depends on its difference being significant, visible, speaking for itself.

Let us again consider the problems of abortion and sexual violence, and ask what sense it makes for women to ask Parliament to legislate on these issues. The sense is clear: women are asking for rules from outside their own gender, thus taking legitimacy away from the will affirmed by many women to manage their own bodies, and miserably devaluating the meaning of that "management." The result confirmed it: what we got was an abortion law that, in essence, takes into account male sexual needs, birth control, and public order (by putting an end to black market abortions). There is no thought of female sexuality. Was there at least a concern for women's health? Not really, otherwise women would not have been *obliged* to abort in public hospitals.

And then, once a law is formulated, its very existence jeopardizes the possibility of better choices and imposes its own logic; this happened when a subsequent referendum to abrogate the abortion law allowed for only two positions: either to keep the law as it was, or to side with those who wanted abortion to be made illegal once again.

The autonomous women's movement started out from the consciousness of the contradiction between men and women, which it analyzed from the point of view of female experience. It was transgressive vis-à-vis the law, even the so-called women's laws, because the political practice of the groups was based on close material and personal relations between women, so that it could bring to light subjective desires and needs which were rooted in different individual histories. And these were concrete desires and needs which could not find representation in the law's simplistic framework of a female condition.

Those groups had come to the conclusion that when a woman stands up for her own desires, when she acts according to her own interest, she clashes with the male world in a more current, less regressive way. When, on the contrary, one starts talking about the needs of all women, one makes an ideological generalization which addresses or corresponds to no one woman's needs. Nevertheless, at the height of the debate among women on the question of legalized abortion, none of those groups had the courage and outspokenness to say: "Your description of a female condition which is the same for all women does not describe me."

In the Milanese group of Via Cherubini, of which some of us were members at the time, an attempt was made to use personal experience as a starting point for discussion and to explain even the personal events underlying our positions so as to identify as clearly as possible the link between our thoughts and their subjective sources. It was not difficult for those familiar with this kind of reasoning to see that those who spoke in the name of the female masses were not referring to their own economic condition, but rather to a female condition which applied to other women and which they were interpreting by means of the spontaneous empathy every woman feels with other women's suffering. However, we did not have the courage to counter that psychological mechanism by simply and openly speaking out on the position of women uninterested in the problem of abortion.

Perhaps it was because they thought that in order to signify the female difference, in order not to be assimilated by men, every woman had to be the same as every other—more exactly, as every other woman in the movement. In this way, diversity, quarrels, and different levels of consciousness could exist among women, but not contradictions, or radical objections like the one stated in an essay on political practice (which we will come back to later): "I don't care at all about the women who must deal with the problem of abortion, and this makes me uncomfortable personally and is a problem for me politically."

That was in 1976. For years, during the long debate on the problem of abortion, this position had never been stated, had never mattered, had never jammed the ideological or psychological mechanisms which falsify women's experience. It was, as we like to call it, *the silent woman's objection,* the objection of the woman who does not want to be described, represented, or defended by anyone. If it is true, as we think it is, that what every woman wants above all is to speak as herself, not to be identified with one problem or another, to speak for herself and be listened to because of what she has to say, and not because of what she represents to others' eyes, then that objection was every woman's objection.

We were afraid of openly stating the position of the women uninterested in the problem of abortion, even though they were present among us, because we were afraid of becoming unrecognizable to one another and thus breaking off our fragile relationship with the world. As it happened, we put that relationship into doubt precisely by doing this, because faking impoverished political confrontation and excluded the women who refused to be forcibly identified with the more oppressed members of their sex.

The image of the oppressed woman won; free relations among women had no symbolic figuration; the wretchedness of the female gender was perpetuated. Of course, it was the abstract representation which was wretched. In actual fact, women were differentiated by very different projects, desires, and needs. They referred to each other in varied ways, not reducible to reciprocal identification; they governed themselves accordingly, defined themselves outside the abstract representation, acknowledged each other as different: one silent, one a writer, one illiterate, another passive, one ambitious. . . .

In the discourse of women, however, there was no representation of this plurality of real determinations of the female gender, of its living specification in singularity. And since language lives off the play of differences, on the social scene, women continued to speak in the inherited languages: the neutral language of the law, of psychoanalysis, of Marxism, etc.

How the law can be changed, in practice

The women writing this chapter are lawyers, and they think it is possible to signify the female difference in the law by weaving a web of significant relations among women and using the structure of the trial to do so. The trial has, of itself, an antagonistic structure: one side is opposed to the other. When the opponents are a man and a woman, it is possible to make it evident that it is a conflict between the sexes, that the sexual interest of the woman is in question there. Sexual difference can be made to speak.

The trial is also a site where several female interests can be intertwined. One is the interest of the woman lawyer, who is aware that she is an outsider in the world of law, which is male-gendered: she realizes what a setback this is for her and no longer wants to appear on the scene as a neutral ungendered professional. So she prefers to associate with other women lawyers and imposes a female-gendered presence in the courtroom. Another female interest is that of the woman plaintiff, who hires a woman lawyer because she knows that her suit will be more effectively pleaded by a woman. The decision to entrust oneself preferably to a woman like herself takes her out of ungendered neutrality, emphasizes the existence of the female sex, and gives it visibility: between herself and the law, a woman chooses another woman as mediator. Conversely, women who propose laws choose Parliament as the mediator between themselves and the judiciary; that is, they choose a male symbolic institution.

Privileging the relation among women in the context of a trial effectively transgresses the rule according to which a client chooses a lawyer on the basis of professional prestige, the same criterion according to which lawyers compare themselves to each other. On the other hand, the criterion of belonging to the same (female) sex refers to a competence more profound than that of professional qualifications and introduces the value of female experience into a field where it was not taken into account before. During the trial, the two women relating to each other can represent and provide the measure of female needs which are usually not expressed, or are expressed incoherently, or are put forward in the form of excessive demands in a context where, even more often, those needs are heard and apprehended through the filter of cultural stereotypes.

Thus, to take one example, in a suit for separation or divorce, the father who says he is willing to take personal care of the child, without, however, asking for custody, since he acknowledges that the mother has educative abilities on a par with his own—such a man gives the judge the impression that he is a sensible, civilized person. If, instead, it is the mother who takes this position, the judge is likely to interpret it as that of a woman who is uncertain and restless. This is so because, while the father's position is judged by what it expresses concretely, what the mother says is fitted into an abstract category whereby a woman is thought not to be a *real* mother if she is not a mother who will go to extremes of economic and personal self-destruction for her child.

The case can be conducted by a woman lawyer in such a way that the needs of her client are presented in a concrete way, outside fixed ideological patterns. The woman lawyer, as the mediatrix between the judicial institution and the woman, can make known the extent and the quality of the client's needs. In this manner, the desires and interests of the female sex, when more adequately represented by female mediation, can be written into law, and modify its structure. This is not a showy but a substantial manner of inscribing into the practice of law a social authority of female origin, which is the first guarantee of freedom for a woman.

As we mentioned before, a women's practice which takes into account a plurality of interests becomes evident here: the women who work in the field of the law—lawyers and judges—can weave a web of attractive, meaningful relations among themselves which rescue them from isolation and from assimilation into the male model, and put into circulation something more, a female plus, which gives them visibility and authority, not as neutral professionals but as bearers of an original knowledge capable of leaving a female-gendered mark on the law. The creation of new social relations among women, which rescue them from isolation and assimilation, can thus become a source of women's social existence, and hence of law.

Against sexual violence: a law on women by women

The mobilization and debates about the abortion law had enlivened the women's movement for years. When those ended, many women felt as if something were missing. Something similar had to be found. It was thus that in the summer of 1979, two organizations, the Mld [Movimento di liberazione della donna] and the Udi [Unione donne italiane], together with some other feminist groups, proposed a grassroots law against sexual violence, the text of which was published in September of that year in *Noi donne* [We Women], the Udi magazine.[8]

The authors of the bill took for granted that other women would back it; the time set aside for consulting and listening to the arguments of other women was, in fact, very short, so much so that the bill was already deposited with the Supreme Court when the debate began in earnest. It was a very heated debate and was not characterized by the partial reticence which had restrained discussion about the abortion law. The criticisms and reservations expressed by women were numerous and radical, both as to the methods used by the groups that proposed the law, and as to the substance of their proposal.

The biggest problem was that some women should have had the idea of dealing with the suffering of their sex and making it the subject of a law. At the Umanitaria Conference held in Milan (October 27–28, 1979), organized by the Women's Bookstore, a woman said it clearly: "I'm interested in understanding why *man's law* should be continually revived again and again among us, now in the specific sense of legislating."[9]

In a political movement whose *raison d'être* was female difference, the issue of the sexual violence undergone by women was always present, and precisely because of this, many women rejected the idea of "formulating in articles of law the experience of and the political practice on sexual violence and, more generally, on sexuality" (Umanitaria Conference). As in the debate on abortion, so here, too, the fact of violence and the social destiny of female sexuality had to be kept united. The proposed law, in fact, singled out only one part of women's overall experience of hardship and suffering; that part only was focused on, to the detriment of other suffering, including abortion, which continued to be shrouded in indifference and silence. Now it was rape's turn to symbolize a human condition and cast a shadow of forgetfulness, almost of denial, on all the rest of women's suffering.

But what was most unacceptable was that some women, in the name of all, offered that specific suffering up to the state for its intervention and protection. The proponents were very likely inspired by a natural indignation at male arrogance, but on a deeper level, they seemed moved by their horror of those women who undergo it. In fact, their proposed law demanded mandatory prosecution, which always prescribes a trial even when the victim does not want it.

Faced by the fact of female forbearance, the authors of the bill took the shortcut that comes from outside, or rather from above, and conceives of women as being, now as always, crushed by a paralyzing need and resourcelessness, literally forced to "progress," in this case *obliged* to stand up in a courtroom and defend female dignity. Whose dignity, in effect? And how defended? This shortcut was also a way of conforming, because it did not question the meaning of female silence and its extraneousness to social rules.

This was a serious omission, a completely mistaken choice, which was rightly criticized. "In the past, and still today, women have been disciplined by the personal authority of men. Women rarely clash with the law in order to affirm their interests. We usually clash with particular authorities, and it is in these battles that we learn to submit. Women are not aware of the law; instead they are very aware of the interests and desires of the people with whom they are in contact," observed a woman during the Umanitaria Conference, and she then added: "the question I ask myself is this: do we really want to go from personal authority to public authorities? Do we really want to switch from the marginality of our official quasi-nonexistence to being citizens equal to men? Or do we want to use this marginality as a starting point for changing our condition and all of society with it?" Some women would like to "change, erase at all costs," the typical female attitude toward the law, because they perceive it as a sign of "inferiority." However, the same woman said, "the freedom for which we are fighting" does not consist in becoming equal to men but rather in "recognizing this inferiority as extraneousness and hence as a starting point for an alternate social project."

The conflict between the supporters and critics of the rape bill brought to light a profound difference in political positions which had already been present in the debates on legalized abortion, although less obviously. The women who had formulated the proposed women's law on sexual violence, and the women who opposed it, stood for political analyses and practices that were mutually incompatible. The former considered women an oppressed social group and, as such, homogeneous and needing protection. The latter considered women a different gender which was denied existence in the actual social system. The second kind of analysis gave rise to the political practice of sexualizing or inscribing gender into social relations, language, and law—in short, of modifying the given social reality so as to impose on it the presence and the voice of the sex which had been negated.

For those who sought protection for the oppressed group, the frame of reference remained the dominant one, and since they trusted the impartiality of the law and acted by means of legislation, they had to introduce into this framework the necessary modifications in defense of women. This was their goal in proposing (1) that violence against women be considered by the state a crime against the person, and be compulsorily prosecuted, regardless of the wishes of the flesh-and-blood woman who had been injured as such; (2) that the punishment be more severe; (3) that the trial take place immediately; and (4) that organizations having as their objective the defense of women's rights in their statute of organization be allowed to sue the guilty party.

The contrast between the two political positions was so great that their confrontation was understandably bitter. The most evident contradiction between the two was that some women wanted to oblige everyone to defend female dignity by using the coercive apparatus of the state. "We are against the article that makes prosecution mandatory," wrote Franca and Luisa in the daily newspaper *Lotta Continua* (11/16/79), and they went on to explain: "the old Rocco Code law allowed a civil action to be filed so that the family of the victim (that is, her father or her husband) could decide whether a public trial would damage their honor. We want women to have the option of filing a civil suit so that each woman can decide if her feelings and interests will be served by a public trial."[10] The decision to prosecute must be left to the woman concerned, reiterates a leaflet put out by the Women's Bookstore, "for two reasons: (1) because we prefer to retain the option of individual choice for ourselves, (2) because we feel it is important for the women's political movement to design its actions on the grounds of what women in the flesh feel, desire, and want."[11]

This second point touched on a basic principle of women's politics, the rejection of political representation. "This legal initiative," said the women of the Bookstore when they first took a public stand," "is a *partial initiative,* just as everything else is: our movement is made up of diverse political practices; no one of them can replace the others. The movement cannot represent women in general. In our view, any form whatsoever of political representation, even if by women, pushes women back into silence and social nonexistence. What is, or should be, women's level of consciousness cannot be decided by legal decree."[12]

The lodging of a complaint by organizations with certain characteristics was criticized for the same reason: "In a rape trial, the individual woman almost certainly needs the support of other women. But who should these other women be? Women in organized movements, or those with whom she has some real tie? As far as we are concerned, only the second alternative is acceptable. Otherwise the organized groups will become women's official representatives. Political representation must not be reconstituted among us, since it is one of the things against which we have struggled in order to attain a minimum of existence and self-expression."[13]

As a matter of fact, the proposed law would have introduced into the proceedings a guarantee of psychological and material support for the raped woman. But its formulation had a darker side. What kind of relationship did the women who wrote this bill anticipate being established between the victim of the crime and the organizations which would lodge the complaint in her behalf? Did they foresee that these organizations might intervene in the trial with defense tactics which conflicted among themselves and perhaps even with those of the injured party? Or did they think that, among women, such conflicts would not arise? Did it ever occur to them not only that the judges could perform their legal rites over the head of the raped woman, but that even the various women's organizations might do so, each one in the name of all women's rights? If, as always did happen, the presentation of every single case was agreed upon with the woman concerned, then one could anticipate that the common struggle would lead to the development of a common consciousness for the women involved. . . . This would make mandatory prosecution superfluous, since it had been justified as necessary in order to obtain justice even for those women who are too frightened to file a complaint against their rapists.

If representation was to be institutionalized, and attributed on the basis of formalist criteria written in a statute, solidarity would become a presumption, regardless of whether it was there or not; the struggle would become a ritual, and the political event of women's attained consciousness would be reduced to the banal recording of a normative procedure.

In an article printed in *Il manifesto* on December 18, 1979, "Il desiderio di essere protette dalla violenza con una legge" [The Desire to Be Protected from Violence by a Law], Maria of the Turin Women's Bookstore writes: "we see a new political perspective emerging ever more clearly: the change over to so-called mass feminism makes way for the women's organizations more or less closely connected to unions and parties to try to run this feminism by institutionalizing some of the issues of the movement. . . . Here is an illustrative example: women's 'separateness,' that is, our decision to unite, to think and act politically as women, has become something else in the interpretation given to it by the Mld, the Udi, and the Intercategoriale (and that part of the movement which supports it); for them 'separateness' has become a dangerous deformation of itself, in a word, a frankly reactionary element. This was brought about by cutting off women's reality from the general political debate and reducing it, therefore, to a separate institution, a kind of ghetto whose condition of social inferiority would warrant extraordinary 'measures,' proposed legislation, etc. . . ."[14]

There was no difficulty in finding the signatures needed for the bill to begin its passage through the legislature. The signatures were well over the number necessary, thanks to the wide-ranging network at the disposal of Udi and the union organizations supporting the bill. But the consensus, which had been called a sure thing, was withheld, including that of the women's movement, which had been actively sought by soliciting the support of some of the oldest groups of Roman feminists. Instead of the hoped-for unanimity, the bill had inspired a most radical controversy. All things considered, that was the bill's greatest merit, as some of the women who had supported it most enthusiastically later admitted.

The debate over the law on rape

The proposed bill on sexual violence made it evident that women cannot be legislators in a society which does not acknowledge their existence. This justified the political work of the small autonomous women's groups, but it also forced them to think about the connection between female difference and the forms of its free social existence. All the criticisms of the bill, however well founded, and if well founded, did not invalidate the claims of some women to legislate. Although one had to take existing social reality into account, one could not say, and no one did, that women's claims should be limited by existing reality or measured by its standards.

It was misleading to think of resolving the contradiction between the sexes by law. This was demonstrated by the direction taken till then by the kind of women's politics which had produced effects of freedom in women's lives. "With regard to the analysis of the man-woman and mother-child relationships, dominated as they are by patriarchal laws, we did not try to impose another law. I believe that the laws of the penal and civil codes are the most abstract creations of the law of the father. Our practice in the last few years had been directed toward women's symbolic and sexual autonomy and toward distancing ourselves from the law of the father, which regulates sexuality and symbolization" (Umanitaria Conference).[15]

It was wrong, besides, to approach the contradiction between the sexes by intervening at the pathological moment of rape and isolating it from the whole of female destiny, from its ordinary forms, which is where the "invisible violence" that robs the female sex of its living unity of mind and body takes place. Rape is the political crime *against* women, someone rightly observed at the time, just as infanticide is the political crime *of* women: the latter spurns the unjust law that imposes the interpretation of woman's human destiny as not free but dictated by anatomy.

Rape is an act of violence against the different body of woman, against that element of her difference which cannot be concealed or erased. Men rape because they consider the female body something available for them, and this availability is conditioned only by the state of relations between men. The law of the father punishes rape only because, and when, those conditions which regulate good relations among men have not been respected. When, therefore, she confronts the causes and when she demands real reparation, a woman cannot count on institutions that were conceived by men in order to bring justice to their relations with one another.

This is confirmed, by the way, by what happened five years after the presentation of the bill on rape. It went to the Justice Committee for examination, and after they got through reworking it, it finally reached the Chamber of Deputies in such an amended form that its own proponents did not recognize it. But at that point, they, as well as all the other women who had signed the proposed bill, had no more say in the matter. They entrusted themselves to an institution which could not represent them; they bet on the impartiality of the law. And they lost.

Many of them, it should be said, had lost interest in the bill long before. One woman reported that a friend of hers, who "took a wheelbarrow with 800,000 collected signatures up to the doors of Parliament," later confided in her: "at that moment everything was over for me, I was no longer interested in that law at all; I only cared about what I had found out along with the other women."[16] The reason for that waning interest may have been, as another woman said, that "women know very well that what is commonly called sexual violence is just the excessive effect of the norm of male sexuality which allows relations between the sexes only when there is disparity . . . disparity in strength and value only on one side."[17]

In spite of what women "know very well," that violence follows from the ordinary state of relations between the sexes, some of them had turned for justice to the custodians of the ordinary state of those relations. And, as the episode of the wheelbarrow demonstrates all too well, women's extraneousness from public institutions was ineffectual, because it manifested itself in abrupt irruptions which, though meaningful in themselves, added more incoherence to a women's history already made incoherent by the intrusion of male authority. On these conditions, an experience splintering into disconnected issues, did it still make sense to talk of a female knowledge?

The debate about sexual violence, because of the very form some women had imposed on others by their proposed law, taught us that we had to move onto the symbolic level, the level of *language* and *discourse,* which is the way in which human reality does, or does not, give itself a reason for being. This had been the guiding idea of the practice of the unconscious, and now resurfaced in a terrain bristling with difficulties.

"No one can deny," it was said at the Umanitaria Conference, "that women have made themselves available to men in ways that cannot be reduced to the imposition of a purely external body of rules, or to an act of violence. . . . It seems evident to me that you cannot talk of violent appropriation of women's bodies if you do not keep in mind the complex history of the relation between the sexes that has historically taken shape in the mother-child relationship, where the availability of women became the coercive condition for their survival: to think of living only by making others live. Women, it seems, have no other way of symbolically legitimating their existence. This is the most dramatic condition, and the most difficult to change."[18]

This idea of justifying one's life by making others live is "known" through and through by all women, from the housewife to the militant feminist to the intellectual commentator on male thought. But actually, it is not true that they know it, because whoever justifies her existence like this does not transform the experience of living into knowledge, and thus depends on others for both life and knowledge.

"We have included internalized violence (fantasies of rape, prostitution, the availability of one's body to all, etc.) in the category of sexual violence. Women have no difficulty in simulating, because the distance between fantasy and acting out a fantasy is so short for them. The woman who actually simulates reveals something that is in all of us, even when we succeed in controlling ourselves"; the woman who imagines she has been raped or "who, after having been raped, makes up the name of her rapist, is laughing at justice, and mocking the good will of those who want to defend women from violence, in order to express her desire for symbolic existence against a reality which does not recognize it.

"For those who backed the law, the simulator, the hysteric, is an enemy: by inventing a crime, the hysteric mocks at the law, and it all becomes ridiculous. Those most mocked at are, obviously, the women who believe in the law. . . . If you pay attention only to physical rape, a law and a trial *might* be enough, but those who care about symbolic rape must ask themselves what practice, what politics could enable women no longer to be raped symbolically."

"This law regulates a contradiction that is internal to men's world. . . . I am interested in modifying the man-woman relation so that I do not have to undergo a symbolic rape like the one which takes place the moment women enter into a relation with the law. In the case of the woman who simulated, which I cited earlier, there was no literal rape, but neither was there purely fantasy. The idea of rape appears in the simulator as the effect of a violent reality which denies or squashes women's desires. That is more or less what I mean by symbolic rape, and it concerns me personally."[19]

The author of this second opinion says she partly identifies with the figure of the woman who pretends to have been raped because of their common feeling of being subjected to the violence of a reality dominated by others' desires. The figure of the simulator, in turn, has a lot in common with the women who wanted to become legislators. Like her, they too were trying to become protagonists on the stage of society, and they all were provoked to act by the seduction of the law.

In the articulation of the three figures—symbolic rape, simulation of the crime, will to legislate—the drastic opposition in analysis and political practice we mentioned earlier became less rigid: they seemed almost to meld, or at least overlap, and hence a third position began to appear. On the one hand, there were those who believed that women were an oppressed social group which needed to be represented, which had claims to make, and needed incisive solutions for at least part of their problems. Others instead believed that women are a sex which wants to give itself social existence, a language, effectivity in social relations, starting from its original difference and its living singularity, so that each woman, two women, several women in relation to each other, must speak out for themselves and find their own way of translating the substance and meaning of their experience into social meanings, without male mediation.

For the women who held the second position, to exclude male mediation no longer meant excluding every form of mediation. They had realized by then that the female difference, in order to exist in the world for itself, had to produce its own forms of mediation, and should no longer be the silent object of others' interpretations and actions.

The supporters of the sexual violence law, who appealed to male authority and used its means as if they were impartial and ungendered, seemed unaware of this need; but it was not entirely so. If we leave aside the way they had approached the problem of rape, and consider that they themselves claimed the right to legislate, we can recognize in that claim their desire to use symbolic forms endowed with social authority.

The intermediary figure of the simulator served to show that this desire of theirs was a common female desire. She, too, in her own way, uses the law as a means of making herself conspicuous because, like the aspiring female legislators, or those who criticize them, and other women, she too needs to signify to society that she exists, a woman in body and mind. In the light of these considerations, the problem became how to free that need of making oneself conspicuous from the subjection to the means of male power and the seduction exerted by it.

The third position was the answer to this problem. Maximum authority had to be given to the means and methods invented by the women's movement—which were essentially the practice of free relations among women—and women themselves had to be made a source of authority, the source of legitimacy, in every sense of the word, of female difference. At the Umanitaria Conference, the third position was concisely formulated in the following words: "Women have learned to speak in these ten years of the movement's existence, and now I do not feel vulnerable. . . . That which has been changed in these years, the nonvulnerability of women, will have to be symbolized somehow, perhaps even judicially, . . . inasmuch as the law is part of the symbolic order. I agree that the degree of symbolic revolution that has been achieved by women should be inscribed somewhere."[20]

The third position was not a synthesis; that is, it was not created to reconcile two conflicting positions. It was something new and not at all peaceful. For what emerged in it was the idea of a female source of social authority, an idea which is disconcerting to female common sense even within independent women's groups.

These groups were, in fact, a source of authority for those who joined them and for others who derived from the groups' existence the strength to change their social behavior and to take liberties that earlier had seemed impossible, or wrong. Women gained in freedom, therefore, by referring to the actions and words of other women, though the meaning of this referring remained vague. These gains in freedom were not seen to be related to the birth of female social authority. The realization of this came rather late—the words quoted above date from 1979—and still today, it must be said, it constitutes a problem for some women.

The problem is not, as might be thought, a fear of entering into conflict with the authority of male origin, or a hesitating to do away with the universality of right. There is a deeper repugnance in facing a female standard of judgment, a repugnance which is present even in women who accept being subjected to standards and hierarchies set up by men. The female standard is the true one for a woman, yet we have been exonerated (by male authority) from subjection to it. Instead of freedom, we have the right to build castles in the air. Feminism has defended this right to daydream, instead of freedom, making separatism the space of a presumed female authenticity which has *no social consequences*.

The instance of the sexual violence law, by representing female difference in the guise of an oppression clamoring for protection, offended those women who wanted to signify their difference under the sign of freedom. But it also served to make them come out of the shell in which they were hiding, probably in order to gain time so as to assemble their forces and acquire more knowledge. The knowledge and strength gained through the practice of relations among women were enough to contend with the world, on the condition that women recognized and accepted the fact that this contention, this confrontation, cannot be carried on in just any old way, for the true measure of female strength and knowledge is basically one, and not an optional one: it is their belonging to the female humankind.

CHAPTER THREE

The practice of doing

Up to about 1975, the autonomous women's groups were groups whose main activity consisted in talking, "speech groups," as they were later called. Around 1975, groups devoted to setting up enterprises such as bookstores, libraries, small publishing houses, and meeting places began to be formed. That was how the so-called practice of doing among women began. It derived, we said, from the practice of relations between women and was a specific instance of it. The second Pinarella conference and the thoughts of Lea (Milan) after her vacation in Carloforte will be helpful in clarifying this transition. The time is late 1975.

According to the records published in *Sottosopra* in 1976, the "main group" at Pinarella ended its work by pointing out the difficulty some women had in productively relating two situations judged to be equally important: that of the political group, the women's collective, and that of their personal relations with other women. Among the women who talked about it, there were those who said they experienced personal relations intensely and, in contrast, felt the collective was rigid or barren, and those, on the contrary, who felt alive in the collective, to which they subordinated personal relationships to the point of crushing them. But they all agreed that in both cases, if one of the two factors was missing, the "dialectic" disappeared and a "splitting" was produced.

What kind of splitting? The same kind which made us say in the past that, because of male domination, the female body is mute and a woman's experience remains separate from social discourses, which she gives herself up to as subjected to others' interpretations and initiatives. Now, however, the splitting appeared to be something that was produced in and of itself in women's experience.

That is the central theme of Lea's thoughts, which were published in *Sottosopra* in 1976. She comes to the conclusion that the splitting depends basically on speech. Women's speech, it was said, ought to be dialectical and to circulate among women, but it was not so: "Where there has always been splitting and denial, it seems utopian to speak of dialectic and circulation. For those who are aware of the fragility of their existence, any political analysis and judgment can be fantasized as a threat of denial or censure." The words we seek in order to escape from silence, from the separateness of female experience, do not address it adequately but, on the contrary, turn against it as a denial more drastic than silence. Silence is a shelter, albeit an uncertain one, whereas speech can end in deadly exposure. "It then seems less important that speech takes on the ways of seduction, omnipotence, or provocation when compared to the deeper mechanism that is *antagonistic opposition,* which proceeds by opposing and negating."[1]

These observations throw light on a situation many women may have lived through unawares, but no less intensely. Thus may be explained how it happened that, in those years, inside a movement without a unified organization, groups independent of each other came to make the same choice of devoting themselves to accomplishing particular projects. Things are not like words; things occupy a limited space and time, leaving some space and time open to do yet other things. And in the process of doing, desire can assert itself with the greatest determination without denying the possibility of other desires, other choices.

The political meaning of that doing, nonetheless, could not do without speech. The above-mentioned thoughts end with a paragraph in praise of speech, a praise which is rife with questions, yet unequivocal: "You say"—Lea's thoughts are in letter form, a letter to a woman—"that the women's movement is extraordinary because there's everything in it. But I go on asking myself: can we forgo speech without giving up the specificity of our practice? I'm suspicious of those who preach the end of speech and fill the silence with the gestures of obviousness. . . . Speech, which expresses the complexity of experience, makes its modification possible."[2]

There were, in fact, women and groups who entrusted the significance of their doing to things they were doing. But more often it was understood that doing, and all it brought to light, should be open to reflection so as to transform experience into knowledge. Besides, the objects of that doing, such as libraries, bookstores, publishing houses, centers for documentation, suffice to show that what was at stake was not so much this or that enterprise but a need or desire for mastery of language.

The practice of doing, by its very nature, lent itself to several possible outcomes. In it, meaning was entrusted to words and things in proportions which could not be decided in advance: "We created situations in which relations between women could be not only spoken or only experienced, but interwoven with forms of mixed communication: we exchanged words, things, work, sexuality" (pink *Sottosopra,* December 1976). The first, surprising discovery of the practice of doing was that it was not natural for women to give speech the material care required for its production. This is surprising whether one thinks of the image of woman as mother—no one more than she ought to know that access to speech is inseparable from material care—or whether one thinks of the image of woman as gifted with concreteness, little inclined to verbal flights.

The first to make that discovery, or at least to have to deal with it, were the women of the so-called newspaper group, in an undated, photocopied document, written most probably in 1975 with the title "Scrivere, pubblicare, fare un giornale e la pratica politica delle donne" [Writing, Publishing, Printing a Newspaper, and Women's Political Practice].³ The newspaper is *Sottosopra*. Its original formulation, which these women went on supporting, required that the powers normally given to the editorial staff be given up. From their special position—which required them to lavish material care on symbolic production without appropriating the power connected with it—they noticed that other women loved being published, and that appeared to be their only interest in the newspaper project.

The women responsible for keeping the Via Cherubini center open made the same discovery, in another undated, photocopied document written toward the end of 1975, when the opening of another, more spacious center was being planned. The document, "I luoghi delle femministe e la pratica del movimento" [Feminist Spaces and the Movement's Practice],⁴ opens by saying that "the stuff of our political practice is the relations among women (as well as the history and body of each)," and that stuff, experienced in private forms in the past, needs "socialized life" to become political. A brief review of the sites of this social life follows, the meeting places and the vacation sites, all temporary, and the permanent space in Via Cherubini. But the political space "most important by far" has been, up to now, "our private places: the comfortable houses furnished by their owners, and free to the group." Further on, the authors note the enormous contrast between these places and the collective's space in Via Cherubini: the latter "is dreary," "a no-man's land, [for] no woman considers it hers to the point of spending money and ideas on it as she would on her own home; on the contrary, they all refuse to attend to even the strictly necessary things like light, heating, rent."

Examples of this indifference to the material side of the life of speech are innumerable. In order to understand the phenomenon, it may be necessary to say outright that it has nothing to do with the well-known division between manual and intellectual labor. The women who were most active in intellectual production were usually most involved in the material side as well. At that time, that is, around 1975, the phenomenon was noticed and countered by the practice of doing. A more in-depth analysis of it would not be made until after the crisis at Col di Lana, the collective's space opened at the beginning of 1976 to replace the one in Via Cherubini.

The theory behind the new politics of doing among women is condensed in a two-page text which appeared on January 20, 1976, as a leaflet signed by the whole Via Cherubini Collective; it was published in *Sottosopra* no. 3 under the title "Il tempo, i mezzi e i luoghi" [The Time, the Means, and the Spaces], and was subsequently widely quoted (or copied) in feminist literature. The document begins by affirming that "there is a specific, *material* oppression of women" and that the materiality of this oppression "is unseen." The words *material* and *unseen* are polemically directed at those who interpreted feminism as a cultural phenomenon of social renewal: at that time, feminism was an object of interest for politicians, psychologists, and sociologists. "Many people still tend to pass off the women's opposition movement as a public-opinion, cultural, or ethical movement."

"Public-opinion movements," the leaflet goes on to say, are not effective in combating "the material exploitation of women." A list follows of social events which demonstrate this exploitation. The list includes events of a symbolic nature (such as the giving of the father's name to children), or psychical events (such as the fear of arousing male violence), economic events (women's double work shift [inside and outside the home]), and others of a mixed nature, like the condition of housewives, the social regulation of births, female prostitution, rape. The list sums up the themes of "six years of practice" spent in "analyzing and overcoming our contradictions"; helps prove that the women's struggle faces "a complex reality" on several levels: "biosexual, unconscious, ideological, and economic." Consequently, "our political practice must confront and engage with all of these levels, and provide the time, the means, and the spaces to transform the reality of our expropriated body (expropriated in its reproductive function and in it sexuality), to transform the social, political, and ideological reality where women are exploited, silenced, and repressed."

Thus a new theme is introduced: the theme of a female politics no longer centered on access to consciousness and speech, but rather on the joint transformation of the female body and the social body. "*Adequate* times, means, and spaces mean that situations must be created where women can be together to see, talk, listen, and relate to one another, and to all the others; it means involving the body and sexuality in these collective situations, in a collective space not regulated by male interests. In this space we assert our interests and engage dialectically with the reality we want to change." The political contents acquired earlier are thus reformulated in new terms. The new terms are *create* and *transform*—create female social spaces in order to transform the given reality. The transformation concerns both the women involved in the project and society. These are not two distinct aims but two sides of the same process whose dynamic element is the conflict between autonomous female interests and generic social interests.

The document mentions experiments already under way, such as the Women's Bookstore, which had been in existence for several months. The "practice of the unconscious" groups are also mentioned, as they too are considered transforming groups, anchored "in *matter*." "We are aware," the document continues, "that since we are dealing with a new political practice, many things must be tried out, discovered, and others corrected." They are cautious, in other words, in the face of a new situation where no longer are only love, dinners, flowers, and dances involved, but also money, deadlines, work, and power.

There is no doubt, however, about its effectiveness in bringing about change, as opposed to the politics of mass demonstrations: "to have daily meetings, build a center, have adequate spaces where the separation between the private and the political can be surmounted—all of this is something more subversive than a showy demonstration." The last part of the document is a polemic against the kind of feminism widespread at that time, which made claims and staged demonstrations within the context of the movement for legalized abortion.

In this context, women's mobilization was very vigorous, almost virulent. It fostered a kind of thinking (which the document calls "ideological") bent on accusations and demands addressed to men and expressed as blatantly as possible. On the other hand, the "six years of practice in analyzing and overcoming our contradictions" had disclosed the all-too-numerous signs of the great difficulty that women have in expressing their desires exactly, and pursuing their own interests consistently.

Hence that explosion of public demonstrations was but a way of "reacting against the feeling of powerlessness"; they were "outbursts, retaliation, anger" which "have always existed but to no use," because "when the outburst ends, things stay the way they were." A "clash" sought as a simple reaction "forces us back into the logic where men dominate." One wants "to rival men" by using some of their forms of social visibility, and this has no more value than the "attempts to convince them." "Our interests and needs" are lost sight of, and "all our strength is frittered away." Therefore, the document concludes, it is essential "to refine and take further our feminist practice in all its specificity." We do have proof, after all, that "things change to the extent that we strengthen and valorize relations among women, and *on that basis* we make our decisions about what to want, what to do."[5]

Against ideological feminism

The polemics against "ideological feminism" was a regular component of the political work carried out in Milan for several years starting in 1975. The French women of Politique et psychanalyse claimed that all of feminism is ideological. Debating with them, the Milanese women expressed a more subtle position: feminism can deteriorate into ideology. Clearly, the term was taken from the language of Marxism. What must be understood is how the term was used in women's political thought during those years.

According to a February 1977 text—a poster entitled *Non esiste un punto di vista femminista* [There Is No Feminist Point of View], which was put up in the Women's Bookstore and stayed there for several years—ideology is "political discourse which no longer has ties with reality." Ideology, it says there, "is very chatty," "produces illusions and consolations over and over again," and "leaves things as they are." Feminism is ideological if it functions as "a pre-constituted, ready-made discourse" which takes the place of the "production of ideas through the collective modification of reality."[6]

The meaning of the term is very close to the traditional one of the Marxist Left. But it does not coincide with the use of the same term in the leaflet "Il tempo, i mezzi e i luoghi." There, it is not the lack of political practice which makes feminism ideological, but rather the lack of a *specific* women's practice, a practice marked, that is, by sexual difference: "In the absence of a specific political practice of our own, an empty space is left open that can be filled by ideological feminism." The latter is sustained by "a unifying goal," while an authentic women's politics builds on "the many experiences, possibilities, and differences" expressed by women.[7]

To complicate things further, the term *ideology* is used with a third meaning in the texts. The so-called *Catalogo verde* [Green Catalogue], published by the Women's Bookstore in 1978, provides a clear example. There ideology is essentially an effect of "stagnation," and stagnation in turn appears when, having found a partial answer, one loses sight of the complexity of the real: "The female condition is entangled in various clusters of problems and contradictions which should not be isolated, denied, or eluded. When this happened in the past . . . there was stagnation, and ideology emerged, with purely imaginary solutions."[8]

According to this third meaning, which was, and has remained, the predominant one, ideological feminism is the kind which simplifies; and to this must be immediately added that the greatest simplification in the women's movement was soon revealed to be its not wanting, not knowing how, to come to terms with the differences which divide women from one another. Like the practice of the unconscious, the practice of doing opposed that simplifying tendency, but with simpler and more effective means. For it gathered together women who were not necessarily bound to one another by affection or familiarity, or rallied by succinct slogans, but who were unified instead by a common project, to which each of them was committed for her own reasons, her own desires and abilities, putting them to the test of a collective implementation.

The identification of ideology with thought that overlooks real contradictions is common to all three meanings, just as it is in the Marxist concept of ideology—with the difference that here the fundamental contradictions are not those which oppose oppressed and oppressors, but the oppressed among themselves (if it be granted that the term *oppressed* is suitable for designating women—at that time it was). The three meanings also have in common the element of ineffectiveness—in the first meaning, because there is a passive acceptance of a world vision; in the second, because mobilization is reactive and does not produce lasting change. In the third meaning, ineffectiveness is demonstrated in a more dangerous way. The kind of feminism which simplifies things, says the *Catalogo verde*, leads one to imagine that things have changed, but "in the materiality of life," the splitting caused by sexual difference in female experience presents itself again in terms redefined by feminism itself: "on the one side there are needs, survival, work, men; on the other, women, tenderness, desires."[9]

This was the picture of a situation which actually affected a limited number of women, but it suggested, if in altered terms, that women's tendency to seek out a marginal security in order to cope with the given reality remained fundamentally unchanged. That this tendency reappeared inside a movement born to make women mistresses of their fate was a heartbreaking sign of the difficulty women have in freeing themselves from their subordinate status. For those who were aware of this, the feminism then triumphant on the social scene constituted an almost unbearable spectacle of female subordination quixotically experienced by many as protagonism.

In March 1977, Rivolta femminile published a short manifesto whose biting prose reveals the hand and the mind of Carla Lonzi. It is called "Io dico io" [I Say I], to make it plain that she refuses to identify herself otherwise—in 1970, she said "I" sometimes and "we" more often.

> Who said that ideology is my adventure?
> Adventure and ideology are incompatible.
> My adventure is I.

Here too, therefore, it is a matter of ideology, with a meaning which succeeds in condensing all those described above.

> A day of depression a year of depression a hundred years of depression
> I leave ideology and no longer know anything
> Bewilderment is my test
> I will never again have a prestigious moment at my disposal
> I lose my power of attraction
> You won't have a safe haven in me.

The remarks seem directed to a woman, an intellectual or a politician, who has been convinced by the success of feminism to take an interest in it as an expert.

> Who said that emancipation has been unmasked?
> You court me now . . .
> You expect an identity from me and can't make up your mind
> You've received an identity from man and don't let go of it
> You dump your conflict on me and are hostile to me
> You tempt and try my integrity
> You'd like to put me on a pedestal
> You'd like to keep me in custody
> I move away and you don't forgive me for it
> You don't know who I am and set yourself up as my mediatrix
> What I have to say, I say by myself.

The issue of inequality among women is articulated at last, very precisely, but with disconcerting severity, because the woman articulating it is proud and alone.

> Who said you helped my cause?
> It was I who helped your career.

The writer, a real expert on femaleness, explains to the other, the would-be expert, what kind of situation she is in:

> By accepting this culture, you have accepted without reserve a request that excludes you
> You wanted to participate without existing on your own
> In the end, you are unrecognizable
> All along, you suffer from inadequacy
>
> You expect solidarity because you exposed yourself to danger
> To my mind you've gotten into a mess
> You've given your life to show that we're mediocre.

And she pounds this message home, because the other woman has been stultified by other insistent messages.

> They keep on saying that mediocrity is temporary
> I view it as perennial in you
> You'll come to envy my nothingness.

In the end, the text takes on tones of joking sarcasm:

> Have you heard the one about "double militancy"?
> And the one about "the personal is political"?
> And the one about "you're not doing enough?"
> I've found my source of humor.[10]

By "double militancy" she meant the situation of women who were militant members of mixed organizations although they also went to women-only groups, either because they were feminists or because they were impressed by the growth of feminism. "The personal is political" was the little formula which, to many men and women, summarized feminist thought. "You aren't doing enough" was the accusation directed at those women like Carla Lonzi who took themselves as the starting point for their politics and did not judge its effectiveness by the criterion of mass mobilization.

In Milan, the practice of feminist demonstrations did not catch on. At the time of the first great demonstration for legalized abortion, in April 1976, some women of the Via Cherubini Collective wrote a critique in the form of a letter to the editor of the *Corriere della sera*.[11] The newspapers had played up this demonstration because of its distinctive characteristics and the high number of women participating in it. It was reported that the banners were pink, the armbands of the guards were also pink, and the demonstrators, some of whom dressed up as witches, clasped hands and danced ring-around-the-rosy in the streets. "We didn't take part in the demonstration," the letter begins. Instead, we want "to analyze and understand together the ambiguousness of this mode of struggle, the discomfort and uneasiness caused us by the descriptions made by some comrades who were there and by the press reports"—which is, word for word, the language the authors would have used at a women-only meeting.

The argument is divided into two parts. In the first, the letter admits that we (always read: women) find ourselves in the contradictory position of having to defend ourselves as an oppressed social group, and yet, by doing so, we miss the fundamental reason for our struggle, which is to affirm sexual difference: "if we accept suggestions from women's present social condition" in order to improve it, we are not affirming anything of what a woman is, wants, and thinks. There is only adaptation, not self-affirmation.

The second part expresses uneasiness with "ideological slogans" and the display of an "affectation of femininity." "For those of us who place sexuality at the center of the struggle, it is as oppressing to be identified with a constructed image like that of the victim, the witch, or the joyful, dancing Maenad as it is to participate in an abstract, symbolic unity." The letter then explains that a public demonstration "has many meanings," especially if it is by women only, because of the position they occupy "vis-à-vis other women and vis-à-vis men." And this must be taken into account while "keeping in mind our basic interests."

Clearly, the letter wanted to affect the hearts and minds of the demonstrating "comrades," in order to convince them that that way of acting politically did not answer to the needs of our common struggle. It worked, at least in Milan, which was the place aimed at. It was not by chance that the text was made public in the pages of the newspaper with the largest circulation in Milan. This procedure, it must be remarked, was altogether unusual for political communications among women, above all when criticism was involved.

The contents of the letter reached Rome, too, which was the capital of the great feminist demonstrations: they were discussed in a meeting on "women's ways of communicating" sponsored by the Maddalena Collective in May of that year. The promoters of the meeting also felt some doubts about public demonstrations: "In taking to the streets," they wrote in presenting the topic of the meeting, "communication chooses . . . breadth over depth and gets overwhelmed because it has to speak to the dominating, male logic."[12]

The second part of the letter to the *Corriere della sera* was understood and appreciated (even though it had no practical consequences in Rome). It was admitted that the demonstrations publicized an image of women as subordinate barely disguised by an alleged otherness. But the first part of the letter was not understood, or was not considered convincing. This came out in a detailed discussion that the women of the House on Via Mancinelli devoted to the pink-armband demonstration and to the Via Cherubini group letter.

The House on Via Mancinelli in Milan, which was occupied by several left-wing groups during the winter of 1975–76, was also the center for a women-only group. Their discussion, recorded and photocopied, indicates that one of them had taken part in the demonstration with full commitment, as she reiterates there. On the contrary, another woman, by the name of Rachele, refused to take part in it. In support of her choice, she cites the letter printed in the *Corriere della sera* and adds: "Before this demonstration, [my male comrades] wanted to know, asked me things, because they felt uneasy; now they need no longer ask, because there are ground rules . . . the role of the feminist has been established," and because the demonstration endorsed "the things we wanted to undermine," that is, the forms of masculine politics.

Others support her views, like Bice, who nonetheless took part in the demonstration: "It has been ages since I had gone to a demonstration, and it was the umpteenth time my reasons for feeling uneasy were confirmed; I just wanted to get out." She heard male comments that embarrassed her; "I don't like being the local color" [in their scenarios]. But the "worst annoyance" was that the male "comrades" said they were "satisfied"—by, that is, this political performance by feminists.

The practice of public demonstration is criticized, therefore, because it only sells out or degrades the diversity of feminist politics. In this sense, the critiques of the demonstration become progressively more severe: "copycats," "mystifying messages," "ghetto culture," etc. Patrizia, perhaps referring to all of the Left, goes so far as to say that "if they prohibited demonstrations, that would be a step forward toward revolution."

Along with the crescendo of criticism, however, a certain dissatisfaction appears, because "our practice," which goes on being opposed and evoked, "didn't produce such things. . . ." This same observation is made about the Via Cherubini letter, which does contain "something more . . . but leaves something unsolved." What follows makes clear what the latter "something" is: "I cannot stand this situation in which you either act like a policeman (this walk-in clinic will not be built . . .), or you wail about the violence done to women."[13]

The reasons, therefore, for *not* going to demonstrate in the streets were clear and were accepted by those who are speaking here, as well as by many other women. But it was difficult to understand, and even more difficult to put into action, the reversal proposed in the first part of the letter. If you reject ideas available in the given social condition—if walk-in clinics are not built, if social services are not provided, if mass demonstrations are not instigated—what do you do, where do you get your ideas? It is 1976; the practice of doing has already begun, and the Via Mancinelli women have adopted it. But the "collective space not regulated by male interests" seems no longer to have relations with the outside world. There is no "dialectic with the reality which we want to change."

The Milan Bookstore and the Parma Library

In October 1975, the Women's Bookstore opened in Milan after about ten months of preparation. Those months were devoted to finding the right place, refining the plans, settling legal problems, getting the women's movement interested, looking for money, learning the bookseller's trade.

A leaflet dated December 18, 1974, states that the place has been found, illustrates the project, and asks for help. The idea of setting up a bookstore (which the women in Milan got from the Librairie des femmes, opened by the Politique et psychanalyse group in Paris) relates to the past and to the present: to the past, because the "practice of our struggle has been to *speak out*," and "early evidence" of this is found in the works of feminist thought; to the present, because the "practice of our struggle is to find the *times* and the *instruments* . . . to disseminate, discuss, go in detail into everything new that women are expressing." The bookstore being planned is intended as a space in which "it—the new—will be gathered and communicated so that it may become collective wealth." The bookstore will therefore be a "center for the collection and sale of women's works." To "(already) existing works" the bookstore intends to add the work in progress of the female mind. As such, it will also be a "gathering place for experiences and ideas to be circulated."

The decision to stock and sell only women's works (in contrast to the French women's bookstore) is accounted for as follows: (a) because knowing what other women before us thought has been, and still is, important for us, (b) because we intended to favor the products of women's thought against the social misrecognition of their value. It is said of these works that they are "an early testimony, even when dimly conscious or mystified, of the need to affirm the difference of one's own gender."[14] In the following years, these two themes would be taken up again and reexamined until they merged into the concept of the "symbolic mothers" (on which the so-called *Catalogo giallo* [Yellow Catalogue] of 1982 was based) and into the concept of a "precedent of strength" (introduced in the green *Sottosopra* with the title "Piu' donne che uomini" [More Women Than Men] of 1983).

In these subsequent developments there is no trace of that presumption with which, in 1974, the role of expressing sexual difference was granted to the writings of women of the past. This earlier attitude derived from the notion of sexual difference and its symbolic expression that was current at the time. We thought that the symbolic expression of sexual difference had to be found in visibly different linguistic forms—and not, as was finally understood later on, that it had to be first produced and hence discovered as well.

We thought we would find it outside ourselves, in black and white, recognizable according to who knows what criteria. At the same time we logically feared we would not find it at all. This helps us to understand another statement that makes us smile today, that is, that the "censoring of female difference" would be "particularly effective in the world of culture and art" (this was written in the first leaflet, undated, that announced the project of the Bookstore). As if the world of industry, of business, of law, of war . . . were more malleable instead. But no one expected anything from them, since they never put their essence down in black and white.

The leaflet of December 18 ended with a request for collaboration. It asked, first of all, for printed political material and suggested that it be produced. Second, it asked for money. According to the calculations made, the "sum needed" to open the Bookstore was six million lira. "We've got one so far," said the leaflet. When the Bookstore opened, three million had been collected, largely by the sale of works donated by women painters. The opening was announced by a poster showing a family group composed of women only and bordered by a long text which explains the project again in terms of calculated simplicity.

The Bookstore is a shop open to the street, says the poster. Anyone can enter. It was made for women by other women. The women who enter are not asked who they are or what they believe. Here they can establish relations with others, "if they so wish." The Bookstore is a political space because in it, women meet publicly and freely. "To be among women . . . is . . . the starting point of our politics." The choice of stocking only women's works is simply announced without any explanation. The intentions of those who started the Bookstore, however, are explained: "We want to bring together, in the same place, the creative expression of some women with the will to liberate all women" (the sentence is in bold type).

Next comes a rather problematic section, unique in this type of poster. It concerns the question of sexual difference in philosophical and literary texts. There is no presumption toward the women writers of the past, but the question continues to be embarrassing. After the discussions leading to the composition of the poster, the conclusion was reached that the difference in being a woman or man is "perhaps" not evident, "but behind the final, visible product there is at work a process that requires time, that requires certain tools, and that implies the body—and the body is sexually marked." In this way, all women's works are meaningfully linked to the female sex: "In dedicating themselves to literary and artistic activity . . . a few women have taken a liberty, in their use of time, of thought, and of their body, a liberty which was judged scandalous and which we want every woman to have, no matter what use she wants to make of it" (the second part, from "and which we want," is in boldface).

The poster then goes on to explain how the Bookstore came into being, how the necessary funds were collected, and that its legal status is that of a cooperative, "the least rigid form of association envisioned by the law." Here the text stops, except for the closing statement: "But from this day forward, the use and function of the Bookstore are no longer the business of the group that organized and opened it," because, in the moment of its opening, the Bookstore "becomes a space belonging to all the women who enter it." The closing sentence is also in boldface.

The sentences in boldface set out the basic theme, the importance of the relation between "all women" and the "few" who work in a special way. The nature of this relation varies. The work of the Bookstore founders is offered for the use of the others, of all those women who enter the store for any reason at all, even, it is specified, "if only to buy a book or ask for information."[15] The work of the writers, on the other hand, is presented as an example of the free use of female time and energy. The idea to be communicated is this: what is shared, and therefore important for the political struggle, that which every woman can make hers, is the will to be free, and not the "creativity" with which some are endowed and which should simply be acknowledged [by the others]. Of the work already done and that which is in the process of being done (political work), the latter is more important.

The publishing house La Tartaruga, devoted exclusively to women's literature, was founded in Milan in that same year, 1975. The first title in its catalogue was *Three Guineas* by Virginia Woolf. Concurrently, in Rome, the Edizioni delle donne [Women's Editions] began to publish literature, criticism, and essays by women. Some of the founders came from the Maddalena Center, which had been open for several years and had a library and a theater. Also in Rome, several women artists got together to form the Via Beato Angelico Cooperative. Following the example of the Milan Bookstore, others would open later in various cities, including Turin, Bologna, Rome, Florence, Pisa, and Cagliari. In 1980, the Women's Library opened in Parma, while in various other cities, so-called documentation centers sprang up. In 1978, the Virginia Woolf Cultural Center was established in Rome, offering regular courses and its own publications.

This very incomplete list is meant only to give an idea of the social process of "deviating" female energies from their "normal" use. This image is taken up by a second manifesto printed by the Milan Women's Bookstore in 1980. The Bookstore, the text reads, "is female energy deviated from its regular social use."[16] The theme of social irregularity goes back to the Pinarella meeting. There, some had spoken of a condition of "abnormality" that was felt when women found themselves outside traditional female roles, and this condition was seen as inevitable "until an alternative becomes a bit more tangible."[17] At Pinarella, the stress was on the difficulty of living in an unconventional situation, whereas the documents introducing the practice of doing emphasize its subversive effects vis-à-vis the social order and its releasing of female energies. This emphasis was imposed by the political polemics with the so-called ideological feminism. And, as happens in polemics, there was exaggeration. The subversive effect was as exaggerated as was the liberating one.

Indeed, as a female social life was developing in more varied forms and with more complex relations, and as things done counted no less than things said, the "alternative" did become "more tangible," but at the price of increasing moderation. At the Bookstore, this moderation took the form of our being satisfied with survival. There was cause for satisfaction: the Bookstore worked out as planned, and better in some ways than had been foreseen; it was open eight hours a day, it was financially self-sufficient, its balance sheet was always in the black, it was frequented by women from Milan and other places, it was a meeting place where individuals and groups exchanged news and ideas.

But the existence of this place, fruit of a project and labor done in common, was also paid for by a considerable reduction of the larger claims which had been made—though often in a negative form—in the speech groups. Comparison with these gave rise to some dissatisfaction. Out of dissatisfaction, some of the women proposed a change in the way the Bookstore was run. According to them, it should continue to exist as a physical and symbolic space, but should be run by one or two experts so that the others could be a more politically active presence in society.

The idea was rejected. Moderation prevailed. This was not, it must be said, anyone's choice: it was the price paid for a politics aimed at keeping the materiality of daily doing joined to the project of transformation of reality. All the women, in some way, wanted that project to be grand and effective, but if, in fact, it was not, then we must endeavor to understand what was holding it up, without severing that connection. The tie which joined the things to do and the things to say, even as it reduced the latter, nevertheless still freed women's desire from its servitude to fantasy and opened the way for it to contend with reality. This necessary verification was not guaranteed by the other arrangements.

The founding document of the Women's Library in Parma says something more about the effect of unwanted moderation. It was printed in October 1979, and on its frontispiece are reprinted the central passages of "Il tempo, i mezzi e i luoghi," the canonical text for the practice of doing. To explain their project more clearly, the founders of the Library chose to "transcribe every woman's opinion," to report, that is, some portions of a debate leading to the "document" which would present their venture. Thanks to their decision to make a document out of the discussion preparatory to the document, we have evidence of something which other programmatic texts do not show.

The reason given for this choice is the need to "compose a political document which may reflect all our points of view," for, as one woman said in the course of the debate, "the diversity of the women in the group and their nonhomogeneity is a political guarantee that no one will be erased and everyone will 'exist.' " Now, however, the reason why they want to found a library must be explained. Various reasons are brought forward. Since its founders already have a "meeting place" at their disposal, they search for additional reasons for the new project, what ought to characterize it and at the same time account for the extra effort which its realization will require.

It is here that an intricate problem appears. The theory is that differences are necessary for the existence of the female sex, but making judgments is not allowed. We know this trope, as it was typical of the practice of *autocoscienza*. In *autocoscienza*, its solution consisted in the possibility of reciprocal modification: juxtaposing women's differences is significant in itself, even without judgment, insofar as it induces each woman thus confronted to change. The practice of doing did not anticipate solutions; it was by definition open to several possible outcomes, since it had been invented just so that female desire could come out into the open. Indeed, it balanced, on the one hand, the natural tolerance of things—I do this, you do that—with, on the other hand, the words that tell the meaning of things and that, in order to tell it, cannot avoid judging.

The Library founders' discussion remains stuck on this equilibrium without a solution. One woman says: "We created a meeting place last year and we still have it. The library requires more commitment, a more reliable political presence." This evaluation immediately calls forth, from the same woman, a qualification which is followed by a return to value judgment: "The document should talk about the library while not excluding the other things we want to do; but we must have the courage to make this venture stand out, we must show our conviction that it is important, and make it an occasion for growth."

The same oscillation turns up a little further on, after a digression in which women's difference from men is loosely talked about. A woman, perhaps the same one as before, says: ". . . but to have a space like this is superior to simply being together." At this, another speaks up quickly: "I'd stay away from terms like *superior/inferior;* I think that it isn't only discussing about books, about women's writing, that makes us think further, but also speaking among ourselves or doing all the other things that interest us." All the other things that interest us . . . how many, which ones, why? Desire detaches itself from the partial object and begins to sail on a vague, limitless surface, exposed to the danger of sinking into depression, as soon as it discovers that among so many yearned-for things, not one interests it really. This danger is not remote: the same woman who evoked the boundless range of things that "interest us" adds that her interest in books is intermittent: "I go for the longest times without reading or discussing books."

After that, the debate was caught up in the problem of whether and how a library would be interesting to oneself and other women. By that time, all the women doubted it, so much so that the debate ended, according to the printed document, with a minimalist declaration: "We need a library because nowadays getting together is difficult."[18]

Having a place to be together, to do something together without any other specification, was the swamp which threatened the politics of doing. As if getting together were a good in itself, for the realization of which only a pretext needed to be found, and in a context where the things truly necessary for the practice of doing—that is, desires and judgments—are absent. Yet, there must have been desires in the mind of the founders if the Library opened and is still open. But the very realization of the object, as we see, makes these desires seem modest and uncertain. This is the effect of moderation that we already noticed in the Milan Bookstore, and that is frequently to be found in the places of doing among women.

In the Parma document, this phenomenon takes visible form: we're doing this, but we could do something else, and we cannot say that this is better than something else. What remains, as a foundation, is that we like doing this. But a desire that is exhibited along with the fear of judging and being judged generates a feeling of superfluousness that damages the foundation. There is almost no pleasure in doing something partial—all things are partial—when desire does not make of that inevitably partial thing its momentary gamble. One goes back to the beginning, to a female desire which would rather feed on fantasy, or fritter itself away between one thing and another, without ever attaching itself to anything.

The politics of doing could not force female desire out of its reticence and induce it to put itself at stake. That was clear from the start. That is, it was clear that, in comparison with the speech groups, the new practice simply offered a better opportunity of knowing and asserting one's own desires. Moreover, this opportunity was expected to work almost automatically in the spaces created out of a common free will. The last idea seemed obvious, but was mistaken. When put to the test, the planned modification was slower than anticipated in some cases, such as the Women's Bookstore; in others, it was blocked, prevented, as in the case of the Viale Col di Lana center in Milan.

Two memorable disasters: the Col di Lana center and the Paestum Conference

We have no texts that set out the project leading to the opening of the Women's House in Viale Col di Lana. None were written. We know that at the start, the Via Cherubini Collective wanted it for reasons which we can gather from the already cited "I luoghi delle femministe" [Feminist Spaces]. In thinking about Via Cherubini and its political significance, the authors of the document note that many women "perceive Cherubini as a stronghold, the cradle of feminism as represented by a small group of women who want to dictate the line . . . monolithically, and ignore its internal dialectic." This image, it is said, has something true about it; that is, it indicates a "convergence on a few basic things" on the part of those who used to meet in that place: first of all, "the centrality of the relations among women as the structuring practice of the movement." As for the rest of it, however, it was a false image and should be destroyed because it promoted attitudes of passive delegation to "a few stable figures," with the further effect of "exorcizing," that is, isolating and weakening the very issues advocated by the Via Cherubini women.

The large Col di Lana center—which was intended for the Via Cherubini Collective and others, and was unrestrictedly open to women—symbolized, therefore, the possibility of a livelier discussion of political positions. The fact that the place was physically larger meant that it would also be more costly. The plans were that it should be pleasant as well, just as the private homes of the first feminist groups were. The document insists on this point again and again. In order to transform women's material experience into political content, the energy and money that a woman spends on herself and her family must be partially reallocated by her to collective feminist spaces, in proportion to their importance for her.

Enough, then, of wretched, small centers that are supported by "charity" like the beggars of the past. There must be a correspondence between the value attributed to collective spaces and the time and money which the women's movement spends on them. According to the writers, only this reallocation of time and money has the meaning of an "alternative, break [with the past]," as did political action by women-only groups "five years ago." At that time, separatist action was enough; today something more is needed.

The theme of reallocating physical strength is closely bound up with that of "responsibility," which is the second point on which the document insists. The model is the same: it is a matter of "exporting" into the collective spaces a portion of what women tend to invest entirely in their personal lives. Thus, "certain habits of responsibility" which women deploy in their own homes must be "exported, taken into our collective spaces," and transformed into "political responsibility." Thanks to this process, it becomes really possible "to invent a different politics which belongs to each woman, is personal, in the plural: that is, a nonmasculine politics," with no delegating one's power to some "recognized authority."

The idea of a necessary subjective transformation which is one with a possible social transformation appears here clearly. It is the pivotal idea of the practice of doing. The text just examined is, in fact, the closest predecessor of the leaflet on "Il tempo, i mezzi e i luoghi" which was printed shortly thereafter.

The Col di Lana House was remodeled in the spring of 1976, and opened in June for its designated purposes. Located in the innermost courtyard of an old tenement building, the place had originally been a factory; it was quite large and attractive, though in bad shape. The considerable work required to adapt it to its new use was entitled to be considered political work, for the reasons mentioned earlier. In this first phase, the "reallocation" plan did not take effect. Or it did only for the few women directly involved; but they were a minority, exactly as in the past.

When the House was put in order, women came in great numbers. The main hall was full on Wednesday evenings when the big meetings took place. And it was soon quite clear that the bigger, more open place did not make for a wider political confrontation either. Its dimensions did nothing but magnify the phenomenon of the passivity of the many vis-à-vis the few. Every time the hall filled up with 150–200 women, they began to chat pleasantly about this and that like a classroom full of girls waiting for the teacher. That state of half-waiting ceased when one woman or another (but they were always the same ones) asked to begin the political work for which they were gathered together. The work then went on with the intervention of one woman or another, always the same ones, about ten of them, while the others listened.

There was no way to change this ritual. If none of the ten started the work, the others went on chatting with immutable vivacity. If, the debate once begun, no one of the ten spoke up again, perfect silence would reign in the big hall. No matter what topics were debated, the situation did not change. In the long run, as is easily imaginable, there was no reason to discuss any topic other than the very situation which had arisen, to try to understand it. Not even this topic had the effect of changing anything. The usual ten speakers brought it up and discussed it in the presence of the implacably silent other women.

It was a total failure, equaled in our history only by the national convention at Paestum, as we will see shortly. All our hopes were disappointed in a bewildering way. Most bewildering of all, the 150–200 women returned every Wednesday to fill up the hall.

In an attempt to save the project, and even more because they needed to understand, in October of that same year, 1976, the ten who spoke decided, with the tacit consent of the others, to stop holding big meetings and to constitute small groups of ten to fifteen people. Each of these subgroups would meet on its own to discuss women's politics in the light of the experience just described. They would have one month's time, after which, together, they would decide what to do. Twelve subgroups were formed, three of which published their thoughts in a special issue of *Sottosopra* which appeared in December and was known as the pink *Sottosopra*.

Even before the Col di Lana experience, we know it had been noticed that the collective spaces survived by the effort of a few women, and yet, many others who were apparently passive clearly showed that they considered them important. This contradiction was explained in the document on "I luoghi delle femministe" as "the conflict between an individual equilibrium attained with difficulty and the questioning that women's practice requires from us."

One of the twelve groups, author of the text "La modificazione personale e l'agire politico" [Personal Change and Political Action], confirms that feminism has produced personal change which is difficult to translate back into a political form. As for the situation which arose at Col di Lana, the text suggested it was principally due to fear of "political conflict," which was perceived as threatening to "the solidarity among women," to the "affective amalgam," the "affective welding" that keeps the collective together.[19]

Group Number 4 (since they all had the same origin, location, and theme, the groups were distinguished by progressive numbers) also points to the phenomenon of a personal change tending to become an end in itself. But in turn, it provides a different explanation for the events in Col di Lana: there is no political conflict in the collective meeting place because that would "keep the women from being nourished symbolically." We quote in its entirety the passage in question, from "Appunti del gruppo numero 4" [Notes from Group Number 4], in the pink *Sottosopra;* and notes they were not only in name, but also in their linguistic form:

> —The fantasy of the collective, insofar as it is one and solidarity-bound, prevents many women from speaking, from taking a position; conflict would keep them from being nourished symbolically.
> —Passivity toward the collective as a resistance to playing a role in the speakers' game.
> Waiting for a reciprocal destruction of the roles. From their dead bodies will arise active beings in peer relationship with one another. The game can go on indefinitely owing to this nonparticipation since in the meantime these roles do not destroy each other but are all confirmed by passivity.
> The solution is not therefore the bombing of headquarters (which was, as some may remember, the Maoist solution), but the breakup of this blockage. *Passivity as need for the Collective as a symbolic place of nourishment for one's own change.*[20]

In point of fact, if the 150–200 women had had their individual equilibrium at heart, as the first explanation maintained, they would not have gone to that place and done what they did. On the other hand, having gone to that place, if they had had solidarity among women at heart, as the second explanation said, they would not have acted that role which, by dint of repetition, became an obvious attack on the common project.

However, even Group Number 4 admits that there is a matter of personal equilibrium involved, in the sense that "passivity contains, as it were, two types of demand: (1) a guarantee of not returning to depend on men, which is offered by the Collective's imaginary nourishment; (2) affective nourishment through women, which permits a return to man's territory (either real or only imaginary) as independent beings."[21] The Collective, if we understand correctly, was then not a place of possible autonomous existence but the empty symbol women have of that existence. This would explain the contradiction of giving an importance to collective spaces which, however, they did not know how, they did not want, to endow with the active power of their own desire.

The absence of speaking desires, incidentally, frustrated the then-recurrent aspiration of "putting (oneself) into question." Who or what could put what or whom into question? And how? Unless it was translated into a guilt trip. We have some examples of this. "In my experience," says a woman deeply committed to the political project, "the exalting of a public role is partly bound up with the denial of personal needs and rhythms, with the tendency to *valorize* the political project more than the individual woman (evidently bound up with the denial of the woman in oneself)." Why "evidently"? Is the pleasure of acting politically by definition male? The same woman goes on: "The dependence which develops in a collective toward certain people"—of whom she is one—"is not reducible to passivity (delegating) but has a sexual connotation . . . : the attribution of power and authority to the women who appear most repressive of sexuality and of need-dependence."[22]

What happened in that "blockage," as Group Number 4 calls it, was that the human power of the individual woman—prisoner of a fixed role, without relation to the other than herself, female desire without interlocutor—deteriorated into something negative and guilty. An old story in women's history, but here we begin to catch a glimpse of the way out.

The "Appunti del gruppo numero 4" are not concerned with this or that woman, with her way of being, with her pleasures and her preferences. Behind the psychological facts there is a problem of symbolic nature. Women need "symbolic nourishment," and that need is satisfied, in actual fact, by casting each women in this or that role, but one that is always the same and therefore limiting, mutilating, and thus reducing to nothing the heap of speeches about the value of differences among women. So much so that the really significant differences became sources of guilt. The same group continued to work through this hypothesis in the following years, away from the collective place. According to Group Number 4, "all the theory we had is used up," and hence new theory must be produced.

Of the three texts published in the pink *Sottosopra*, the first is the one which most closely reflects the thought of the 150–200 women, even in the title: "Osando finalmente dubitare . . ." [Finally Daring to Doubt . . .]. While the other two texts attempt a theoretical analysis, this one tries above all to express a feeling of uneasiness and to get to its roots—an uneasiness which seems to date from quite a few years earlier, according to some statements: "After a very nice start, we realized that power roles were cropping up" even "inside the small *autocoscienza* group." Then, with the passage over to the practice of the unconscious, "I caught glimpses of the unconscious which provoked great anxiety in me without giving me the possibility of changing myself"; "I had the feeling that the interpretation of behavior was delegated" to some of the women, and that "the overall plan was clear only to them."

What the others say about personal changes and gains which we do not translate back into political content takes on quite another sense here. The splitting complained about is between a personal condition of restlessness and search, on the one hand, and a female politics which does not seem to take it into account, on the other. One woman said it outright: "At this point, I wonder if our practice will allow us to remain ourselves, with our specific characters; I wonder whether there is any space for these things in relation to ideology." In this passage, as in the entire text, "ideology" means women's political project, without any other connotations except that it is a political project. One woman acknowledges this openly: "I wonder what is the borderline between political project and ideology." Perhaps there is not any, when the expression of a desire is confused with the imposition of a norm. "For example," the same woman goes on, "last year I felt that our obligation (the norm) was sexuality among women. Therefore, on the one hand, I experienced it as a new moral code, but on the other, it also had the more profound significance of showing me change."[23]

The same thing, therefore, could have two opposite meanings, or one double-edged meaning, restricting one's freedom or instigating one to use it. How long could such a predicament last? We do not know, because the ambiguity was solved by abandoning the project of a collective space for "confrontation."

Instead of confrontation, which ambiguity could make everlasting along with the site in which it took place, a few of the women decided to privilege the term excluded by the confrontation, and that was "the silent woman's objection." This phrase, which is the title of a "Postilla" [Postscript] to the Group Number 4 notes, does not designate oppressed woman, but rather the woman who will not play when the game is between one who dominates and one who is dominated. Thus the term did not refer to the women who attended the Col di Lana meetings, involved as they were in that kind of game. It referred, as the "Postilla" states, to that "part" of a woman, of every woman, that "does not allow herself to be described, illustrated, defended by anyone." If this part talked, it could say, for example, that it "didn't care at all about women who have abortion problems."[24]

But it did not talk, because in the political model followed until then, the one which had in fact favored women's speaking out, there was no place for female indifference toward the oppression of which many women are the victims. So that everything which came up during discussion ended up rearranged and stuck into a dichotomy—set up no one knows how or by whom—of just/unjust, innocence/guilt, victim/oppressor. In this model, everything female had to be defended and defensible, and could not be otherwise. Even those women who called every political project ideology wanted to stick to this position. Indeed, they above all wanted to. It was the way in which women gave each other confirmation of their existence as women (that is, symbolic nourishment), a poor way but ancient and safe. The Col di Lana experience demonstrates this. The female symbolic had no autonomy. Every failing or lack had to be blamed on someone, man or woman.

The "silent woman," therefore, portrayed the female difference which is silent until women speak it by setting forth the injustices of which they are the victims. As such, it is related to the figure of the "autonomous mother" that appears in the practice of the unconscious texts to indicate the symbolic authority which female speech acquires when it is free from the need to be accepted and from the fear of being rejected. These are the first figures of an autonomous female symbolic, which sees outlined in failing or lack, not the wrongs of others but the something more which a woman wants to be and can be.

The national convention at Paestum, in December 1976, was a success insofar as the number of participants was concerned, and a failure in every other way, yet so grandiose as to be memorable. Everyone knows Paestum in the summer as a luminous archeological and tourist attraction; in the winter, it is transformed into a rainy, desolate plain. More than fifteen hundred women gathered there, lodged in hotels reopened for the occasion, each one far from the others and some so far that their guests were confined there not knowing where to go to attend the meetings. There were two main meeting places, a shed which doubled as a dance hall in the summer, and the main hall of one hotel.

Those were exhausting days. What was intended to be a confrontation between different political practices turned out to be merely the attempt of some to convince others that women's politics should not address itself to male society by means of demonstrations, demands, or accusations. We know the arguments, all of which centered on the specificity of women's politics, and many of the women gathered in Paestum knew them too; for they derived from the practice of relations among women, of the unconscious, and of doing, and had already been expounded in numerous texts. Hundreds of copies of the last of these texts, the pink *Sottosopra,* were sold at Paestum.

The idea that female politics is marked by an irreducible difference was shared by many, and thus everything that helped reinforce it was welcomed by the majority of the women present—just as had happened, on a smaller scale, in the Via Mancinelli House. But the belief that female suffering should be the prime consideration in women's politics withstood all those arguments. The figure of the women who have abortion problems was fading and being replaced by that of the women who are victims of male sexual violence. At Paestum rape was much talked about and abortion very little, even though no particular social events occurred in those days to motivate this shift in attention. It was, apparently, a phenomenon internal to the political imagery. We know that to solicit identification, one must vary the images. Those that are overexploited become ineffectual.

The mechanism of a politics whose leverage consisted in a mass identification with the suffering of some was quite evident at Paestum. And even though many arguments were made against vindictive politics, no one made the only argument that could tackle that mechanism, the argument of a real confrontation, which was the silent women's objection: the failing or lack that is nobody's fault, but is rather the desire for something.

New perspectives in the thinking of women who attend adult education classes

It was, as we said, a problem of symbolic nature. To realize this, all we have to do is read what was written in 1977 by a woman who had gone back to school to get her middle school diploma, in commenting on an article she was assigned to read, "Quale cultura per la donna" [What Kind of Culture for Women] by D. M., a feminist writer:

> The first impulse I get from reading this is to reject it: I refuse to accept as true the theory that we women have lived, and go on living, used and managed by man and his history. I realize that I am trying to defend myself with this protest, but let's at least acknowledge how dramatic it can be for a woman who has already reached midlife, and has always thought she was doing her best, to hear someone say (I'm putting the concept into my own words): "You've been completely wrong about everything in your life; the values you thought were good, like the family, children, fidelity in love, chastity, your own work as a housewife: all wrong, all the effect of a subtle strategy transmitted from generation to generation to continually exploit women." I repeat: it's enough to appall anyone.[25]

The text delineates the limits of feminist thought perfectly, and, although it needs no comment in itself, analyzing it will help us finally to understand the obstacle which made women's politics tilt toward vindictiveness or, alternatively, withdraw into itself to defend its own specificity—and which we attributed summarily to a weak symbolic or, more precisely, a subaltern one.

As will have been noticed, the writer, who signs herself Maria Pia, does not raise the question of true/false. She would like to reject the "theory" as untrue, but she knows that is "a defense." She therefore does not defend herself from the truth, because in that case she would call it false, but from something else, and that is from a representation of her life which—to say something which she does not exclude could be true—annihilates her position as a human subject capable of wanting and judging. However, this position is one she necessarily occupies, if for no other reason than to know what the other woman wants her to know. But if what the other woman says is true, then that means ("I'm putting the concept into my own words") that up to that moment she has gotten everything wrong. A thinking subject can come to no other conclusion when she discovers that all she has done and thought was not really her own thought and will, but some other subject's thought and will. She was not altogether a victim, then, as the writer wanted to depict her, but rather, altogether mistaken.

In the subaltern female symbolic, to speak the oppression suffered was to speak the essence of the female sex, everything else (for example, rebellion) being a consequence of that. It was an absurd representation, as Maria Pia well understands. If, until that moment, her thought was nonthought, her will nonwill, how does she know that now her thought is really hers and her will (for example, her decision to go back to school) truly hers? If that representation is true, and the person who produces it is a woman, where does *she* place herself as a woman who wants to tell the truth to her fellow women? And where does she place her fellow women whom she addresses so that they may know the truth? So there must be female thought that is free for a woman to be able to know that she is oppressed. A representation which says nothing of free female thought—whom can it possibly represent?

"However, if I calm down and I stop to think a little and remember," Maria Pia goes on, "I see my mother again and so many women of her time; I remember the conditions of their life, inside and outside the home. Then I have to go back on my convictions and admit that there is a lot of truth in it." Projected onto another woman, the figure that no woman could make her own becomes once again probable, nay, true. We know this process; it is the same one that made female politics need housewives, women with abortion problems, raped women—not flesh-and-blood women, desiring and judging, but figures of the oppressed female sex and, as such, avatars of everything female.

The opponents of the politics of victimization were against the element of complicity. They asserted, and demonstrated by strong arguments, that women play a part in keeping sexist domination alive. This was a step closer to verisimilitude. They emphasized, moreover, the element of personal gain. This too was a step forward because it introduced the idea of a female economy and thus made it be acknowledged.

But these were partial corrections which did not get to the bottom of the question—which is that the women's movement lacked a representation of free female thought as that which comes before consciousness and makes it possible. It was believed that freedom came from consciousness. The logical order was reversed by an error the nature of which can be glimpsed in Maria Pia's final words: the figure of the woman enslaved by man is true for the past; it is her mother. It must be understood that this is not a question of factual truth, but rather of symbolic forms: that is to say, a question of the way things are represented, on which, however, depends whether the truth is or is not speakable in words—which is exactly the question raised by Maria Pia.

The conceptual confusion about the origin of female freedom could be observed, as well, in an incongruity: all the women tended to represent themselves as freer than their own mothers, but this did not dislodge the myth of an ancient past in which women had been freer. On retracing the course of past generations, the mind perceived greater freedom and stronger shackles. This falsified the accounts of even the most recent and best-known events, such as the determining role that some women had in the formation of groups or common projects. This role was passed over in silence. Otherwise, it was resented as an impediment to the full expansion of each woman's freedom.

The female symbolic lacked autonomy because it lacked an origin. The knowledge gained by women about sexist domination was without foundation. It was not false in itself, but neither was it true, because it lacked its own principle. That is what disconcerted Maria Pia. She cannot recognize herself in that image which does not show her her ego capable of freedom and knowledge.

The numerous women who, like her, signed up for the 150 hours of adult education courses granted by law, taking time and energy away from their families, do not try to justify themselves with arguments about a generalized justice, such as their right to education or to leisure time. In returning to school, they knowingly break with a constituted order—that of female dedication to the good of others—because they are searching for symbolic existence, they want to give meaning to their life. They show they know very well that, in reality, the constituted order is stronger than the so-called rights of human beings. Their transgression, which was giving less time to their family and more to themselves, had to be justified on its own terms. For these women, to know about oppression is not enough.

Santina, a classmate of Maria Pia's, writes the following: "What I expect, and above all hope for, in going back to school is this: because it has been so many years since I stopped studying, I feel as if my brain has gone to sleep, and I would like to be able to wake it up." "It isn't easy," she then says, "to talk about the insecurity I've felt inside, since I was born, I'd say." She talks about it, to say that perhaps it is innate: "I wanted to say this because I don't feel like blaming others for my nature; certainly I became an adult, wife, and mother, but my character hasn't changed much," and later she adds: "I feel happy that I found the courage to go back to school after so many years. I consider it an act of courage toward myself, the first after so many years of dedication to my family. This return to the schoolroom has served to convince me of how wonderful it is, for three hours a day, to think that my ego exists."[26]

For all these women, going to school is an act of freedom and courage which valorizes them and in the light of which they examine their human condition. Their judgments on the past vary, but usually the pleasure of telling about it (which sometimes elicits wonderful stories) prevails over polemics, even though quite a few have lived lives of frightening harshness. Polemics prevail, instead, in the analysis of the present. The 150-hour adult education experience illuminates by contrast their domestic isolation, their feeling of being cut off from social life, their disappointed efforts to participate in it (for example, parent-teacher meetings), and, above all, their "habit" of not doing anything for themselves.

Many women return to this last point using similar words. At the end of the course, Antonia, "over forty, with three children," realizes that, though it cost her "some courage" to start, her "drama" is that now, at the end of school, she does not know how to go on devoting herself to the things that have awakened her interest: "To meet with other women, without the pretext of school or work, is not at all easy." It is not so much a question of material obstacles (the others agree on this); though they do exist, they are not the real problem. The "worst" is that, "once you steal a few hours from housework, or at any rate from your usual routine," you find yourself "somehow impeded, blocked by what I call, very simplistically, the habit of not doing anything for ourselves, which increases our anxiety."[27]

On the same subject, Teresa writes: "I believe that we women have never thought of having some time at our disposal to use as we like best. . . . We are always at our family's disposal, tied with bonds of flesh and affection. . . . We women know that our work is extremely valuable when it is about making sacrifices and dying for others, but in itself it is nothing." From what follows, we infer that the intrinsic lack of value of female work keeps a woman from participating in social life inasmuch as it is not encouraged by her fellow women: "We are often hesitant to get involved in things that are useful to society for fear of other women's judgment, women who are also slaves to the same prejudices."[28]

A similar observation is to be found in "La traversata." While reasoning about solitude, Franca writes: "Solitude is above all a problem for a woman because she is not free to decide, even if her husband grants her this freedom. She has to take care of the children, the housework, which increases when the family gets bigger, and there is her difficulty in entering into society. It's more likely that she will be excluded and gossiped about."[29]

When a woman tries to enter social life, Amalia and Emilia write, "she discovers a closed, diffident society governed by male laws," where, for her, "everything is so difficult, so complicated. . . . She must continually show that she understands, is rational, worthy, and equal to man, because she really isn't equal." Then they interrupt the accusation: "But let's stop the polemics," and state the need "to fight for a mass revaluation of women."[30]

The names of the two authors are to be found again on the pages quoted earlier from *Lotta Continua*, but in a different setting; Emilia is dead at fifty-three, and Amalia devotes her contribution about the 150–hour experience to talking about her. "At the beginning, this woman was pretty boring: she went on telling her story umpteen times a day, and both Teresa and I were tired of listening to her." Amalia is a great storyteller, and this simple, blunt beginning is proof enough of it. Further on, Amalia tells how she learned to understand and help Emilia. She began helping her when she understood that, of the entire class, Emilia "was the person with the heaviest burden of problems to bear." Her life had been spent "without even the smallest satisfaction," and now she was married, poor, and childless. She herself said to Amalia: "My life has always been a no." Something began changing for her at the 150–hour school:

"This course did her a lot of good; she almost seemed younger—at last, after so many years, she was doing something for herself and meeting other people with whom she could at least let off steam. She trusted me a lot. . . ."

A close relationship developed between the two women, one wholly centered on writing, because Emilia needed to organize her thoughts and Amalia had the gift of expressing things well, both orally and in writing: ". . . she was always making me read the sentences she wrote at night and even on the bus on her way to school . . . when I let her read what I had written, especially when I was talking about my hometown, about the farmers and particularly about my life, she cried. . . ." Emilia cries for a reason which her friend explains thus: she too needs to tell about her life, "but she wasn't able to connect any of it up, and so she let herself go."

Amalia then tries to console Emilia by telling her what she thinks of her, the opinion which she repeats in this memoir: "that woman really understood things; she wrote a lot of sentences that were unconnected with each other but were very profound and true. She underestimated herself only because she couldn't connect her thoughts properly in writing." Amalia, at the end, finds the way to solve Emilia's problem: "Once I wrote the story of her life, because by then I knew it by heart, and she always carried it in her handbag and read it again and again, overcome by emotion."[31] The gift of the written story which connects thoughts and saves one from letting herself go is an exquisite image of what we have tried to explain, that is, that in women's struggle, the symbolic revolution—the representation of oneself and of one's fellow women in relation to the world—is fundamental and must come first.

The women who returned to school in order "to believe that my ego exists" do not need so much to know the fact that they are oppressed as to know that they are not oppressed by definition. In different but substantially concordant ways, their texts indicate that the necessary symbolic modification consists in privileging the representation of female freedom over the criticisms and accusations of society, no matter how well founded. It is a matter not of psychological need but of a symbolic one. They want female knowledge to represent their present experience of freedom and understanding, and they want it to have the place it deserves, the essential place. In fact, even if my life is ninety percent not mine, the ten percent that lets me know that gives it all back to me and is therefore the essential part.

In the women's movement, the importance of the symbolic was known from the start. But there was no idea of doing political work on the symbolic. In many respects, the practice of the unconscious was this kind of work. However, since it was confined to the female sex and aimed at the transformation of each individual woman, it provided political knowledge useful in developing relations between women, but not between women as members of the social body. It was commonly thought that relations would consequently change in that direction. In actual fact, as we saw, the division was between a female experience which has no social inscription, and the social services which a woman conforms to doing according to prescribed roles, if she accepts taking them on, or else as a neuter if she can evade the female roles and wants to.

For years we had devoted ourselves to understanding female experience, our experience, in order to transform it into a principle of strength and knowledge with regard to the world. As it went on, this task appeared ever longer, or better, endless, like Penelope's weaving. Everything new and original that came to light only accentuated women's extraneousness to society, as if they were two incommensurable things. And on the other hand, when the two incommensurable things were put together, as in work and other forms of social intercourse, or even in the spaces of women's doing, the result was female self-moderation. Change was not translated into social contents. Or it was, but then they were miserable contents of vindication and survival that did not correspond to the change.

In the meantime, by different paths—like the practice of doing, the 150-hour school, the crisis of the collective political spaces, the debate on the law against sexual violence—a stream of thought was reaching its conclusion: that if female experience does not translate into free social forms, it is because women enter society without having either the idea or the possibility of being there on the strength of their own sexuality. Women enter society as a losing sex.

It was therefore necessary to sexualize social relations, to drive home the point that behind its apparent neutrality, society is a place of sexual games and conflicts. I, who am writing this part of the book, remember that when I first heard expounded this idea of sexualizing social relations, I was terrified by it, as I was when, as a little girl, I dreamt of being in a crowd and realizing that I was in my slip or barefoot.

The political work on the symbolic will consist of dividing in two the unity by which the functioning of the social body is represented, and thus showing its gendered nature; it will consist of legitimating the presence of female sexuality in the social, and the female desire which will find satisfaction in taking part in the knowledge and the governing of the world.

The women who engage or would like to engage in social intercourse bring within themselves a desire seeking satisfaction. No one doubts this, but it is something which has no legitimacy and which therefore cannot be shown openly. The work on the symbolic will thus consist in thinking through or constructing the symbolic figures capable of translating the fact of belonging to the female sex into the social measure of all the freedom a woman can desire for herself.

The first of the figures we found was named the *symbolic mother* to indicate the source of social legitimacy for female difference, as concretely embodied for a woman by those women who validate her desire and support it in the face of the world. With the rise of this figure, the regime of female self-moderation wanes, and a new time begins, a time whose history we cannot tell because it is our present. We will, then, talk about it in this form, about what we think and what we want today.

CHAPTER FOUR

There is yet another story that we want to tell, the story of the Yellow Catalogue [*Catalogo giallo*]—because of the color of its cover, this was the name given to a pamphlet entitled *Le madri di tutti noi* [The Mothers of Us All] published in 1982 by the Milan Bookstore and the Parma Library. It is a story wholly bound up with its theoretical results, and these constitute the introduction to our present. It is about disparity, about the simple fact that women are not equals even among themselves, and about the possible social interpretation of this fact by women themselves.

From women's literature, the first figures of freedom

The work of the Yellow Catalogue began with the aim of finding "a female symbolic." It was not the first time that this line of research had been attempted, nor was this the only group that worked on it in those years. We had already tried with the 1978 Green Catalogue *(Catalogo di testi di teoria e pratica politica)* [Catalogue of Theoretical and Practical Texts]. There had also been a "writing group" which had published a pamphlet entitled *A zigzag, Scritti non scritti* [Zigzag, Unwritten Writings] in that same year. In the preface of the latter, the purpose of the research is thus explained: "Uncertainty about our sexuality separates us from any order of discourse . . . we don't have a language of our own, and are forced to use the words of others if we want to express any part of our new knowledge." The "contradictory ambiguity of our knowledge" derives from this.[1]

This research, in other words, grew out of the need for a female gendered language. Lacking this, women's politics was weak. It oscillated between justifying itself with others' reasons, i.e., with the politics of victimization and vindication, and an attempt to speak starting from itself, which often resulted in a confining, unwanted, and unsatisfactory moderation. All this went along with the fact that, in the meantime, because of the effect of women's politics, female emancipation was making great progress in both national legislation and social reality. A politics intended to give expression to female difference was actually contributing to speeding up the process of women's assimilation into male society.

At the beginning, the project of the Yellow Catalogue was unlike others of the kind because it privileged literary writing, especially novels, and because it took the reader's side, that is, the side of the person who wants to find and not invent. When the Bookstore was founded in 1975, women expected to find that sexual difference expressed itself in special linguistic forms in the writing of female authors. In 1980, this expectation became a need and a pressing demand. But as far as linguistic forms were concerned, they were no longer thought of in any special way—except that we thought women writers could help us in one way or another. Their production did not interest us as an example of women's contribution to human culture. It interested us, or rather we needed it, if it served to signify what human culture does not know about the difference in being a woman. It was the most difficult measure, for which we had no criteria except our need to find what we needed. What it was exactly, we could not know then, because what was missing was a "language," that is, a symbolic structure of mediation. And that had to be found before we could know, along with the answer, the content of the question itself.

This situation gave rise to a procedure which would have to be called wild had it not already been tested in our politics. Literary texts were treated as we treated our own words, that is, as parts of an enigma to be investigated by taking them apart and putting them back together in different ways along with nonwords: places, facts, feelings. The result of this total experimentalism was to wipe out the boundaries between life and literature. Women novelists, their biographies, their fictional characters, and we ourselves exchanged roles, giving birth to new, strange novels: we kept searching for the right combination, the one which would give us the answer and reveal the meaning of the question. In the end, we found it.

It began with our choice of women writers and novels to be read. We immediately decided to read our favorites. It was the only decision possible, since more objective criteria did not exist. But it was not the innocent decision it seemed to us at that moment. If we had thought more about it, we could have intuited this right away, but the thing seemed so very banal that we did not. The fact of one woman's preference for another woman outside a relationship of friendship or love was not something for which we were prepared. We were prepared, rather, for its opposite, that is, to know nothing about it.

This preference was not innocent in another way as well. With it, in fact, we intended to pay in advance for what we would take for ourselves either by love or by force. These were the signs of gendered difference, signs which we had decided to find in women who had often defended themselves from any gendered interpretation of their work. The favorites, as they were called in the initial title, which was changed in the end to "the mothers (of us all)," proved to be Jane Austen, Emily Brontë, Charlotte Brontë, Elsa Morante, Gertrude Stein, Silvia Plath, Ingeborg Bachmann, Anna Kavan, Virginia Woolf, and Ivy Compton-Burnett.

The act of preferring, with its latent "harmfulness," was destined to unbalance that schema of female politics which kept every female desire in a tormenting equilibrium, as if crucified. In order to assert itself, it was always forced to balance itself against the weight of its opposite, of sufferings undergone, or injustice endured, of energy given away and written off. The unbalancing effects of preference acted little by little until they became obvious. As was natural, the preferred writers were not the same for all the readers in the group, and some had no preferences. It was precisely this circumstance, which one would tend not to consider at all, that brought about the crisis. For the strong preferences shown by some called forth a divided response in the others, between those who supported and those who opposed this phenomenon, identifying it as precisely that which prevented them from making a personal choice.

The quarrel broke out over the figure of Jane Austen, venerated by some as Aristotle might have been by the scholastic philosophers, and identified by others, as this veneration grew, with the figure of a mother who prevents her daughter's freedom. The dispute then shifted to Silvia Plath's (biographical) mother, and then to mothers in general—each woman having in mind her own—finally to return to Jane Austen or her fictional characters, especially Emma, the protagonist of the novel by that name.

We have already explained that this way of proceeding was the group's method and that, along with a place in a female tradition, it had a rationality of its own in spite of appearances to the contrary. It was a question, in fact, of finding a language, and the order of things depends on language. In the absence of language, one is forced to try every possible combination with an open mind. In the abstract, it could be objected that this is a never-ending undertaking because the combinations possible are innumerable. But in the concrete, we were guided with an iron hand by the need for language, or rather, by the need to find a meaning for the things that concerned us most directly. When this appeared, we would not fail to recognize it.

This happened when the number one opponent of Jane Austen, in the middle of a discussion where she was again in the minority—caught between the "scholastics" who were pressing her and the others who were watching and waiting to give an opinion until everything was over—stopped arguing and said, as if she were making an observation: "The mothers are not the writers; they are really here among us, because we are not all equal here." When this simple truth was put into words that first time, the words had a horrible sound, in the literal sense of the term: sour, hard, stinging. But their meaning was crystal-clear. No one doubted that they were true, and everyone understood that they had a close relation to our research.

Indeed, that was its first result. We wanted a language to signify the unspeakable of gendered difference, and the first words we found served to name the "injustice" present in our relations. It did not take long to accept what for years we had never registered, though we had it in front of our eyes. We were not equal, we had never been equal, and we immediately discovered that we had no reason to think we were. The horror of the first moment changed into a general feeling of being a bit freer.

Mentioning the disparity present in our relations apparently freed us from the constraint of representing them according to an ideal of neutral, genderless justice, and cleared our minds of the image of this kind of justice as well as of the guilt feelings and the resentment that this neutral authority introduced into our relations. Because of an ideal of equality which neither grew out of our history nor corresponded to our interests, we had forced ourselves to imagine what did not exist and had forbidden ourselves to take advantage of what did. As if our problem had ever been that of finding a remedy for a possible rivalry between strong competing desires. Our problem was, on the contrary, the uncertainty and the reticence of our desires, which were recognizable underneath the so-called power conflicts between women as that which made them painful and endless.

The liberating effect was felt immediately, right there in the basement of the Bookstore, where the work on the Yellow Catalogue was going on. But it took months before what had caused it was understood. At that time, we thought that we were freer simply because a regime of pretense had ended along with the obligation to maintain it. However, this first result of our research, seeing that we were not equal and we had no compelling reason to think we were, was an important result, but an incomplete one. What was missing was the realization that, having released our minds from subjection to a neutral symbolic, we had released the symbolic power of the maternal figure. It was not by chance that the disparities among us had been named in relation to the mother.

It was a short step, in theory, from accepting the fact of inequality to thinking that we get value from a female source, the mother, in a symbolic sense. It was not simple, however; it is not simple. We can see and say that women are not equal among themselves because we are sure that the lacking experienced by one woman with regard to another directs her toward a "plus" of female origin, a "more" of which she is capable and which appears in her precisely with the experience of that lacking. This means that we are in the presence of a female source of value. It must be named; but there was, there is, the danger of representing it as a female duplicate of the authority of male origin.

It must be named in order to indicate clearly that a woman's female-sexed humanity, her belonging to the female gender, constitutes the first reference for what a woman is, wants, thinks. But it must be named in a way which befits its appearance to us, which is different from the way the authority figures of male origin—God, father, God the father, city, state, party, etc.—are instituted, and destituted. The authority which legitimates female difference as an originary human difference is engendered in the context of political practice through the words and gestures of daily life, in one's relationship with this or that woman, in the quickening of desires, in proximity to everyday things.

Naming the origin of female difference was necessary, then, for the symbolic inscription of reality modified by women's politics; but it was, it is, just as necessary to understand the female meaning of that name. Under the specific circumstances, in our work on the *Catalogo giallo,* our way was again to go through our favorite women writers who, during this phase, were named "prototypes."[2]

It was not an attractive name, but it served to characterize the position of that which comes first and offers us the means by which to know and differentiate ourselves. Our favorite authors helped us to represent the female source of authority and to represent it together with the revelation of our diversity. Reference to the words of other women who preceded us gave our relations the structure we had searched for in the practice of doing in order to overcome the "antagonistic comparison" between one woman and another. Insofar as they were included in the common horizon of sexual difference, different female words could be affirmed, and even clash, without fear of destroying each other.

In this way, we approached an understanding of why gendered mediation is necessary. Attributing authority and value to another woman with regard to the world was the means of giving authority and value to oneself, to one's own experience, to one's own desires: "In defending Stein, I am defending myself." The work of the Yellow Catalogue ended with this result, achieved in the last phase, which was dedicated to the finding of a title. The title was *Le madri di tutti noi* [The Mothers of Us All]. What comes before a woman is her mother; there is no other name.

Naming the fact of disparity among women was certainly the decisive step. It meant breaking with the equalization of all women and their consequent submission to the distinctions set by male thought according to its criteria and the needs of men's social intercourse. It meant that among women there can and must be established a regime of exchange to make that plus of female origin circulate, that plus which acknowledged inequality introduces among them. From being objects of exchange, as they were in the male world, women can and must become subjects of exchange.

We were searching for a female-gendered language. But this cannot evolve if what is lacking cannot be signified by it, if it excludes the signification of the plus of an unrealized desire. The egalitarianism of our political groups precluded the symbolic power of our differences. When compared without taking into account the lacking, our differences appeared inert like things offered to one who has no desires. But it is not like that among us. In our relations any lack is sorely felt. We know, for example, that a woman can suffer when she meets a fellow woman endowed with a good that she herself desires. It is an experience that usually is not looked into because it already has a name, envy, which functions as an explanation. But that name, at least in this case, does not contain the explanation. That painful feeling, as we understood in the practice of disparity, arises from the need to put oneself in relation with the female source of one's own human value.

Even in a society where all the measures of value are male and where the wealth of female origin circulates under a neutral sign, women among themselves, though they lack measures, do not fail to feel that what they desire for themselves is so much the more desirable and convenient in itself when they see it realized in a woman. This correct perception remains in the rudimentary form of envy only because she who is touched by it does not find among the approved kinds of social behavior the appropriate way of putting herself in relation with the gifted woman.

Naming the disparity required—as does every thought capable of assessing an imbalance—thinking the horizon which includes that imbalance without being unbalanced by it. As long as the imbalance registered was one of woman compared to man, the horizon was neutral. A neutral justice ordered women not to compare themselves to one another, promising to bring them to equality with men, with the result that female experience stayed imprisoned in itself, without social translation.

Our search for language was a search for gendered mediation. But this cannot take form if the individual woman does not admit in practice that someone like her might possess something that she wants for herself, and if she claims instead that she is equal to every other woman. The fact of disparity proves this claim false. And only after acknowledging this did the deeply felt female need of language discover of what it was the need. For only from acknowledged disparity can an exceptional female position take shape, one that is unmeasured measure, unjudged judging, principle of knowledge of the world, and of legitimation of desire.

The "symbolic mother," a gendered figure of origin, signifies simply that truth and justice are not indifferent to gendered difference. The farthest horizon of thought is gendered, as is it subject, and a woman can venture outside herself with her desires, projects, and claims, having the guarantee that her female experience will be valorized by all which yet surpasses it. The guarantee comes from the mediating figure. Every symbolic structure of mediation is made more powerful by being used, and the more powerful it becomes, the more extended and refined it makes the area of the expressible. And so on, in a circle of unlimited power.

Without the symbolic mother, or rather without gendered mediation, the wealth produced by women circulates in the social body under a neutral sign and does not benefit the female sex. Most of the time, recognition of its true origin comes, if it comes, from envy among women. Without gendered mediation, the wealth possessed by one woman may be resented by another as something stolen from her. The symbolic mother puts an end to this sad state of poverty. Because of her, disparity, made recognizable and usable, becomes a means for enrichment.

The green *Sottosopra*

The results described above were obtained with the work of the Yellow Catalogue, but almost as if in a dream. That is to say, they were all set out in images, and at the time had almost no other form. The title, for example, was suggested to us by Gertrude Stein's naming a theatrical work of hers about Susan B.

Anthony, the American feminist, *The Mother of Us All*. Or another example: the new wealth that women acquire in their relationships by referring to an original female standard was first signified in a comment on *Menzogna e Sortilegio* [Lies and Witchcraft] by Elsa Morante: "The immense, sumptuous place that thus opens up has a charm which makes us recognize it; it is the maternal place. In that place, criteria of measurement which make us seem poor are not operative. There abundance lies, and nothing is measured out to anyone."

Then came the awakening. That is, the moment arrived to repeat what had been said in images and derive consequences from it. The awakening came in 1983 with the publication of the green *Sottosopra*, *"Piu' donne che uomini"* [More Women Than Men], this, too, a title taken from a woman writer, Ivy Compton-Burnett. But it is the image of a concept which the text elaborates and reelaborates with complete self-consciousness. The green *Sottosopra*, in fact, uses a female language which relies on arguments, according to the working method of its authors, the above-mentioned Group Number 4, which was formed out of the Col di Lana crisis.[3] The group achieved results which agreed with—they were not the same, but matched—those of the Yellow Catalogue. The results of the latter, therefore, were inserted into the discussion of the contradiction between female extraneousness and wish to win, which is the central theme of the green *Sottosopra*.

This contradiction is experienced by women in different ways. The green *Sottosopra* analysis privileges the experience of defeat and female moderation or mediocrity in social performance. The analysis reveals that the female will for social existence fails because of the absence of an adequate, faithful, symbolic mediation. The difference of being a woman, therefore, remains excluded from social discourse, like an irrelevant particular, which is significant only if the woman takes on the roles bound up with her anatomy. But the difference in her is part and parcel of her humanity, and hence with her aspiration to be useful, to be acknowledged, to know, decide, and judge. In a word, to be free. A social role based on anatomy is not freedom, just as there is servitude in a social freedom paid for by the erasure of one's sexed body.

The first part of the argument raised only one difficulty in its readers, who were very numerous, as the green *Sottosopra* was very successful; they found it difficult to admit there is something in the female sex which can be called "the wish to win." We still get messages today, years later, from women who tell us that, after having thought about it for a long time, they have arrived at the conclusion that, yes, one can talk of a female wish to win, which they have finally discovered in themselves, some of them as a thing now buried in their past, others as something still alive and present. But it must be said that it did not take so long for many women to recognize themselves in the green *Sottosopra* analysis. And for some, the recognition was so immediate and moving as to make them cry, as Emilia did when she read Amalia's memoirs: "She said I was writing the things that she too would have liked to write, that she had had a life like mine but she couldn't connect any of it up, and she let herself go."

There exists, however, an undeniable female hesitation in admitting that a woman, like every human being, deep inside does not want just something but everything—and in admitting it to herself. The immensity of our desire frightens us when we do not have the means to satisfy it in part and up the ante for the rest. It all too often happens that a woman is pushed ahead by an internal impulse that is too strong for her, and when she turns back, there is no one behind her like Bryher, H. D.'s friend, to tell her without hesitating, "Go ahead." And all too often it then occurs to her to interpret as disapproval that absence of necessary support, as Teresa of the 150 hours observes: "Often we hesitate to attend to things which are useful to society because we are afraid of other women's judgment."

One woman, just one, would be enough to give the necessary support for a whole life; no need to spell out who she is. It is on her, in fact, on the real mother, that we blame the weakness of our desires, with a bitter resentment that the right intuition (mother is whoever supports my desire) does not save from being sterile and unjust. Since she, the real mother of each of us, basically demands of us, or hopes for us, only that we will succeed, in spite of everything, in interpreting in her favor and ours what she has done for us. In the first place, having made us of her same sex.

This hesitation in acknowledging the immensity of desire and in claiming it as a legitimate part of one's own or of other women's female experience, provided an easy opening for a series of criticisms put forward by professional female politicians. These were women who, because of their existential position, could not be without knowledge of the human wish to win; but, perhaps because of their insufficient familiarity with the practice of *autocoscienza*—which teaches one how to take note of the contents of one's experience without censuring them—or perhaps because they were too used to thinking up ideological solutions, these women rejected the language and contents of the green *Sottosopra* as something repugnant to authentic female nature.

As for the contradiction there analyzed and illuminated by the experience of defeat, they resolved it by saying that the wish to win was unknown to the overwhelming majority of women, present only in a tiny minority, and induced by the male world (or by the worst part of it, since in their eyes there also exists a male world that aspires disinterestedly to the triumph of truth and justice). It was, obviously, an ideological solution. But it had, and continues to have, a certain hold on women's minds because of the real difficulty which a woman encounters in acknowledging the immensity of a desire she has no way of putting forward, openly, in full sight of society, without the disguise of some female virtue.

Female difference is indecent. That is the title of a text, "L'indecente differenza" [The Indecent Difference], which appeared shortly after the green *Sottosopra* in the 1983 Program of the Virginia Woolf Cultural Center in Rome.[4] Female difference is indecent as is everything which cannot present itself in its proper social habit. And such habit is not, as philosophers have wrongly taught, a rule of action, but rather is language itself—or better, the symbolic apparatus which makes what is, sayable, thus giving meaning to that which a human being experiences inside her/himself and which can become death to her/him if s/he cannot externalize it by signifying it to others.

There are women who are dying of being different unaware that they are different; they are ever more numerous in a society where traditional female roles, no matter how hypertrophically stretched, do not succeed in filling their lives. Many women wither and die emotionally, as Sigmund Freud noted, though he could not discover the cause:

> I cannot help mentioning an impression that we are constantly receiving during analytic practice. A man of about thirty strikes us as a youthful, somewhat unformed individual, whom we expect to make powerful use of the possibilities for development opened up to him by analysis. A woman of the same age, however, often frightens us by her psychical rigidity and unchangeability. Her libido has taken up final positions and seems incapable of exchanging them for others. There are no paths open to further development; it is as though the whole process had already run it course and remains thenceforward insusceptible to influence—as though, indeed, the difficult development to femininity had exhausted the possibilities of the person concerned.[5]

The great success of the green *Sottosopra* is principally due to its first part, which accounts for the obscure suffering it caused in women by their searching for a reason for sexual difference and not finding it. The last part explains the way to overcome the contradiction, by making use of the theoretical contents gained with the *Yellow Catalogue*: it is necessary to make the maternal figure significant to the female as a figure of origin so that female difference can signify itself for itself, in full view of society, and be for every woman a principle of knowledge and transforming power with respect to the given reality. The originary significance of sexual difference, read the green *Sottosopra,* is activated by practicing disparity among women and entrusting oneself by preference to a fellow woman in facing the world.

The separate group of women, a political form invented by feminism, is already a form of gendered mediation and has given visible and autonomous social existence to the female gender. But it is no longer this mediation when it functions as protection and shelter for an otherwise insignificant difference, and in the group one thinks in terms of an inside and an outside, which is the sign of the recurring separation. The protective function removes the maternal image from its place of origin, because it puts limits to its symbolic power. The relation of entrustment gives it back whole, because it establishes itself precisely where a woman experiences her extraneousness toward the world together with the wish to win. And there is nothing between her and the world that can remedy this utter contradiction, except the acknowledged necessity for female mediation.

The reference to one's fellow woman in this context puts an end to the symbolic sterility of the female sex. Ruth has a son and her neighbors say: "Naomi has had a son." The symbolic fruit of the relations between women enters the world and shows its origin. It shows that the before and beyond, with regard to a woman, is yet a woman, and so on, up to the origin.

This second part of the green *Sottosopra* surprised women; even the many who found the first part clear and just thought this was a strange and difficult idea. Agreement and disagreement followed. To judge from the reactions expressed in public, disagreement was more frequent. Many of the criticisms brought forward were without foundation. For example, it was said that the authors were against solidarity among women, while the text simply says: "Solidarity is a precious element, but it is not enough." Or it was said that the authors wanted to establish disparity among women, whereas the idea obtained from the work of the Yellow Catalogue was that disparity already existed and should be recognized.

A detailed analysis of the initial criticisms is not as interesting as understanding what inspired those criticisms, that sense of anxiety at the thought of practicing disparity among women in order to give oneself value. In our opinion, the anxiety came from the economy of survival which characterizes the social existence of the female sex, and from the role that fantasies have in this economy. The social status assigned to the female sex is such, wrote Carla Lonzi in *Sputiamo su Hegel*, that ". . . a man would prefer never to be born if he had to contemplate it for himself." Women have borne it, bear it, helping themselves in part—a part difficult to measure—with fantasies. It is difficult to know at the moment to what extent fantasies help us to bear our difference when we find ourselves exposed to the exhibitions of the male sex. Usually one finds out when it is too late, when, that is, the power to fantasize diminishes. Then the female mind surrenders and falls into that state which psychologists call depression. One could quote Freud on this point too—to be precise, his last work dedicated to the unresolved question of sexual difference, *Analysis Terminable and Interminable*, where he states that psychoanalysis is impotent in the face of feminine depression.

When the ongoing investigation of Group Number 4 reached the formulation of female inadequacy in social intercourse and named the experience of defeat, many women in the group reacted by asserting that they knew nothing about it personally, that their experience was of either tranquil indifference or complete satisfaction with social measures, and that their problems were of a very different kind. But one woman, who had been in a state of unsurmountable depression for years, broke her habitual silence to deride their assertions and confirm that inadequacy and defeat are the daily bread society feeds to women. She did not express herself in these terms, but the idea was the same, and without her intervention, perhaps we would not have gone on investigating in that direction. A depressed woman does not fantasize anymore and sees things. But she sees them only from the side that negates, and is therefore desperately incapable of planning any change that is not the destruction of herself.

To practice disparity among women and to entrust oneself to another woman in order to deal with the world is a project which found support in the lucid knowledge of a woman who was desperate because she could no longer dream. Said in this way, it is a paradox, because projects arise from a lively claim in relation to the world. The paradox no longer appears such if we consider that in the economy of survival which characterizes the social existence of the female sex, fantasies are nothing but the legacy of dead claims, whose places they take. When the fantasies die in turn, the claims do not come back to life, but they do at least get their places back.

Female fantasies are a way of sustaining the difference in being a woman when she discovers that, socially, she is a loser. Then the task begins, the task of making up—in her mother and father's love, in adults' esteem, in her peers' consideration, and so forth—for that peculiar disadvantage which is not having been born a man. It is then, too, that fantasies begin. Claims diminish; sometimes they completely disappear, and fantasies take their place, fantasies which no longer measure themselves against anything.

The first measure which disappears, the true measure of every woman, is her belonging to the female gender. The woman who fantasizes does not know how great a need, and *what kind* of need, she has of her kind. From this point of view, there is no great difference between the young woman who watches soap operas and the intellectual woman who models her life on the projects of male thought. Both avoid turning to their like in order to find out what to think of themselves and of the world. Both use fantasy to feel like protagonists in a world where, in fact, they act with moderation and respect for the sexual hierarchy.

The experience of defeat reveals, however, that female claims are still alive. The women in Group Number 4 who protested that they were satisfied, intended to reject the idea of having to submit to a social judgment which, for women, is not a true measure but a deforming constriction. The experience of defeat is not that, however. The experience of defeat is having oneself measured, if this can be said, according to old infantile claims which never died, or which were reborn. More precisely, it is the impossibility of adapting oneself to social measurements owing to the irruption of excessive claims in the given reality. The evocation of those ancient claims deeply moved women; but the necessity of submitting to a female social measure in order to support those claims and make them count in reality was, and still is, a bitter pill to swallow.

Perhaps what was really disconcerting in the green *Sottosopra*, what disrupted the economy of female survival with its many fantasies and few claims, was the gendered thinking about the world. Clearly, this way of thinking is new, but not absolutely new for the female mind—in the first place, because there are women who made it theirs well before us, women fully aware of needing other women in order to face the world, and ready to draw all the necessary conclusions, practical and theoretical, that derive from this need. And second because, in the existence of every woman, there was a time, however remote and buried, when she looked to one or another of her kind as the depositary of knowledge most important to her. That was the same time when a woman ingenuously thought—she was a child—that the world was waiting for her and needed her. Female fantasies speak of nothing else—except that they lack the constraints attendant upon the confrontation with reality and hence lack their necessary complement, the idea of learning from their like in order to meet expectations.

The most disconcerting things are not those which were never known before, but those first known and then forgotten. The negative social value of the female sex is the brutal experience that makes a woman forget what she knew in her ancient ingenuity: that to become great or to grow, in every sense of the word, she needs a woman greater than she is.

When we were discussing the way to resolve the contradiction between extraneousness and the wish to win, and the idea came up that a woman can succeed by entrusting herself to a fellow woman, this idea seemed very new to us. Later on, we realized that other women had had it before us, from the earliest times, and that we had been led to it by a logical reason—i.e., one does not confront an outside which is other than oneself without a mediating structure—as well as by a memory of the past. What we thought we had invented, had actually preceded us. In the text of the green *Sottosopra*, the relation of entrustment is talked about but not taught. Here we shall go on doing the same thing. The only new thing added is having said that it was not invented by us, but only discovered.

We can explain the political project and its reasons, but insofar as the relationship itself is concerned, with its concrete setting and its own particular reasons, we can only give an idea of it. In other words, we can repeat how we have learned it, but we cannot teach it. Naomi had two daughters-in-law: one decided to entrust herself to her, and Naomi, after trying to dissuade her, accepted her. We have learned from them, and we have learned as they have: by necessity, from calculation, from love.

Women's politics proceeds with an experimentation that involves individual women without reservations. One of the criteria used to ascertain its correctness is personal gain, which allows us to ascertain as well that individuals were not sacrificed. But this criterion has a limit in the fact that thought is revolutionized by a mental act which takes no time, while all the rest must be gained through a process of modification and rebalancing, which takes time and much more than time. In the interval thus created, it is difficult to say what is personal gain, because this is, more exactly, a time of personal risks, of energy spent without a guaranteed result, and of attempts which do not always produce the expected result. For some women, to find themselves experiencing such a situation is already a gain; for others, it is the promise of a gain; for others still, it may be too difficult a task. At this point, the gains cannot be calculated unless the element of personal choice is included as well. The individual woman must make her accounts and decide by herself what she wants, what is worthwhile for her, what she is willing and what, instead, she is not willing to risk.

Perhaps we ought to remember that the revolution brought about by female thought does not leave behind a world destroyed so that going ahead is unavoidable. The revolution of gendered thought has a logical irreversibility insofar as it is a form of thought that surpasses that of neutral-masculine thought. It is also constrained, to some extent, by the human condition of the female sex. But it does not have the historical necessity attributed, perhaps mistakenly, to social revolutions, and which these sometimes assume in destroying the world that precedes them.

Social revolutions destroy in order to force one to think the new. But destroying is of no use to the revolution of female thought because the new to be thought is a difference and what that difference makes thinkable for the knowledge and rule of the world. Subversion has to do with the way things are arranged, that is, their meaning. There are new arrangements which render a given reality meaningless, and thus change it by making it *deteriorate*. In this operation all violence is concentrated in thinking and putting into effect new arrangements, in contrast with the ones which a given reality presents as the only ones endowed with meaning and value. Physical destruction would not be as effective because there are arrangements which, even if destroyed, retain their meaning, and one can be sure that they will turn up again.

The new, then, cannot be forced into being. On the contrary, the first effect of women's politics is to show that the constraints borne as if they had no alternative really do have some; and that, as a rule, social impositions are always less powerful than one imagines them when she (or he) submits to them. The women's movement is particularly and originally marked by this knowledge. Think of the notion of female complicity with sexist domination, and even more, of the necessity to modify oneself as the other side of each project to modify society. Female political thought has emphasized that the symbolic order has a material effectiveness not inferior to that of the natural order, an idea which is not new in itself, but which the women's movement translated into political practice.

Even without knowing it, perhaps, all social revolutions are essentially symbolic in nature, as Simone Weil thought. The revolution brought about by female thought knows it is symbolic. The disruptive element in it is not acquired over or against the continuity of material things, the continuity which links together all things bound up with our being-body. Think of the way in which female symbolic authority took shape: from the new arrangement of free relations between and among women, through words and gestures of everyday life, bringing together particular needs in different combinations so as to make them a vital vehicle for the signification of female desire.

The liberation of the woman oppressed more by the figure of the oppressor than by the flesh-and-blood oppressor is still unfinished, and will not be irreversible until she herself finds the way to replace external constraint with internal necessity—until she herself sees that the world needs her freedom. Therefore, all the reasons we can adduce to urge the entrustment of one woman to another within the system of social relations, all our reasons, no matter how valid, cannot replace her own choice in each woman's mind. On the contrary, when we got to the bottom of those reasons, we understood that they cannot stand without the choice made by each woman in the ways and for the reasons that most suit her. The authority by which we are empowered must be close to, and consonant with, individual reality.

Within the horizon of sexual difference

The introduction of the relation of entrustment into social relations, so that the female sex may find in itself the source of its value and its social measure, is a political project born from the knowledge of sexual difference. Its basis is the necessity of gendered mediation. Its reference point is the female human experience, its past history, its present needs.

The objections of neutral (male) thought, all sterile and predictable, fall by the wayside: for example, the objection that any "plus" which emerges in human relations would be destined to become the object of private appropriation for the purpose of dominating others. This possibility, which of course cannot be excluded *a priori,* imposes itself with the force of an objection only for historical reasons. But history itself would be enough to refute it; the system of appropriating another's goods in order to dominate, instead of letting them circulate within the body social, was established, history shows, not by women but indeed against them.

Equally unfounded is the objection of those who say that the practice of disparity would go against an ideal of equality felt to be unrenounceable by every human being. The idea of equality, which once upon a time was not common sense, became common sense as a universal human goal by virtue of a political thought which, in theorizing it, with supreme inconsistency did not include human beings of female sex. This supreme inconsistency is explained by the fact that the idea of equality was arrived at through a history of relations among women. Women were included in it, and the inconsistency was remedied, when women themselves sought free social existence. They were then thought of as equal to men in their aspiration to equality, as if that were an appropriate response to their demands. It was not, but this aspect of the issue is secondary to another consideration—and that is, the ideal of equality did not, and does not, have anything to do with the history and the present state of relations among women. So much so that the equality meant when speaking of women is the equality of women to men.

We know that there can be a need for equality in the relations among women which is stronger than that of the male in certain aspects. But it is of a different nature. A woman can resent the negative social value of her sex so strongly that she cannot bear for herself, or want to inflict on another woman, this having to be less than her like. But it is precisely from this feeling that we learn about our deeper need to find, in our own gender, the source and measure of the social value of women, and of each individual woman. To recognize the fact of disparity between women and to practice it in the form of a relation of entrustment satisfies this profounder need. There probably are, or will be, other possible answers, better ones, for that matter. But it is certainly not an answer that women must constrain and regulate their relations so as to compensate for the injustice they suffer in relations with the other sex.

We have neither the desire nor the ability to answer this type of objection, because we conduct our lives according to the factual premise that our belonging to social life is determined by our belonging to its female component. And because our political practice is to transform this factual premise from a social cause of unfreedom into the principle of our freedom. There are, on the other hand, objections which affect our project directly and which should be taken into consideration because they are located within its range of thought, within the horizon of sexual difference, or because they reveal the difficulty a woman may encounter in locating herself within that horizon.

When Mademoiselle de l'Espinasse took to organizing meetings with the *philosophes,* without Madame du Deffand's knowledge, she knew she was going against her patroness's wishes but did not understand why the latter refused to encourage the fledgling party of the *philosophes* even though many of them were her friends and admirers. Mademoiselle de l'Espinasse had the naïveté of the young woman of talent who faces the world with élan and ambition, and does not perceive the extent to which all social intercourse is, in fact, male homosocial intercourse; or else she does not perceive it at all and thinks it is neutral, explaining the few female presences as the sign of a backwardness which will disappear with the general progress of customs.

There is more than one justification for this intellectual naïveté, often found in otherwise intelligent women: seduction by those who most obviously excel, the youthful presumption that she can succeed where others have not, the natural repugnance to thinking that being a woman may be a social disadvantage. . . . All these circumstances are overtaken by another, i.e., that being a woman and having claims on the world—though both in themselves are normal in a human being—form a combination which human society will not validate in its symbolic order. Thus, the woman who has grown up without losing her claim to counting for something in the world finds it more natural to turn to male individuals in order to get ahead. That is the obvious choice so long as the symbolic order is not changed and the difference of being a woman is not signified as a principle of value and a legitimation of female claims, capable of providing a measure of their worth with respect to the world.

The other reasons which are commonly adduced are less important. When the ties between women who have every interest in helping one another are not formed or when they are broken, it is not so much a result of excessive rivalry, or envy, or mistrust, or other, supposedly deeper motives of an unconscious kind. Before these reasons, a symbolic order must act which admits of relations of mutual aid between women (and these are, in fact, the ones usually practiced: every woman in need seeks out her fellow women with the most spontaneous feeling of trust) but does not foresee any relations which confer value.

If it does not revolutionize this order, the awareness which brought many of us to feminism is not useful to a young woman of ambition. It is knowledge valid in itself, but belated. It bears the marks of defeated claims, frustrated expectations, enthusiasms that came to naught, realizations dearly bought. A woman venturing into the world rejects such bitter knowledge because it threatens her good, which is to want and hope for the best she can have. If her still-intact claim and our awareness do not communicate with each other, there will be nothing but a succession of ingenuous hopes and bitter knowledge between one generation of women and another, without change or exchange.

The absence of exchange between these two moments of female humanity, between the woman who wants and the woman who knows, is not something whose cause should be searched for in female psychology: the cause is in the symbolic order that underlies the system of social relations. The alliance of old women with young women frightens men. Many of us may remember having been courted in our youth by men whose primary aim was to keep us from frequenting "older" women—older in either a literal or a figurative sense; women, that is, who were more aware.

The relation of entrustment is this kind of alliance, where by old is meant having the consciousness that comes with the experience of defeat, and by young is meant having one's claims intact, the one and the other entering into communication to empower each other in the face of the world. In fact, it sometimes happens that both things coexist in the same woman, who thus finds herself both old and young at the same time: though young, she is already warned that her difference has no worth in social intercourse; and however old, she is still attached to the wish to count for something in the world. This coexistence does not yet constitute a social relation, but it does prefigure it. If that relation is established between two women, a new combination enters the system of social relations which modifies its symbolic order.

Difference in age favors the formation of such a combination, because, on the one hand, it offers disparity the most easily acceptable arrangement, while, on the other hand, it makes what is involved explicit. What is at stake is the revolution of a symbolic order. The young woman needs to be told what is at stake so that she can make her choice. She recoils from knowledge that threatens her confident expectation, but not from making it available in order to accede to great human claims.

But the idea of practicing disparity and tying oneself down in a relationship of entrustment disconcerted even women who are aware of their difference and who do not look for ungendered measures of value, either in fantasy or in practice; women who, in fact, easily attach themselves to another woman and are ready to acknowledge her worth. For them, nothing they are or do is an obstacle to that project, which actually fits in very well with their personal way of being, except that it is presented as a political project.

This objection may seem very strange. In reality it is the most common, most diffuse one, since it concerns the visibility of female difference, its showing itself as such in the social body. Whoever has read *Cassandra* by Christa Wolf may understand this. To signify the female plus, since she could not imagine it circulating in the social body, the German writer represents it in the form of a community of women hiding in the caves of Mount Ida.

We have come across this objection more than once, often in courageous, sensitive women; it seemed to arise from their difficulty in grasping the political project of sexualizing social relations. Each time we repeated that we simply propose to translate into social forms their spontaneous behavior toward other women, until we finally understood what the stumbling block was. To give social and symbolic existence to female difference seemed just to these women, but not enough. In their eyes, female difference appeared to be a way to succeed in making society better, and for them, only this second goal would have the dignity of a goal, and hence the capacity to inspire a project worthy of our political struggle.

A similar view is held by those who, faced with the idea of a female plus to be recognized in relations between women so that it may be visible and circulate in the social body, objected that this plus is not qualified; it does not express positive values, and hence it cannot qualify, give value, either to female difference or to a female politics. The answer to the objection thus formulated is also simple: the female plus expresses nothing but the concept of the irreducible difference owing to which being a woman is neither subordinable nor assimilable to being a man. And therefore it cannot be qualified, for the only essential qualification is expressed by the adjective *female,* a horizon of humanity which is enriched by all that a woman is and becomes. The comparison refers only to this strengthening of oneself insofar as it is possible while remaining faithful to oneself.

These objections apparently confuse being different with being better. But a closer look reveals that it is not a question of confusion at all. The female difference that wants to be signified in contents already qualified, and wants to have the social good as its goal, seeks to attain that true and just transcendence which patriarchal culture denies women, binding them to an anatomical destiny, outside which even the most liberal society does not attribute any end or *raison d'être* to the female sex. The woman who wants to break the chains of this servitude, for herself and her fellow women, and at the same time wants— as is just or, better, necessary—to find a new, freer social interpretation of female difference, may believe she has found it in demonstrating that female difference is consonant with the social good, and may think that only this demonstrated consonance gives a women free social existence.

It must be said that very often this reasoning is crystalized in a spontaneous mental attitude, whose implications are more easily perceived in women's reactions to gendered transgression, that is to say, when a woman lets herself be guided by the interests of her sex rather than by interests considered common to all (which are usually male). Thus, to take a concrete example, the schoolteacher who theorizes a preferential relationship with her female students frightens the colleague who thinks she ought to assert her female difference by giving proof of her professionalism, and hence of impartial neutrality toward her male and female students. It is almost no use reminding her how much and in how many ways the male students are favored anyhow, merely by living in a society full of images which valorize their sex. She needs to prove her moral superiority as a woman, and seeing the exchange of privileges that goes on between men all but confirms her intention: she will oppose her superior justice to male injustice.

For many women, this is the only way female difference can signify itself in the world. So we understand why they ask for the female plus to be qualified, just as we understand their indignation at the idea of a social practice whose primary aim is to promote the interests of the female sex without investing them with some positive social quality. Consequently, we also understand why a gendered thinking about the world proves difficult for women who are not tempted by male thought and who sincerely desire a language marked by the feminine. They actually reason and speak in the feminine, but only within the specific context. When the topic becomes general, their experience passes through a filter which eliminates, often even before they realize it, all that clashes with an idealized image of the female sex. Female experience thus receives a simplified interpretation, and thought is weakened accordingly as it loses its grasp on reality.

This effect is noticeable even in the splendid prose of *Cassandra,* whose vigor wanes perceptibly when the test shifts from the description of the city of men where Cassandra lives to the description of the community on Mount Ida. It should have been the description of a feminine extraneous to the violence of male history, but instead it is the emblematic depiction of a feminine rendered insipid by the need to think itself better. The cavewomen who withdraw to model clay vases or to fuss over their handlooms are a thin ideological symbol of women's extraneousness to war; for a more concrete, material idea of it, one ought rather to think of the advantages, power, and pleasures women have seized for themselves, in the absence of men engaged in waging wars.

But thinking in this second, material way appears inferior to many women because it mixes up the special advantages of their gender with the higher interests of humanity; they would like to prove that they are seeking the latter for their own sakes and never want the former without them. They are ready to devote themselves unconditionally to female interests as such when women are oppressed and discriminated against. And one can understand the reason why, for in that case there is a higher good to defend, that of justice affronted.

A female politics has been grafted onto this mental attitude, a politics planning to change the social order by invoking the values embodied in female, rather than male, behavior such as doing volunteer work, taking care of the weak, shunning the use of violent means, etc. The splendor of these values, in which some of us firmly believe, does not prevent us from seeing the fundamental error of such a plan. To make the significance of female difference depend on contents of an ethical nature, or on any other content, is as politically ineffective as it is humanly wrong. Those who come into the world with a female body have chosen neither to be born nor to be born female. Being a woman, then, cannot depend for its existence on something which, by definition, has value only if it is freely chosen.

Sexual difference is an originary human difference. We must not enclose it in this or that meaning, but must accept it along with our being-body and render it significant: an inexhaustible source of ever-new meanings. If this difference is denied, every subsequent attempt to valorize it by showing that it corresponds to this or that social interest, even the noblest, is practically equivalent to forcing one of the two sexes—needless to specify which—to justify its being what it is: different from the other sex.

Our politics does not aim at bettering society, but at freeing women and their choices—that is, freeing them from the obligation of justifying their difference, with all the forms of social servitude that obligation entails and which have been well illustrated throughout human history. But though it is easy to criticize the politics of ethical values, the mental attitude it appeals to is deeply entrenched. Even when we have convincingly demonstrated that the ethical interpretation of female difference does not bring women freedom, the individual woman still has, on the one hand, the problem of freely integrating her own interests with those of society, and, on the other hand, her fear of gendered transgression.

All we can add is that no true, just transcendence can exist for women without gendered transgression. A woman must take her experience as a measure of the world, her interests as a criterion for judging it, her desires as a motive for changing it, so that the world may then become her own responsibility.

The action of those women who met only with other women, and consequently changed the methods and contents of their politics, is an example of liberating transgression. Their example legitimized others, but nothing and no one guaranteed that what they were doing was right. The value of female difference is not inscribed in the system of social relations, nor does anything which has to be done so that it will exist appear with a guarantee that it is the right thing to do. We, in flesh and blood, have to take the place of the missing guarantee, of the justice still to be done, of the truth still to be learned. It is an inevitable passage.

We must investigate this passage which we call inevitable, but which proves to be so difficult for women: it is to give oneself the authority to decide for oneself what to think, and what to want. A woman who has this authority makes the female difference visible and significant. Clearly, we do not think that to give oneself authority is an individual act. Authority is received originally from another human being who is in a position to give it, who has the authority to give it. But she cannot have it if the person who needs to receive it does not acknowledge it in her. "Go ahead," answers Bryher to H. D., giving back to her, in the form of symbolic authorization, the maternal authority which H. D. had attributed to her by turning to her.

The lack of female authority in and over the world is the result of an unfortunate mirroring between women. My sisters are my reflection, and what I cannot see in any of them is denied me as well. But why is this so? Why does a woman want to find in another woman the reassurance that she is not less, instead of searching for the possibility of being more? Where does this insecurity generating more insecurity come from?

To answer this, we investigated among ourselves, eliminating the easy arguments with which the lack of valorizing relations between women is usually explained away, and we were able to reach that level where social matter intersects its symbolic organization. In investigating our own selves, we saw that the disparity between women, with all that it signifies, evokes a maternal figure that may prove crushing when there is no social measure of value for the individual woman as well, that is to say, when practicing disparity valorizes her gender but not her personally.

The knowledge that no human value accrues to a woman without the value of what makes her different, this knowledge by itself (not accompanied, that is, by a female social economy) would (and does) lead to idealizing those women who from time to time come to embody female superiority. Actually it more often leads women (or those who are most insecure about their personal destiny) to look to male society for a measure of their value in order to counterbalance a maternal power which they feel cannot be appropriated. Male society has at its disposal a symbolic economy where, except in drastic cases of illness, old age, or marginalization, the individual has ways of asserting himself and exacting respect. It is true that this economy is supported and determined by the negative value of the female sex: to look for a measure of herself in it is a bundle of contradictions for a woman. But this problem may be lesser than the problem of being crushed by a female plus perceived as an excessive measure of the self.

We can now understand why, for years and years, the separate group of women did not acknowledge the fact of disparity within itself, although it was under everyone's noses. The separate group evokes the maternal figure with a power that no individual woman can equal, no matter how strong she may be; and individual women, even the strongest, have defended themselves from it by imagining themselves as equals, that is, as all equally partaking of that power. It was an expedient with a high price, as we said; its price was a limitation of the symbolic power of the maternal figure, thus reduced to the function of reparation of a female difference which, outside the group, was left without mediation, and therefore silent and ineffectual. . . .

Women need maternal power if they want free social existence. The mother is the symbolic figure of gendered mediation that puts women in relation with the world, opening a vital circuit between the self and the other-than-self in their experience, which otherwise remains divided between an unspeakable intimacy and an extraneous exterior. Maternal power, in itself, is not something from which the individual woman should defend herself, but the contrary. However, it mays seem such to her in a social-symbolic system that does not teach or show her in practice, that does not contemplate, but actually excludes, the way in which the individual can relate herself to that power and draw from it, as from a source, the sense of both her value and her freedom.

In the social order thought up by men, there are no forms of symbolic bond between a woman and the woman greater than herself, who is her mother. Only a natural relationship exists between the two, variously overlaid with affect and loaded with emotions, but without symbolic translation, that is to say, without figures or rules. If no one chooses to be born, for someone born a woman there seems to be no possibility of enfranchisement. In the social-symbolic order thought up by men, to be born a woman is an accident that conditions all of life. She has no personal destiny in life; there is no way for her to make freedom and necessity coincide. For her necessity means to submit to the social use of her anatomy (maternity, virginity, prostitution, the "chains of the flesh" mentioned by Teresa of the 150 hours), while her freedom merely means to evade all of this.

Outside the roles which give social meaning to female anatomy, a woman's destiny hangs in the void, dependent on personal choices which today are easily accepted but are not valorized by the knowledge that they answer to some objective necessity. So much so that in societies where women are not heavily engaged in the work of procreation, women's biographies become mostly chaotic, dragged hither and thither by the most casual circumstances. The female-sexed being, if not procreating, is not bound to anything. Freed from servitude to her anatomical destiny, a woman does not automatically become free, but rather superfluous.

Not unreasonably, some women interpret this superfluousness as a social direction that they should become neutral, ungendered, sexless human subjects, and they make this their destiny. Their biographies are consistent with this. In order to have a personal destiny, these women rid themselves of the "casual" datum of being female. They are said to be like men, but mistakenly, because men have a sex that determines them in what they are and do as social subjects.

Few women choose a consistently neutral or ungendered position. Many, perhaps the great majority, come and go restlessly between emancipation and feminine roles, combine the most disparate tasks, pass from one project to another, try one thing, try another, like someone pursuing something which exists only in her mind and nowhere else. This order cannot be changed without paying a price. The road toward change requires just such a payment.

The price of freedom which men pay in passing from nature to culture does not free women, whose natural servitude is extended into social servitude without solution of continuity. Nor should anyone believe that progress in societal life will provide freedom for them later on. Societal progress may make up for the social disadvantage of being born a woman, and this is the most it can do. But it does nothing, even less than nothing, toward female freedom: as long as a woman asks for reparation, no matter what she may obtain, she will know no freedom.

All of us, either personally or from our relations with other women, have experienced that female feeling of damage suffered which makes us ask for reparation. The demand is spontaneously addressed to women and men indifferently, but perhaps more often to the former, or those among them who may appear better endowed in some way—luckier, as that feeling suggests. We have also seen the demand for redress become a sort of female politics; in this version, on the assumption that they are all equally victimized by male society, women turn to the latter for redress. The response to such demand is usually positive; society has no problem in admitting that women are victims of a wrong, although it then reserves the right to decide according to its own criteria how they will be compensated, so the game may go on forever. But we well know that the demand is so indeterminate, the feeling of damage so deep, that there can be no satisfaction unless this consists precisely in the right to recriminate forever.

A similar attitude fits in the poor economy of female survival and perpetuates it along with its characteristics, subordination and irresponsibility. If we do not feel responsible toward a world thought up and governed by men or by their god, it is also often the case that a world toward which we have no responsibility appears to us to be governed by the will of others. The state of irresponsibility has its advantages. One is that society easily tolerates the mediocrity of female work. Contempt for the female sex also means that society does not expect the individual woman to do her best. In spite of the general discontent over the state of the educational system, for example, and in spite of the fact that primary and secondary schoolteachers are mainly female, no one blames women, and with few exceptions the latter do not feel addressed when the school system is criticized.

Obviously if a woman puts forward a claim for personal self-affirmation, then the standards become more rigorous, that is, closer to those applied to men—more rigorous, but also vicious, because inappropriate and improper for a woman. This is not, this cannot be, the price of female freedom. This price—the only one society makes explicit to its female members—is doubly senseless. First, because a woman might never stop paying it, since those standards will find her inadequate most of the time. Second, because it does not give her freedom since it is paid to the wrong creditor.

Women do not owe anything to men. To think otherwise would be moralizing. In modern societies, marked by the emancipation of women, a great deal of moralizing of this kind is done concerning women. There is no social contract between women and men. Men have never wanted one. It would be moralism for me to pay for what I take from someone who has found it more convenient for himself not to come to an agreement with me on the exchange.

In this sense, female irresponsibility is right. The mistake of many women and of the whole politics of victimization is to think that a woman, therefore, owes nothing to anyone, and not to see what she owes, instead, to other women—to the one who brought her into the world, to those who have loved her, those who have taught her something, those who have spent their energies to make the world more comfortable for her. . . . The female price for freedom is the payment of this symbolic debt.

If a woman does not see this debt, if she does not learn to pay it, she will never be free. The world will always be for her a thing thought up and governed by others from whom she can extort one advantage or another, but in the forever subordinate position of one who petitions. And her right to freedom, even when it is socially acknowledged, remains empty because she herself has not won the freedom of self-determination. If she does not see and pay for what she has received from other women, her possessions are not really hers. It may be "male" possessions—including her freedom—that she can thus display. Or else female possessions that she will not be able to display, like stolen things, with the insurmountable feeling of being forever poor, lacking, dispossessed, or incapable of bargaining for anything at all.

Treasures of reassurance have been poured in vain into the bottomless pit of female insecurity, whose first cause is not wanting, or not knowing, how to acknowledge the symbolic debt toward the mother. Simple gratitude in the relation between women is what female freedom is practically founded on. Everything else, in theory as in practice, is either a consequence of that or has nothing to do with freedom. One woman who is grateful to another for giving her something is worth more for the liberation of the female sex than a group or a whole feminist movement in which this kind of gratitude is missing.

By acknowledging the good received—life and sex, love, friendship, solidarity, knowledge, encouragement—a woman learns the way toward relating to the female source of her value. By taking on an obligation toward those women who have given her something, she puts an end to a furtive relationship. Maternal superiority will then no longer seem crushing to her, and her plus will become something which she can appropriate for herself to use in the world as she sees fit. The lack of gratitude between women impoverishes the individual and all women more than sexist domination does. Moreover, if we move to that symbolic level which underlies social relations, it is easy to see that the two causes of poverty coincide. Men cannot make a woman's riches his when she knows their female origin and displays them with the sign of their origin.

Moving to the symbolic level which structures social relations is also necessary in order to give gratitude its proper weight. It cannot be said that the current meaning of the word takes it away; the word *gratitude* in current use has, indeed, great weight. But among women, perhaps because a woman finds little correspondence between her feelings and social rules, it often happens that gratitude is reduced to an inner feeling or to private behavior. A woman can be full of gratitude toward a fellow woman, but when she enters into social intercourse, she is likely to feel confronted by a game where there is no way to signify gratitude. In that case, her gratitude remains without any consequences, and everything unravels again—inside/outside, subjective/objective, etc.—splitting the female mind in two and driving it back into its insecurity about the world.

That is why we say that the relation of female entrustment is a social relation, and we make it the content of a political project. The symbolic debt toward the mother must be paid in a visible, public, social manner before the eyes of everyone, women and men. The positive, liberating sense of this payment, on the other hand, like the sense of maternal authority itself, can hardly be grasped without a political practice of relations between women. This, in fact, removes the maternal figure from masculine representations and re-presents it to us in forms which answer to our needs and interests.

A woman, for example, needs to think that her desire can legitimately leave the sphere of the family and be directed toward social objects. The maternal figure as constructed by the male social-symbolic system often causes terrible guilt feelings in the woman who looks for satisfaction outside the family, and makes her invent hypocritical or neutral motives, or in any case, motives which are far from her real desire. There, a woman pays a toll of servitude to the mother. However, from her political bond with other women, from the responsibility she assumes toward other women out of her belonging to the female sex, a woman learns that the mother never asked her to pay that toll.

Earlier on, feminists thought that the mother is content with any position whatever. This is not true, as we now know. The egalitarianism of our political groups only covered up conflicts and emotions deriving from the ancient relationship with the mother, which could not be openly acknowledged. The practice of disparity between women is not optional: the mother demands to be recognized because of what she has given. This necessity, it must be added, is not separable from its fruit of freedom for the individual. By gaining freedom and strength in the eyes of the world, we come to know that our desires are legitimate and legitimated by a female social authority. The symbolic forms of this authority are the concrete gestures which produce freedom and self-respect in a woman's life. Otherwise she does not speak.

Taking care of qualitative differences

Someone may object that there are, however, instances of social injustice as well. And indeed there are. It would be stupid of us not to acknowledge that the existing disparity among women is determined or accentuated in part by an unequal distribution of social goods. But if we really confront it, if we do not bring it up only to disguise the paralyzing effects of envy, this fact need not vitiate or prevent the practice of disparity between women. In any case, the first injustice a woman suffers is the social disadvantage of not being born a man, and this concerns us all; aside from this elementary consideration, it must be said that the perpetuation of that injustice also depends on the lack of a social representation of possible female greatness.

It will be recalled that Maria Pia of the 150 hours decried the kind of feminist thought which did not offer her that representation of herself. She did not want to, could not let herself, be reduced to the figure of the oppressed woman. Other students affirmed that lack of self-assurance had counted for more in their lives than social injustice; these were women who had intimate, not hearsay, knowledge of social injustice. Their view presages a concept of justice which is different from the masculine one.

Both experience and women's politics show that the social valorization of differences must precede the issue of rights and the whole question of justice. Value is not bestowed along with justice; it comes before or does not come at all. But in that case, justice may not come either. Unless society values differences, justice proceeds by uniforming everything, and we see that this procedure more often succeeds in removing individuals from their own resources of originality than in eliminating injustice. In this way as well, a social class, the bourgeoisie, was able to bind the other classes to itself, to its interests and its projects, to its ways of reasoning and behavior. With a substantially identical procedure, nations which have been long industrialized bind the destinies of agricultural countries to their own—that is to say, by ignoring differences in ways of thinking and acting, and at the same time, by offering a dream of possible equality with those who, by now, present themselves as a model of development.

The women's movement is against this tendency to assimilation. It started with women who rejected the prospect of becoming men's equals, and chose to give preference to relations with other women in order to know themselves and how to act in the world. In this sense, the women's movement, no matter what the social location of the women themselves, is an antibourgeois movement.

The difficult thing to realize is that the need for justice can play into the hands of the tendency to assimilation when it tries to compare what is not comparable. In emancipated societies, the female search for free social existence has been too often interpreted and measured according to goals achieved by men, as if that were the most appropriate interpretation. It was indeed appropriate for the kind of justice aimed at eliminating disparity, but women thus found themselves divided from each other and separated from their original resources, which lie in their belonging to the female gender. We can escape this contradiction by proposing that justice does not come before everything else. Fidelity to what is, to what one is, comes before everything else. The practice of disparity among women is not justice or injustice, but something which comes before and concerns the interpretation of sexual difference.

Disparity in social relations appears in intricately confused forms. Our need for others is confused with exploitation by those who have more power; unjust forms of disparity are valorized, or at least resist elimination by piggybacking on those differences which we feel are unavoidable and even beneficial in certain cases. The practice of disparity is a necessary test. It will make it possible to distinguish unjust forms of disparity from others which are in any case unavoidable, as even male thought admits without, however, the verification of an explicit political practice. There are disparities between human beings, like that between men and women, which take the place of a qualitative difference that is not interpreted as such. In this case, eliminating injustice does not mean instating parity but rather making the difference speak in free social forms.

Among the productive forms of disparity, the one between adult and child is the only one which can be cited as an example in our culture, but others exist or could exist. There are forms of disparity, in beauty or health, which often cannot be eliminated; it is senseless to call them unjust even if they unfortunately provide the occasion for some of the worst injustices—think of the condition of the sick or of the old who do not have the power of money.

An egalitarian politics does not have the means for evaluating injustice and never succeeds in eliminating it. Egalitarian projects have regularly backfired as a result of the conservative whiplash they receive from outside, as well as from inside, when an unavoidable disparity between human beings becomes the vehicle of the social privilege of some over others. The events of 1968 are an example of this; just think of the educational or social selection revaluated by the very people who had denounced it unequivocally at that time, in a moment of generous enthusiasm for eliminating injustice. The problem is to prevent the measures taken by those in power from ignoring those qualitative differences within which the original value of a human experience is preserved. And to know that even the search for social justice often tends to ignore them.

When the green *Sottosopra* came out, where the practice of disparity and entrustment between women was proposed for the first time, its authors were accused of supporting entrenched social hierarchies—an accusation which sounded like a compliment in certain versions because of the realism they showed. It was a laughable accusation and an undeserved compliment. The woman who is truly respectful of entrenched hierarchy, in this society, entrusts herself to a man or to a male enterprise.

But, as we later understood, this accusation, ridiculous in itself, originated from the difficulty of attributing authority, in acknowledging superiority without associating it with domination, with the sanction of power, with the form of hierarchy. Thus, the proposal that we should bring to light the feelings aroused in us by admiration for a woman was understood by some women, not as the possible attribution of social value to what takes place between women, but as an obligation to be consistent: if you do not hide your admiration for a great man, learn to show your admiration for a great woman as well; if you accept the hierarchies established by men, respect them even when a woman is in a superior position; and so forth. Not, therefore, entrustment as the social instance in which the qualitative, living substance of female experience—the ancient relationship with the mother, gratitude for the good received, desire searching for its fulfillment—leaves its mark in a human relation; but a transferring to women of the model of male power which thus imposes itself as universal, ungendered mediator and sole standard of human superiority.

If the original value of difference is not safe, if there are no qualitative differences, if everything can be compared with everything else, and if one sees a struggle between power and right in every difference, then the only differences, the only measures, that end up being dominant are those set up by the objectivity of power. This gross but easily made equivocation illustrates the problem we have with justice. Introducing the relation of entrustment between women into social relations can save female difference from being absorbed into a system of neutral measures. But the sense of entrustment must be saved.

When the hierarchies of power threaten us, or tend to be reproduced among us, we oppose them neither with the ideal nor with the practice of equality, but rather with the practice of disparity in its given forms so that female desire may surface among them and become primary. An ardent desire is enough to create a possible disparity between human beings; it is a disequilibrium, vital, dynamic, and, under certain conditions, capable of counterbalancing any form of inevitable disparity (sickness, old age, physical ugliness . . .) and combating the unjust ones.

But when hierarchies are set up with objective criteria, no matter which (even those of compensatory justice), the criteria end up replacing the original indication of desire or need and its dynamism. When need and desire lose their qualitative contents and are translated into a vague demand for power, then, of course, everything may seem to be a question of rights and justice. But then subjective experience is lost, along with its original content and its potential riches.

For us, the original quality of female experience must be safeguarded before justice can be. And that experience must signify itself openly in the form of a desire which is no longer reticent or imitative; it must have authority in the knowledge and governing of the world, and, therefore, in what concerns social justice as well. It is this sequence which alone makes us competent to argue about justice.

Class and national differences also exist among women, and involve much injustice and many just reasons for conflict. We can deal with these in a productive way if, and only if, the interests at stake and the reasons adduced bear the mark of gendered difference. Otherwise the contradictions will call up men's interests and authority, and the polemics between women will revert to the patriarchal paradigm of the daughter's hate for the mother.

Doing justice starting with oneself

We think that there will be no justice for women as long as they know it as the thing which has been denied them and must be restored to them—as long as they do not know it as something they can, and must, do starting from themselves in their own relationships. Society has absolutely nothing to teach us about this. Regulated from the outside in the interest of the collectivity, women were left among themselves like a herd out to pasture. Which, since it is a question of human beings, would anyway have given rise—and in certain circumstances did give rise—to rules and measures. But women were a herd on the symbolic level, not in social life. In the latter, in fact, they were mostly isolated from each other.

The end of this isolation, which was the birth certificate of feminism, enabled us to discover that the system of social relations always functioned, and goes on functioning, without a single thought concerning women's relations with women. From this point of view, too, putting the practice of relations among women at the center of female politics was a wise decision. It was thanks to this that a state of affairs which neutral (male) thought left in the dark of the unthought, and which ideological feminism tended to beautify simplistically, became an extraordinary opportunity for getting to the gendered foundations of the social contract. Without rules and measures of exchange with other women, a woman never learns the rules of social exchange.

Imagine you are at the beside of a dying woman. You will find out from her words that what she has not had and what she thinks she can still give are tangled up in a knot lacking any expression of regret for what she has received and must not leave behind. There is no feeling of death in her, but the final desperation for a life in which accounts never square. We have encountered this regime of accounts which never balance, if less dramatically, in the practice of relations between women. We tried to put them in order; our attention to personal gains should have served this purpose too.

A specific political treatment was required even for something as simple as the appreciation of the advantages of a situation improved by our collective political struggle. The advantages were enjoyed, but not evaluated. A tendency prevailed of thinking of oneself and other women as if swayed by the whim of the moment, disinterestedly, without calculation or obligation. Furthermore, if we had to make accounts, quite a few liked to portray themselves as women who had given up other great opportunities, the more indeterminate, the greater. We later realized that enjoyment without obligation and the emphasis on personal sacrifice sprang (spring) from our ignorance of our symbolic debt to the mother and of ways to pay it.

This is also the cause of the more strikingly ungrateful behavior of those women who get ahead in the world by relying on what they have received from other women, and while doing so, feel the need to underscore their distance from them. Such behavior, despicable but not rare, is justified considering that the unpaid symbolic debt leaves a gap which must somehow be filled. Usually, women remedy this by creating a bond of unifying complicity, of commonality or sameness among themselves, which defends them from male hate as well as from hate among themselves. This defense works as long as no one tries to distinguish herself from the others. On her part, the woman who wants to leave this commonality, and who does not know, does not want to acknowledge, that she needs her fellow women, will solve the problem by denying any debt, especially toward those women from whom she has received something precious for herself.

These are two sides of the same question. The judgment on female solidarity depends on it. The solidarity which must make up for the absence of rules of exchange between women is a poor defense against the contempt of society for the female sex. Perhaps there is no woman who, from infancy, in her relations with her mother, her sisters, her friends, her schoolmates or fellow workers, has not known about the difficulty of reconciling the female demand for commonality with the need for her own personal distinction.

This knotty problem also appears in the writings of the women in the 150-hour courses mentioned earlier. According to Teresa, women are reluctant to draw attention to themselves in social life "for fear of other women's judgment." She attributes this reluctance correctly not to a personal lack of courage, or to the maliciousness of other women, but to a collective state of servitude which is symbolic in nature. The individual woman hesitates, and the others do not give her the encouragement she needs because, outside the domestic sphere, everything a woman does runs the risk of seeming like a repudiation of her gender. Consequently, many women give up the hope of fulfilling in the outside world "what they are inside themselves," with the result that "many spiritual and psychic values are buried."[6]

We would search in vain among the age-old male pronouncements on the relation between individual and collectivity for an answer to the problem each woman encounters in reconciling her wish for personal distinction with her sisters' demand that she not leave the women's commonality. The social-symbolic order, which men believe to be universal, does not provide this problem with an answer, whether just or unjust, acceptable or capable of improvement. Everything that takes place between and among women—life, words, feelings, sexuality, love, knowledge—was left to chance in that order, regulated only when it interfered with the regulation of men's relations. It is precisely this blind spot in male political thought that proves how the social contract was conceived on the sole basis of male human experience.

The first wave of feminism used words and slogans which were judged from the outside to be extremely individualistic. Freedom, as a feminist questioned on this subject answered, "means freedom to be . . . *to be*. Freedom to be different . . . in spite of the law, even beyond what you called 'natural laws.' To be able to relate to people on the basis of what one truly is. Freedom is being able to choose without erasing any part of oneself: one's own intellectual being, one's own material needs, one's own innermost self." To this a woman engaged in the class struggle responded that she, who "had been born to reason," had instead "tried very hard not to be different." Different, for her, meant privileged, separate, making her way without waiting for anyone else, etc. Years later, comparing the two answers, a third woman finds the first less ideological, more sincere, but she does not hesitate to classify it among positions "of a liberal-individualistic, explicitly elitist kind."[7]

This is an altogether extrinsic judgment. If a woman cannot reconcile what she experiences in herself with the norms that regulate collective life, and if, aware of this disconnectedness, she identifies her freedom with the possibility of being herself, that is, "different" (what else could she say, from the perspective of an experience lacking representation in society?), then individualism is as little to the point as collectivism, that is, not to the point at all.

The answer of the feminist, of the first wave of feminism, reflects the position of a human subject without freedom, subordinated to the interests of societal life. The answer can be, and has been, criticized, but for a completely different reason. It was an abstract answer; it did not take into account the necessary mediation between the individual self and the self formed by her human identification with the female gender. In the early years of feminism, female difference blended with individual differences; both the former and the latter had the same absolute *raison d'être*.

Self-criticism began in feminist thought with the Pinarella meeting in 1975, where it became clear that in order to have free social existence, the individual woman must work through a mediation between herself and her fellow women, so as to be able to get out of her "psychological prison"—in the words used by Teresa in 1977. The first feminist groups had met the demand for a commonality based on gender, in a form we can call elevated, if we compare it with the lower commonality typical of spontaneous female groupings. But it was obvious at Pinarella that the problem had not been solved. On the one hand, there were women who said they were excluded and who clearly showed by their fantasies ("we are all insecure") that there was still a very strong demand for a commonality based on negativity and defeat. On the other hand, there were feelings of guilt. A woman who distinguished herself in some way with respect to the others was threatened by the idea of renouncing, repressing, or censuring (the terminology varied) her own gender—that is to say, betraying the mother.

We must also add to the above the position—which did not appear in our groups for obvious reasons—of those women who shrink from associating with their fellow women in order to escape their demand for gender commonality which they know, or rather fear, tends toward negativity and defeatism. These all seemed to be, were presented as, facts of a psychological kind, but they were the signs of the savage state of female humanity.

Women may appear to be the most civilized part of humanity in many ways. The absence of civilization appears, and we recognize it, when a woman enters into conflict with another woman and finds herself having to face emotions that nothing and no one has taught her how to handle in a socially appropriate form. A savage state, then, in every sense of the word, determined by the fact that a woman's relation with another woman has no place among the forms of relationship wanted by the collectivity. This is why the personal search for distinction is experienced by many women as something incompatible with the female demand for a commonality based on gender: do not forget that you are a woman like all the others.

Actually, these are two irreconcilable aspirations in a society where authority and value are masculine in origin. The search for distinction separates one woman from the others insofar as neither she as an individual nor they all together know the female origin of that plus, that something more which allows the individual to distinguish herself. We can reread the ancient myth of Proserpine in this light. An authority of masculine origin intrudes into the relationship of the daughter with the mother, giving the daughter a social status which she did not win from the maternal authority. Thus she will end up imprisoned in the realm of the petrified symbols of male power, in need of other women but incapable of negotiating with them for what she wants.

There are women experienced in social negotiation who nevertheless demand to be accepted as they are by other women with an arrogance and an ingenuousness which are attractive only in a child. One's own sex is denied just as well by conceding nothing to the generic female demand to "be like all other women," when, that is, I do not do what is necessary to make other women recognize a fellow woman in me.

The symbolic debt to the mother can be paid in this way too. But it is not optional. It may seem to be, but only because society, as it is, functioning and founded on male freedom, does not present it to us; on the contrary, it forces those women who aspire to personal self-affirmation to follow the rules already set down by the male part of the social body. In one way or another, the social exoneration from the obligation to pay one's debt to the mother always falls back on the woman in the form of servitude. Without gratitude to the mother, belonging to the female sex is a destiny that weighs us down; it is a *misfortune,* a *dis-grace.*

We are not free with regard to payment of the symbolic debt, yet its payment is liberating for us. It represents the internal necessity which replaces the external coercion and dependence on others which have shaped women's choices. Thus, the random chance by which one was born a woman can be converted into personal destiny, and mischance revealed to be a *grace,* in the classical sense of the term, familiar to anyone who knows Simone Weil's thought. In other words, a woman is free when she chooses to signify her belonging to the female sex, well knowing it is not an object of choice.

The paradox of this formulation of female freedom is resolved when we consider that woman has been enslaved socially because of her anatomy. One could act like an animal caught in a trap who frees itself by biting off its trapped paw. But the body in which patriarchal society entrapped us was lovingly formed by a mother. We can, or rather we must, free ourselves from her without ferocity, humanly. That is to say, symbolically.

This whole discussion brings us inevitably to the conclusion that, for a woman, the freedom earned in relations among women is her freedom, and that the social contract by which she freely binds herself to her fellow women binds her to the whole world as well. A woman, in other words, is responsible for the world inasmuch as she must answer for herself to other women; she has no social obligations which are not derived from the obligations to other women. We realize that these statements sound terrible, just as the words which named the "injustice" present in our relations did. These statements, too, are "unjust" in comparison with conventional ideas of justice. For indeed they are suggested by a thought previously unthought in the social organization of relations between human beings. It is, however, a just and necessary conclusion in which facts agree with reasoning.

The facts show that society does not hold women responsible for collective life; that some want to be responsible, and want to participate in it, is absurdly assigned to the category of what they have a right to. Other arguments could be adduced, but this one is sufficient to demonstrate that women are not concretely present in the contract that founds societal life. If the latter depended on male good will in the same way that it depends on female good will, it would go to pieces tomorrow. A man in the fullness of his strength, ousted from collective responsibilities, is a mine floating around in the social body; the innumerable women who are in that same situation serve the common good without creating any problems.

A woman participates in social life in the same way as those who join volunteer organizations, with the difference that if she does not like being in this life, she cannot go to another, but can only remove herself, erase herself. And quite a few women, incidentally, join social enterprises as volunteers with the notion of thus participating in social life: what they are and do in their daily existence does not seem a proper social life to them. Actually, it is not, and neither is that imitation of life which is their volunteer work: both lack the element of negotiation, which is wholly replaced by their good will. Thus when they try to imagine freedom, women will often use words which seem extremely individualistic. If they take on responsibilities concerning the collective interest by a voluntary, personal decision, and if they contributed substantially to the common good by physical and affective bonds, where are the social terms to signify women's freedom?

These are not extraordinary discoveries. Men know that male individuals are sufficient and necessary to the contract needed to sustain social life; women are superfluous. On their part, women know that men's society needs their presence but not their freedom. They know it only too well, and they tend to imagine their freedom as a right to be claimed, without considering that, and to what extent, they themselves have already renounced it in order to make up for the social disadvantage of having been born women—in psychological terms, to be accepted. A woman uses up part of her human potential in her efforts to make up for the social disadvantage of belonging to the female sex, and socially, she shows she has used it up.

Events and reason tell us that claiming freedom as compensation for a freedom one has renounced cannot bring the results one hoped for. Nor can one suppose that they will be attained by those women who, in their search for freedom, estrange themselves from their fellow women whom they see as not free. A woman belongs to humanity insofar as she belongs to the female sex: the one signifies the other, and there are no alternatives which are not interpretable (and, in fact, are always interpreted) as a denial of oneself.

We therefore say that the tie of gratitude and acknowledgment toward her fellow women is essential to a woman's social bond. It makes the bond real through her responsibility, and strong in her negotiating power. Everything else is either subject to that bond or worth only what joining some volunteer organization is worth. Female freedom, in short, does not come from admission to male society, or from a claim made on that society, but from that elementary negotiation in which a woman exchanges with other women the recognition of her own existence for the signified acceptance of their mutual belonging to the female sex.

In itself, our conclusion would in no way clash with common sense, if one only considers that women are half of the human race. To derive the social form of one's own freedom from one's kinship with the female sex is surely not a small bond with the world. Certainly it is a more shared, more social bond than the one traditionally established for a woman through the few male individuals who, as bearers of their own personal interests, effectively ensured that she conformed with the interests of all men. Similarly, it is a bond more consistent, more exacting, than the one some women assume toward the collectivity by embracing so-called universal projects which actually are extraneous to the female subset of that collectivity.

But the bond we are formulating, based on our symbolic debt toward the mother, is a *gendered* one, and signifies the female difference within the social contract. It introduces that difference into a system of social relations that bases its universality on the insignificance of female difference, and that is enough to conjure up horrible specters of social disorder. Whoever has a more than superficial knowledge of witch hunts (at least enough to know they are a matter of modern, not medieval, history) knows what can happen to the male mind when faced with the prospect of an alliance among women.

But the female mind itself retreats or reels before the host of possible, as yet unthought implications of that conclusion. And if it hesitates to acknowledge that it is an inevitable, just conclusion, it is because it has not yet evaluated all of its possible consequences or found the way to reconcile them with what it already knows. The problem of gendered transgression thus returns, and trips many women up, in spite of their desire for freedom, when they must move conceptually to the site of freedom, which is to give oneself the authority to judge and decide by oneself.

Historical events indicate that it may be less difficult for a woman to move there bodily than conceptually, thus leaving to others the responsibility for the consequences, which are always unpredictable to some extent. One sees that numerous women have often participated alongside men in the great human quests for freedom, and have taken liberties for themselves which, however, they did not know how to keep after the quest, as far as the men were concerned, had ended. We think of the women who took part in the Italian Resistance or in the struggle for Algerian liberation, as if defying the Nazis and Fascists or the torturers of the OAS were an easier thing to do than questioning the family hierarchy or changing the process of holding a political meeting.

We have said that gendered transgression—that of the woman who does not respect the established order for reasons dictated by her female experience—is an inevitable passage, and we presented it as a personal choice. We are, however, aware that the strength consciously to transgress is possessed by few among women, no differently than among men. But an analysis of that passage necessary for female freedom revealed that the other side of transgression is conformity to an order.

Female politics, as we understand it, consists in bringing to light for every woman this other side of female transgression, so that every woman may understand, evaluate, and appropriate the reason behind the irregular behavior of her fellow women who do not conform to the rules prescribed by society, and on that reason may base her behavior in the world: the reason of the mother who kills her child, of the woman who does not marry, of the lesbian poet, of the selfish daughter . . . and so on, until one understands the many ways in which female humanity tries to signify its need for free existence, from the child who falls from her arms into the boiling wash, up to the impulse to shoplift in supermarkets.

The countless instances of a sought-for freedom will remain fragmented, brilliant at the moment and then destined to go out, if they hit a social body which has neither the will nor the way to translate them into a coherent meaning. It is the task of female politics to show in practice, and demonstrate in theory, how those fragments can combine among themselves and with the world in an unheard-of yet sensible form; this would connect an apparently meaningless transgression, not negatively, to the oppression undergone by the transgressing woman, but positively, that is, connect it to the reasons of the woman who transgresses consciously. The first *autocoscienza* groups which gave rise to our politics were aware of this and worked in this direction, toward a new social combination and a positive bond.

There are women who have the strength to personally violate the universality exhibited by male thought, and who do not use male or ungendered measures to act in the world, to judge it and decide; they use only that measure—female human experience—of which they are sure and competent to make use. What comes to light in such women as Madame du Deffand, Jane Austen, or Carla Lonzi is not disorder, is much more than rebellion: it is fidelity and consistency.

The light of a rationality that is not extrinsic, not superimposed on one's own experience, has the power to orient the female mind in its search for free social existence. One can explain the emerging sense of gendered transgression, and its effect on those who yet lacked the personal strength to transgress, by considering that, by virtue of gendered transgression, the passion of sexual difference—that blind endurance of one's own difference from which no woman can entirely escape—is transformed into knowledge: consciousness of self and competence vis-à-vis one's given reality, competence to judge it and to change it.

We name female politics the project for changing our existing reality by utilizing the possibility, which every woman, every human being, possesses, of transforming what she suffers from reality into a knowledge of reality. Whoever comes into the world with a female body suffers, from the natural and social reality, the pain of her sexual difference. The transformation of that reality into knowledge about nature, society, and their relations is both her human possibility and her social plus.

Some men and women think that female difference should have no place among the things of this world, and that its fate should be to stay among utopian things—utopia literally means *nonplace*. We do not share this view, first of all because abandoning the social translation of female difference equals letting women stay in the place where society puts them. The Olympus of the Greeks was populated by marvelous female divinities, but the women in their cities and villages were undernourished and prematurely pregnant servants. Second, we do not share this view because we cannot theorize things in contrast with our experience, and we are seeking social existence. We judge negatively those women who want and secure for themselves a social position in political parties, on newspapers, etc., and from there then theorize about the utopia of female difference.

But our positive experience counts for more. In actuality, our functioning in society is aided by relations with other women, and we suffered when those relations were missing. We are open to exchanges with other women and feel that their judgment, whatever it may be, is the most important social judgment for us to take into account. Indeed, our existence in the world has improved since we followed the rule of taking care of our gender's interests, and of other interests only insofar as they are compatible with the former.

In actuality, then, we had a bond with the world, the bond of an unnamed social contract which was based on the principle of gratitude and exchange with other women. Now we have named it, and not without consequence. Since it is named, it ceases to be something practiced in this or that context according to the convenience of the moment, and becomes an acknowledged, explicit form of female sociality, and hence a measure of judgment to which we submit ourselves and other women.

A woman can and must judge other women. A woman can and must face the judgment of other women. In the social regime which elided the relations between women, the individual woman feared the judgment of her fellow women as a threat to herself, to her wish for affirmation, to her originality—so much so that early feminism had nearly prohibited the judging of one woman by another without, however, being able to prevent the expression of some judgments, though mute and unappealable, uttered and rejected with the violence of things that touch us without the interval of thought. A woman's judgment on her fellow woman always impresses her and can have an enormous importance for better or for worse, whether it is acknowledged or not. We do not propose to submit to it but, on the contrary, to acknowledge its weight, and therefore to think through and actualize a regime of social relations where female freedom is guaranteed by women themselves.

Suspending all judgment, as early feminism desired, is not liberating, aside from the little consistency of such a proposal. In actuality, as we have shown, it produced unwanted moderation in female social undertakings. Inhibiting the female measure of judgment was supposed to show regard for a desire which dared not signify itself, but the only effect of such regard is to preserve the reticence of female desire, for indiscriminate acceptance is never felt as valorizing, not even by the one who needs it. If the need for approval prevails among women over their desires, if they do not dare subject their desires to judgment, sensing that short of unconditional acceptance there would be only denial and death, then our social undertakings will be what satisfies that need and placates those fears each time they surface. But they will be nothing else. They will not leave behind the conformism unwilled, unchosen, yet not imposed from the outside.

As for the women who had courage enough to defy Nazis fascism, but not to rebel against a domestic life without freedom, or against a political practice which was extraneous to their way of being, this strange phenomenon—a phenomenon recurrent in human history—may be understood by going back to what some women said to explain what holds them back from exposing themselves in a social context without the protection of male choices. They are afraid of other women's judgment, afraid of falling into a void of meaning; they try to tell themselves that doing something for themselves is their right, but it is not enough.

It is not the severity of their oppression that explains the failure of female freedom, but the lack of authority, of symbolic authorization—that authorization which a woman can receive only from a female source because it is the only one which legitimates her in her difference. And which she receives only if she agrees to submit to a female measure of judgment. The latter, as we know, is the decisive, difficult step of female freedom, which determines whether female difference will issue alive from its historical imprisonment, inside and interior, twice inside: inside the social order which keeps her locked in an unspeakable experience, inside the experience of the individual woman who does not know how to get out of it without denying her sex.

Survival or freedom

Instead of tearing up the social contract and measuring themselves against the world according to their difference, one might think that it would be better for women to wait and encourage the progressive social validation of their sex by eliminating the forms of discrimination which still persist, from the most apparent to the almost invisible, more insidious kind rooted in family life or in less controlled social behaviors.

This moderate perspective, upheld by people sincerely concerned with righting the relations between the sexes, would be unobjectionable were it not that in the social order those people have in mind, though it is capable of progress, nothing has been thought of to allow a woman to take another woman as reference and gain self-confidence, self-validation, in return. This kind of relation is essential. Without it, the elimination of discrimination is an endless process. When this kind of relation is introduced and at work within the system of social relations, things will be exactly as we say now; that is, a woman will be guaranteed free social existence primarily by her fellow women, or she will not be guaranteed it at all.

Tearing the social contract in half is not too great a cost to secure that guarantee. It takes but little historical knowledge to realize that the progress we are promised together with the rights already guaranteed is, in fact, dependent on a geographically limited social wealth, which is historically recent and endangered besides: by economic crises at regular intervals, and by a possible atomic war, or ecological disaster in the near future.

Freedom on these conditions would already be very precarious. But it is not freedom in any case, because even someone with very little imagination cannot help looking back in time or closer in space at poorer countries, and realizing that her existence as a woman is threatened by a negating violence that will tear her to pieces if that is what society needs. The threat is not external. Within a society marked by female emancipation, when she does not work in the service of man, a woman notices immediately that her human difference is a detail as visible as it is irrelevant. She is a woman, but she could be a man, and society lets her know in a thousand ways that it would be better for her if she really were one.

The progress promised is that one day society will no longer send her this signal, so that she will be a woman without any reason for being one, but without feeling that it would be better for her not to be one. Progress would then mean for me to be divided in two—on the one hand, a female-sexed body, on the other, a social and thinking subject; and between the two not even the bond of a sensorily perceived uneasiness would exist any longer: rape perfected as a symbolic act.

For female freedom to be guaranteed by itself—without which it is not freedom, but emancipation, as it is rightly called—it is indispensable that the historical circumstances which favored our liberation from the outside be rendered superfluous, so to speak; that they be translated into, or replaced by, a freedom which reproduces itself parthenogenetically and produces the material conditions necessary for its exercise. If, as has been written, it is true that the pasteurization of milk contributed more to giving women freedom than did the struggles of the "suffragettes," we must act so as never again to let it be true. Similarly for medicine, which reduced infant mortality and invented contraceptives, or for the machines which made human labor more productive, or for the progress in societal life which induced men no longer to consider women inferior beings. Where does this freedom come from that arrives in a bottle of pasteurized milk? What roots has the flower which is offered to me as the sign of a superior civilization? Who am I if my freedom lies in this bottle, in this flower someone placed in my hand?

It is less the precariousness of the gift that we question—though it should not be neglected—than its origin. One must be the origin of one's own freedom in order to have sure possession of it, which does not mean guaranteed enjoyment, but the certainty of knowing how to reproduce it even in the least favorable conditions. The purpose of sexualizing all social relations down to their foundations is to put women at the origin of their freedom, before those pieces of paper called laws or constitutions, before the organization of material production and scientific research which now gives me a bottle, then a pill, then who knows what, and before social conventions ordering men to respect the other sex. Before. That is, at the time when sexual difference receives its first interpretation.

We do not reject the fruits of civilization when they are useful to us. On the contrary, we appreciate them greatly, the more so since behind them there is not only the work of free men but also a great deal of work by women who desired to be free. We appreciate the medical science which reduced infant mortality, the machines which replace or lighten manual labor, the social rules which inhibit man's sexual aggressiveness, the reforms which open every career and profession to women, the philosophical and scientific theories according to which the anatomical difference between women and men is not to be interpreted as inferiority of the former.

But these are only the fruits, and freedom, as we have always known, or at least known since the time of the French Revolution, is a tree. If a woman's freedom is not rooted where social life begins, in the first relations which tell her who she is and introduce her to the world, if she does not develop in keeping with her origin, if she does not base her social existence on the strength of this fidelity, then she will be "free" by chance, a chance that made her be born in this century and on this piece of earth. But chance did not make her a man, and her poor freedom without roots is mocked by this final misfortune.

We cannot really go back in time to the moment before our difference from man was interpreted as being something less. But we can go back to that before with a mental act which we endow with the reality of its consequences in the present. We will not make female freedom, ours and that of our fellow women, depend on the progress of a culture which, from time immemorial, has nourished itself on contempt for our sex. We will do the opposite. We bind ourselves in a pact of freedom with our sisters, and through them with the world, and hereafter, our social existence having been guaranteed, we will do what remains to be done so that society may free itself from contempt for the female sex. The politics of sexual difference does not come *after* the equality of the sexes has been achieved; it replaces the much-too-abstract and often contradictory politics of equality in order to fight against every kind of sexist oppression from the place of an achieved female freedom, founded on social relations between women.

There is a low register of female survival which confirms what we say here both positively and negatively. In order to survive, women have given, and give, each other material and symbolic help which is so basic that if it is lacking, there is no social guarantee that can take its place, no religion, or laws, or etiquette. This fact, easily seen when we must face the great necessities of life, reappears, if less evidently, even in mundane circumstances—for example, in that mental attitude which makes many women expect or demand unconditional acceptance on the part of other women, that attitude which we said reveals the savage state of relations between women. But it also reveals that a woman cannot live in the world unless she is accepted by her own kind, and that she needs this more than the guarantees offered by the law, religion, or good manners, not to speak of sterilized milk and bunches of mimosa.

This way of helping each other, excluding negotiation and not signifying exchange, is useful for survival but nothing more; in this limit is the cause of the social weakness of the female sex—a weakness which appears precisely in advanced societies and which one then tries to explain by appealing to insidious, hidden forms of antifemale discrimination. Entering social intercourse, without taking into account the good received from other women, without acknowledging the social nature of the need one has of them, and without reference to female models, gives rise to incompetence in the unwritten laws of give-and-take in social relations, to a lack of self-confidence paid for by extra effort at adapting to dominant models, and to the feeling that every plus one gains in society is gained against or over one's fellow women, that is to say, one's own sex, and therefore oneself.

There is no question that there are forms of continuing antifemale discrimination even in advanced, emancipated societies. But this is not an explanation; on the contrary, it needs explanation. If, in social relations, female difference is exposed to evaluations which damage women, the cause is to be found in the gendered nature of social relations. There is no ungendered social subject who will wish for and effect the end of all discrimination; if the social translation of the human value of being a woman is not done by women, it will be done by men according to their criteria. Criticizing these criteria and trying to better them in favor of the female sex, whatever the result may be, cannot fill the gap left if a translation done by women themselves is missing.

There is a low register of female survival. We propose to convert it into a high register of freedom by naming and giving social form to what went on between women without name or form. Clearly, it will not be the same, either for women or for the whole of society, if the help we gave one another to survive becomes an alliance which guarantees our social existence. But it will not be the end of the world. We are splitting in two a social contract which already worked in a divided manner: in negotiations between men, in solidarity among women. This splitting will not give rise to chaos.

It will give rise to a society thought up and governed by women and men, where their difference will find the way to signify itself freely, from dress to the administration of justice, the organization of work, the education of children. Just as today there is no problem in signifying sexual difference when it is a question of clothing a nude body or singing opera, but on the contrary, we like it because it interprets and enriches nature with humanity, so also there will be no problem in administering justice, organizing work, planning society according to the difference in being a man or a woman.

When? Now. There are no possible or necessary intermediate stages. Putting things off in time is necessary when one must reach ends which differ from their means, like sowing grain in order to eat bread, whereas in the work necessary for attaining free social existence, the means is the same as the end. Freedom is the only means for attaining freedom. To find out what society will be like when female difference can express itself freely, we need only to know how we can make belonging to the female sex the surest guarantee of freedom for each individual woman.

A few years ago, in our country, a courageous poor girl named Palmina refused to obey her fiancé, who wanted her to become a prostitute; he punished her by dousing her with gasoline and setting her on fire, and she died. The monstrousness of male behavior must not prevent us from seeing the other, less spectacular but more tragic side of this drama: Palmina, who was fourteen years old, did not get from the older women around her the help she needed to make her desire for freedom triumph over male imposition. In her environment, prostituting oneself for men was an accepted practice, and one may easily imagine that the other women would have helped her to bear this common condition if she had accepted it.

This recurs in an identical manner in other social environments as well, and will continue to recur again and again if women do not find among themselves the means to be free. Literally, not figuratively speaking, Palmina died in the place of female freedom, along in a place left empty by a female solidarity which stops short before a woman who wants something more and better for herself, a place not reached either by abstract freedom, which is supposedly guaranteed to women without any reference to their sex.

We cannot make up for that death, for that void, by insisting on female solidarity, on the one hand, and on the reinforcement of neutral guarantees, on the other. The pattern of female nonfreedom remains unchanged: on the one hand, female relations without social form, for survival, for signifying among ourselves that part of us which remains insignificant in social intercourse; on the other, women unrelated to each other who measure themselves with reality as given. The society in which female difference can express itself freely is a society where this double regime no longer exists, and the individual woman confronts the world preceded and helped by the social authority of her gender.

Often a woman evokes freedom as a remote goal from which we are separated by obstacles of all kinds which she may specify as being men, other women, her neighbors, the context in which she lives, Catania, Milan, the province, the capital, or else, if she wants to make her argument appear more objective, she cites institutions, capitalism, the South, the economic recession. Most of the time, with this declaration of impotence, she is only declaring her inability to attribute authority to another woman. She is unable to give value to the most elementary relation which defines her socially, the relation to another woman, so society is contemptuous of her; unable to conceive that a woman like her might have authority, she suffers from being without authority. Whatever she says is all true because external reality will never fail to send her back the judgment she has already made within herself, and that is, what a woman thinks or wants has no value.

Before feminism, many women were ignorant of the fact that there was a mediating structure between them and the world. And even later, having seen and rejected male mediation, they went on being unaware that a mediation between oneself and the world is always necessary. Understanding this necessity was an important turning point in female politics, equal only to the subsequent understanding that the necessary mediation must constitute the content of a political project. To the individual woman struggling with her desire and fear inside a personal experience, it is not enough to say: get out of your psychological prison. The way must also be found for her to get out of it alive and free.

The first, natural mediator for every woman who comes into the world should be her mother. Actually, she does not often succeed in being one because she is intimidated by paternal authority or absorbed in her love for her son, and used and interpreted by men according to their needs. Female entrustment is the social practice which rehabilitates the mother in her symbolic function for women. In this sense, the relation of entrustment is more than a political proposal or a personal choice. Its deeper meaning is the restoring of maternal greatness and the foundation of a female social authority.

Against this background, entrustment assumes the nature of a *ceremony*. Luce Irigaray has lamented the lack of female ceremonies in the life of a woman, in contrast with the numerous male ceremonies, ancient and modern, which help the individual man in his socialization.[8] Now, entrustment can assume this function in the life of a woman, provided that one modifies the current sense of the word. In the current sense, a ceremony always has something repetitive and ritualistic, because the ceremony serves to legitimize the new by symbolically carrying it back to the authority of the old. But the new has entered, and will enter, our lives already legitimized by male will. Think of the conflicts between mother and daughter about so-called sexual freedom, conflicts which concern the interpretation of male will, the mother remaining attached to what she has regulated her life by, the daughter tending toward new, more advanced interpretations.

Ceremonies are not needed for such conflicts, and in general, ceremonies are superfluous without an autonomous symbolic order. Reconciliation will come by itself, necessarily, when, for example, the daughter realizes that this so-called sexual freedom satisfies neither her interests nor her desires. But when a woman accepts her belonging to the female gender, learns about the necessity for female mediation, and recognizes therein the true reason for woman's authority over woman, she cannot but feel the need to make her peace with the woman, her mother, who had this authority and should have exercised it, not others, over her. In this sense, entrustment is also a ceremony. When a woman ousts the authority of male origin from her relation with the world, and agrees to give authority to another woman, or to assume it for her, with this act she honors her mother for what she knew how to be and for what she ought to have been but did not know how to be, and she makes her peace with her.

There is a tendency among women to exaggerate the subordination of the mother to the father's will. This tendency reflects an internal fear of transgressing the limits set by man on his property. We have met women who accept entrustment provided that it is with someone who has a female consciousness of self and does not subordinate herself to male measures. On this condition, entrustment is a sensible, surely useful alliance, which, however, is kept within limits which women's politics can and must surpass.

The consciousness a woman has of herself depends on the means she has, or has not, found for situating herself in the world, and on what she has, or has not, invented to make up for the social disadvantage of being born a woman. Both the constrictions suffered and a female wish for existence make up a woman's consciousness of herself. Women's politics, on the other hand, has never been a collection of good consciences or correct representations of oneself. From the start it has been a struggle against all that divides a woman from her kind, depriving her of her fundamental resource of freedom, which is belonging to the female gender. It was not a war against men, but it was, and is, a war against male interference in relations between women, and between women and the world. Male interference, as we know, does not prevent women from being grouped together as a losing gender. It prevents the kind of relation which gives value, esteem, authority.

This polemic is not about opposing the value of being a woman to the value of being a man. Being a woman rather than a man, or vice versa, has no value in itself. Sexual difference is partiality; it is a sign of finiteness, the most powerful sign marking thought as corporeal. Its value can come only from what the fact of being a woman makes possible when this limit is recognized, accepted, not denied, but changed into a pathway. We know this idea; it is the true and just transcendence of the first feminist texts.

In order to know what a woman is, then, we must also look at what she makes possible. In order to know what she thinks, let us consider everything that her thought makes thinkable; to have an accurate idea of her experience, let us think of what we can experience thanks to her. If this is the true measure, as we think it is, the measure applicable to the little Palmina and to the great woman scientist, and the measure we want applied to ourselves, then we know the reason for entrustment. Entrusting oneself is not looking to another woman as in a mirror to find in her a confirmation of what one actually is, but it is offering and asking from female human experience the means of signifying its true and great existence in the world. In the relation of entrustment, a woman offers to another woman the measure of what she can do and what in her wants to come into existence.

Female difference does not ask to be described. In order to exist, it needs mediation so as to be able to come out of itself and become in turn the mediator in a circle of unlimited power. Entrusting oneself actually starts this movement which frees female energy. It starts with a relation between two women, but it is not a couple relationship, and very soon we see it branch out into other relations stimulated by the new possibility of putting into play the whole of one's humanity, one's female mind and body.

Many times, in our politics and in this book, our arguments have ended with the discovery of the meaning of things we had in front of us. It is best that way, because knowing how to discern what is, is more important than planning changes, and the best projects are those dictated by things, when we understand what they mean. The political proposal of entrustment was born this way too, and we hope it will be accepted in this sense.

There were long debates among us to decide if we could, if we should, present the relation of entrustment in the form of a necessary conclusion. No answer satisfied us. An answer in the affirmative took away the precious, delicate component of personal choice. Outside the relation with the mother, one cannot give or receive value without a personal preference, a subjective feeling.

An answer in the negative, however, took away something even more important. It made the relation optional, and this contrasts with its *raison d'être*. Entrustment is the form of female gendered mediation in a society which does not contemplate gendered mediations, but only male mediation endowed with universal validity. As such, we think entrustment is necessary and must say so.

But, considering the way by which we came to this conclusion, we see that it is not made up solely of arguments or constraints; there were also events, which occurred partly by chance, partly by free choice. And we see, besides, that the conclusion, with all of its internal force, does not make the pathway superfluous. What does that mean? That we see the necessity of entrustment because it appeared to us, but we cannot demonstrate it completely because we do not see it completely. This admission does not weaken our arguments. It means that our arguments have partly been dictated to us, to an extent we would not know how to measure, by the power of things which are not under our control, but which are favorable to us. Many women have abandoned the way of emancipation, and our minds are open to the meaning of ancient female behaviors.

There are things which do not come by historical necessity, but because they have been favored. Among these is female freedom. There is an ancient Greek word, *kairós,* which serves to name this favor, this form of necessity which shows itself and can be read, but not actually demonstrated. It means that many disparate things combine together and realize the goal, earlier and better than could those working toward that goal. It is neither pure chance nor iron necessity, but a mixture of both and, better still, something you can enter into, on your part, and the whole will answer you.

Notes

INTRODUCTION

1. Cf. Émile Benveniste, *Le vocabulaire des institutions indo-européenes*, 2 vols. (Paris: Minuit, 1969), especially Livre 2, "Le vocabulaire de la parenté," vol. 1, pp. 203–276.

2. Cf. Luce Irigaray, "Une chance de vivre," in *Sexes et parentés* (Paris: Minuit, 1987), pp. 203–207.

3. Cf. Claude Lévi-Strauss, *Les structures élémentaires de la parenté* (Paris: P.V.F., 1947).

4. Virginia Woolf, *A Room of One's Own* (London: Hogarth Press Ltd., 1929).

5. Ellen Moers, *Literary Women* (1977; paperback ed., London: The Women's Press Limited, 1989), p. 61.

6. Book of Ruth, King James Version.

7. Cf. Jane Austen, *Jane Austen's Letters to Her Sister Cassandra and Others*, comp. and ed. R. W. Chapman (London: Clarendon Press, 1932).

8. Cf. Benedetta Craveri, *Madame du Deffand e il suo mondo* (Milan: Adelphi, 1982).

9. Cf. George Eliot, "Prelude," *Middlemarch* (1871–72; paperback reprint ed., Middlesex: Penguin Books Ltd., The Penguin English Library, 1975), p. 26.

10. The quotations that follow are taken from H. D., *Tribute to Freud* (1970; paperback rev. ed., Manchester: Carcanet Press Ltd., 1985), pp. 40, 41, 44, 45, 47, 48–49, 51, 55–56.

CHAPTER ONE

1. The "Manifesto" was originally a mimeographed text, date: December 1, 1966. The quotations are taken from Rosalba Spagnoletti, ed., *I movimenti femministi in Italia* (Rome: Savelli, 1971), pp. 38–40. (The date of the foundation of the group, 1965, is found in the manuscript notes and recollections of Daniela Pellegrini, a founder of Demau.)

2. Demau, "Alcuni problemi sulla questione femminile," ibid., pp. 41–48; originally a mimeographed text, date: January 1967, Milan.

3. Cf. Demau, "Il maschile come valore dominate," in Spagnoletti, ed., *I movimenti femministi*, pp. 49–63 (the essay appeared originally in *Il manifesto*, no. 4, September 1969).

4. "Manifesto di Rivolta femminile," ibid., pp. 102, 104. (The "Manifesto" originally appeared as a manifesto on walls in Rome and Milan, date: July 1970.)

5. Carla Lonzi, *Sputiamo su Hegel* (Rome-Milan: Scritti di Rivolta femminile, 1970), p. 37.

6. Spagnoletti, ed., *I movimenti femministi*, p. 102.

7. Ibid.

8. Lonzi, *Sputiamo su Hegel*, p. 4.

9. Ibid., pp. 36–37.

10. Gruppo Anabasi, "Editoriale," "Donne è bello" (Milan, 1972), no page number. (The first pages in the leaflet are not numbered; numbering starts from the page which should be page 7.)

11. *Sottosopra. Esperienze dei gruppi femministi in Italia*, also called *Sottosopra* no. 1 (Milan, 1973), introduction, no title, page number, or author's name.

12. Ibid., p. 24.

13. Ibid., p. 25.

14. "Contributo al dibattito," *Sottosopra. Esperienze dei gruppi femministi in Italia, 1974,* also called *Sottosopra* no. 2 (Milan, 1974), without a page number (actually it would be page 2, but the numbering begins from what would be page 3), signed: Florentia—in the name of the following groups: Movimento femminista triestino, Lotta femminista, Comitato femminile.

15. Antonella, Daniela, Giordana e Marina, Graziella, Sandra, and Silvia, "L'esperienza del giornale," ibid., pp. 1–3.

16. "Esperienza alla Feda," ibid., p. 90, unsigned.

17. A comrade from Milan, "La nudità," *Sottosopra* no. 1, pp. 19–22.

18. Lea Melandri, "La violenza invisibile," *Sottosopra* no. 2, p. 59.

19. "Manifesto di Rivolta femminile," in Spagnoletti, ed., *I movimenti femministi,* p. 103.

20. *Sottosopra* no. 1, p. 86.

21. "La Tranche: un incontro internazionale, una vacanza al mare," ibid., pp. 18–19.

22. "Dalla registrazione di una discussione collettiva," ibid., pp. 30–38.

23. Ibid., pp. 35–36.

24. Ibid., p. 34.

25. Lillith (Demau group), "Madre mortifera," *L'erba voglio,* no. 15 (February–March 1974), pp. 10–12.

26. "Dalla registrazione di una discussione collettiva," *Sottosopra* no. 1, pp. 31, 38.

27. "Noi pratichiamo l'auto-in-coscienza," *Sottosopra* (also called *Sottosopra* no. 3) (Milan, March 1976), p. 22, unsigned; this is the tapescript of a debate.

28. Maria (Turin), "La parola, il silenzio, e la distruttività," ibid., p. 58.

29. "Pratica dell'inconscio e movimento delle donne" (Milan, 1974), fourth page (the pages are not numbered; it is a large sheet of paper folded in half), signed: Some Milanese feminists. The same text is to be found in *L'erba voglio,* no. 18–19 (October 1974–January 1975), p. 23.

30. The letter was never published. It is in Luisa Muraro's private files.

31. "Per Pinarella," *Sottosopra* no. 3, pp. 3–4.

32. "Noi pratichiamo l'auto-in-coscienza," ibid., p. 23. This text is the tapescript of a debate. It is the source of all the passages quoted from here to the end of this subchapter, "The meeting at Pinarella."

33. "Esistono dei traumi piacevoli?" ibid., p. 62.

34. "Noi pratichiamo l'auto-in-coscienza," ibid., p. 17.

35. Ibid., p. 19.

36. *Catalogo di testi di teoria e pratica politica* (also called *Catalogo verde* [Green Catalogue] because of the color of its cover) (Milan: Libreria delle donne, 1978), p. 14.

CHAPTER TWO

1. Later printed in AA.VV., *E'già politica* (Milan: Scritti di Rivolta femminile 8, 1977), pp. 115–122.

2. Mimeographed leaflet (Women's Bookstore of Milan Archives, Milan, Via Dogana 2).

3. Rossana Rossanda, "Considerazioni sull'aborto," *Il manifesto* (Milan, February 23, 1975), p. 1. Reprinted in Rossana Rossanda, *Anche per me* (Milan: Feltrinelli, 1987), pp, 35–38; mistakenly dated November 1975.

4. "Noi sull'aborto facciamo un lavoro politico diverso," a mimeographed leaflet which was reprinted in *Sottosopra,* special issue (Milan, 1975) (known as the red *Sottosopra*), pp. 43–44.

5. Ibid., pp. 44–46.

6. Ibid., pp. 38–39.

7. A group of women from Col di Lana—Milan, "Autodeterminazione: un direttivo

ambiguo," *Sottosopra,* special issue (Milan, December 1976) (know as the pink *Sottosopra*), p. 1.

8. "Una legge che sarà di tutte," *Noi donne,* no. 35 (September 7, 1979), pp. 22–34.

9. All the Umanitaria Conference (October 27–28, 1979) remarks were transcribed in a mimeographed notebook: "Contro la violenza sessuale, le donne . . . la legge" (Milan Women's Bookstore Archives); four contributions were published in *Il manifesto:* on November 18, 1979, those by Lea Melandri, Luisa Muraro, and Nicoletta Gandus, and on November 20, 1979, the one by Lia Cigarini.

10. Franca and Luisa of the Milan Woman's Bookstore, "Stupro senza orario," *Lotta Continua* (November 16, 1979).

11. Mimeographed leaflet (Milan Women's Bookstore Archives), undated, later printed in *Il manifesto* (October 8, 1979) and in *Quotidiano donna* (October 24, 1979).

12. Undated text for the press conference (which took place at the beginning of October 1979) held by the Women's Bookstore to make known its position on the proposed bill against sexual violence (Luisa Muraro's personal files).

13. Mimeographed leaflet, undated, later printed in *Il manifesto* (October 18, 1979).

14. Maria of the Women's Bookstore of Turin, "Il desiderio di essere protette dalla violenza con una legge di donna," ibid.

15. Lia Cigarini, "C'è differenza fra iscrizione simbolica, giuridica della non violabilità delle donne, e una legge repressiva," *Il manifesto* (November 20, 1979), p. 3.

16. Roberta T., *Il manifesto* (November 25, 1984).

17. Alessandra B., *Il manifesto* (November 3, 1984).

18. Lea Melandri, "Un' acquisizione importante della nostra pratica politica è l'impossibilità di tracciare un solco netto tra violenza e amore, tra consenso e costrizione, tra felicità e infelicità," *Il manifesto* (November 18, 1979), p. 3.

19. Cigarini, "C'è differenza. . . ," *Il manifesto* (November 20, 1979).

20. Ibid.

CHAPTER THREE

1. "Esistono dei traumi piacevoli?" *Sottosopra* no. 3, p. 63.

2. Ibid., p. 64.

3. "Scrivere, pubblicare, fare un giornale e la pratica politica delle donne." This was a leaflet of only a few photocopied pages. (Personal files of Luisa Muraro.)

4. "I luoghi delle femministe e la pratica del movimento." This was a leaflet of only a few photocopied pages. (Personal files of Luisa Muraro.)

5. "Il tempi, i mezzi e i luoghi," *Sottosopra* no. 3, pp. 59–60, signed: Collective of Via Cherubini Feminist Groups.

6. *Catalogo di testi, di teoria e pratica politica* (or *Catalogo verde* [green Catalogue]), p. 1.

7. "Il tempi, i mezzi e i luoghi," *Sottosopra* no. 3, p. 60.

8. *Catalogo verde,* pp. 9–10.

9. Ibid., p. 10.

10. "Io dico io," a manifesto which later was printed as "Secondo Manifesto di Rivolta Femminile," AA.VV., *La presenza dell'uomo nel femminismo* (Milan: Scritti di Rivolta femminile 9, 1978), pp. 7–9,

11. "Lettera" di alcune donne del Collettivo di Via Cherubini, *Corriere della sera* (April 25, 1976), in the Letters to the Editor column.

12. Photocopied letter (personal files of Luisa Muraro).

13. Typed text (personal files of Donatella Massara).

14. Photocopied leaflet (Milan Women's Bookstore archives).

15. Printed manifesto entitled *Si è aperta a Milano, in via Dogana 2, la Libreria delle*

donne (undated, but certainly from the last months of 1975; Milan Women's Bookstore archives).

16. Printed manifesto entitled *La Libreria delle donne di Milano esiste da cinque anni* (Milan Women's Bookstore archives).

17. "Noi pratichiamo l'auto-in-coscienza," *Sottosopra* no. 3, p. 23.

18. Printed one-page declaration (Parma Women's Library archives).

19. "La modificazione personale e l'agire politico," *Sottosopra*, special issue (December 1976) (pink *Sottosopra*), pp. 4–5.

20. "Appunti del gruppo numero 4," ibid., p. 6.

21. Ibid.

22. "La modificazione personale e l'agire politico," ibid., p. 4.

23. "Osando finalmente dubitare," *Sottosopra* special issue (December 1976), (pink *Sottosopra*), pp. 2–4.

24. "Postilla 1. L'obiezione della donna muta," ibid., p. 7.

25. Maria Pia, "C'è da restare sbigottite," in "La traversata" (Milan: Scuola Media V. Gabbro, adult education 150 hours group, ca. 1977–78). Like "Più polvere in casa meno polvere nel cervello" and "E' sparita la donna pallida e tutta casalinga," this is a leaflet written and mimeographed by the women registered in the course, undated and without page numbers, but the quotations come from the actual pp. 1–3 (Milan Women's Bookstore archives).

26. "Dove sono finita io?" "La traversata."

27. "L'uovo terremotato," *Lotta continua* (December 21, 1977).

28. "Le donne e la scuola," "Più polvere in casa meno polvere nel cervello" (Milan, March–April, 1977), p. 5.

29. "Pregiudizi," "La traversata."

30. "Una moda o una rivoluzione," "E' sparita la donna pallida e tutta casalinga" (Milan, 1976–77), p. 2.

31. "L'uovo terremotato," *Lotta continua* (December 21, 1977).

CHAPTER FOUR

1. Preface, *A zigzag. Scritti non scritti* (Milan, May 1978), p. 3.

2. Libreria delle donne—Milano, Biblioteca delle donne—Parma, *Catalogo n. 2—Romanzi. Le madri di tutte noi*, also called *Catalogo giallo* (Milan: Libreria delle donne, Parma: Biblioteca delle donne, 1982), p. 55.

3. "Più donne che uomini," *Sottosopra*, special issue (Milan, January 1983) (also called *Sottosopra* verde [green], because of the color of the print).

4. Alessandra Bocchetti, "L'indecente differenza," *Programma 1983* (Rome: Centro Culturale Virginia Woolf, 1983), pp. 7–23.

5. Sigmund Freud, "Femininity," *The Standard Edition of the Complete Psychological Works*, vol. 22, ed. James Strachey (London: The Hogarth Press, 1964), pp. 134–135.

6. "Le donne e la scuola," "Più polvere in casa," p. 5.

7. Cf. Edoarda Masi, *Il libro da nascondere* (Casale Monferrato: Marietti, 1985), pp. 101–104.

8. Cf. Luce Irigaray, *Sexes et parentés* (Paris: Minuit, 1987), pp. 87–102.